Pra 

BARBARIANS IN THE GARDEN CITY

"Any British Columbian could write a book listing the vast patronage, ideologically driven stupidities, savage class warfare, casual incompetence, numb arithmetic, breathtaking waste and grim repression of free speech of the most scoundrel government in the province's history, the disastrous Mike Harcourt-Glen Clark New Democratic Party regimes. But while we await the exhaustive 26-volume chronicle of these abuses of power, we're unlikely to be treated to such a comprehensive, solidly researched study as Mark Milke's, certainly not written with as much style and wit. A must for the thoughtful, and a stimulus for the forgetful." *-Trevor Lautens, Vancouver Sun columnist*

"There are two reasons to read this book. The first is to remember the recent political past, which otherwise fades so quickly from our memories. The second is to consider ideas to reform our system of government so that no matter which party might be in power, the horror show of the Nineties cannot easily happen again." *-From the forward by Gordon Gibson, columnist, author, and former BC Liberal leader*

"Mark Milke provides a hard-hitting analysis on the rise, stumbling and fall of the Harcourt and Clark governments. The political and economic mismanagement of British Columbia by the NDP provides lessons that no aspiring politician nor informed voter can afford to ignore." *-Michael Geoghegan, former NDP Ministerial Assistant to the Honourable Bill Barlee*

"Mark Milke zooms in on the NDP's fiscal fumbles with precision and clarity. If there's little time in your life for reading about BC politics, make Barbarians in the Garden City your one selection." *-Joey Thompson, Editorial page editor, the Vancouver Province*

"If there is one thing present-day politicians — especially those in power or near it — dislike talking about, it's the real issues. Making up issues and fighting elections about them are what the BC NDP do especially well. Mark Milke tells us what the real issues are and it's our fault as voters if we ignore them and consent to being bribed with our own money." *-Rafe Mair, author, host of CKNW's Rafe Mair Show, and former provincial cabinet minister*

Thomas & Black Publishers

Steven

Best regards and enjoy the book!
— Mark

Copyright 2001 by Mark Milke

All rights reserved. No part of this book may be reproduced or transmitted in any form or by any means, electronic or mechanical, including photocopying, recording, or by any information storage and retrieval system, without permission in writing from the Publisher.

Thomas & Black Publishers
Victoria, BC

Printed in Canada

Canadian Cataloguing in Publication Data

Milke, Mark, 1967-
Barbarians in the garden city

ISBN 0-9687915-0-6

1. British Columbia—Politics and government—1991-* 2. New Democratic Party of British Columbia. I. Title.
FC3829.2.M54 2000 971.1'04 C00-911158-1
F1088.M54 2000

Contents

Appendices

Acknowledgements

If writing is a solitary act, the creation of a book is anything but an experience in isolation. Those who helped answer my queries on specific subjects included Vaughn Palmer, Ken Drushka, Terry O'Neill and Suromitra Sanatani. Mike Geoghegan helped provide insight into the mystery wrapped in the enigma that is a New Democrat mind. Those helpful in other areas included David Gratzer, Michael Taube, Mike Jenkinson, Nick Loenen, Rafe Mair, John Nelson, and Febe Galvez.

Trevor Lautens, Joey Thompson, George Gibault, Fazil Mihlar, Gordon Gibson, and Troy Lanigan all suffered through a first draft of the book. Their insights, suggestions, and criticisms have, I hope, made the chronicle that the reader holds more enjoyable; any lack thereof is entirely my fault. An extra thank you is owed Gordon Gibson for his very thoughtful forward, and to Troy Lanigan for going beyond the call of duty on his suggestions, and indeed, for bringing me on board with the Federation three years ago.

Many, *many* thanks to Faith Farthing for her sharp proofreading skills; if errors yet exist in the text, they are due to an author who just couldn't resist including another thought at the last moment. Dean Smith spent many hours formatting the book, lining up the cartoons and pictures, and making it a pleasant experience for the eye. I only hope my writing engages the reader's mind to the same degree. And if pictures are worth a thousand words, I figure the cartoons from *Victoria Times Colonist* cartoonist Adrian Raeside have saved me many thousands of words and six months of writing.

It should be noted that any mistakes and opinions contained herein are those of the author.

I offer a final thank-you to the late Mel Smith, to whom I dedicate this book. He would not have known it (though perhaps he does now), but he was one of the sparks for this chronicle. Mel, I wish I had known you longer.

VICTORIA TIMES COLONIST.–DIST. BY KOKO PRESS INC. www.raesidecartoon.com
RAESIDE
B.C.
ECONOMY
Bates
MOTEL
OFFICE
1
NO, NO. MA'S DOING
FINE... JUST A LITTLE
SLOW THESE DAYS,
THAT'S ALL.

Foreword

There are two reasons to read this book. The first is to remember the recent political past, which otherwise fades so quickly from our memories. The second is to consider ideas to reform our system of government so that no matter which party might be in power, the horror show of the Nineties cannot easily happen again.

While the main audience will be British Columbians, anyone who is interested in Canadian politics can learn something here. British Columbia's experience with dreadful government has been unusual, but not unique. The process abuses of the federal Liberals over roughly the same period have been less egregious but still important, and they demand the same sort of democratic reform for the future protection of the public.

The Nineties were terrible years for this province. We seriously underperformed compared to the rest of the country. From 1992 to 1999 our personal disposable income per capita grew only by 4.8 percent, as compared to 12.1 percent for the country as a whole. Our GDP per capita dropped below the Canadian average for the first time, all the way down to the 95-per-cent level. Our relationships with central government – which extracts so much tax revenue from the province – went from bad to disastrous, to our great economic cost.

Directly due to the climate established by the provincial government, investment dried up – the very investment needed to finance social programs and infrastructure for our growing population (though by the end of the decade even our growth had plummeted by about two thirds). The Edmonton Chamber of Commerce thanked the BC government for being the essential engine of Alberta's growth.

The author provides an invaluable compendium of details. This has two merits. In the first place, our memories are all too frail. With the departure of the detested Premier Clark, his replacement by the soothing Ujjal Dosanjh, a slight upturn in the economy and the passage of a couple of years, the Nineties easily could – and will, hopes the current government – easily fade away as a bad dream, best forgotten. That would be a mistake. Bad government happened, and it didn't happen by accident.

Therein lies the second merit. The perspective afforded here demonstrates that the government of the Nineties was furnished as part of a pattern – a pattern that flowed right through the time of the bland Premier Harcourt, exacerbated during the Clark years, to the present. For example, Ujjal Dosanjh may be the Premier as I write, but he was the Attorney General, the man responsible for the integrity of our legal system, when Judge Glen Parrett so excoriated the government for the concealment of evidence and the obstruction of justice in the Carrier Lumber case, reported herein. Was Ujjal Dosanjh's response an inquiry to root out the truth as to who was complicit? Not on your nelly. The response was to lodge an appeal, safely putting the matter beyond the next election. It is too easy to personalize error, and pretend it is over when this or that individual is replaced. The error here has been systemic.

The author takes us through the incredible escalation of taxes and of debt. He outlines the damage done to our major industries of mining and forestry, and how the manipulation of labour legislation tilted the scales of industrial relations, raised public sector costs and damaged employment. We get the essential primer on the wasted pork of Forest Renewal BC, the scandal of the "fudge-it" budgets, and the (not so) fast ferries.

Process is treated as well. The election gag law and the Human Rights Commission mess illustrate an attitude of attack on democracy and due process. The author and I disagree on the bubble zone legislation, but he makes a strong case. And the manipulation of the legal system – Carrier above all, but many other examples – is revealed.

The failure of the Treaty Commission process is one of the tragedies of the era, and stems directly from fuzzy-minded, politically correct and vote-seeking government approaches. The net result was a loss of votes where they had hoped to gain, but that is of little comfort to the people of BC. The author details the NDP government's disgraceful abandonment of sound legal principle in instructions to its new lawyers once it had control of the appeal process in the Delgamuukw case, and the ongoing problems caused thereby for all British Columbians.

The hugely controversial Nisga'a Treaty has its own section, and deservedly so. It was passed over the clear opposition of a majority of British Columbians, with no mandate to proceed in this way. The legal ramifications of this adventure have only just begun. The toll in terms of damage to a civil, democratic and equal society has yet to be reckoned, as with the ultimate damage to a group singled out for special treatment on the basis of race, apart from other Canadians. One would think the years since 1867 would have provided a sufficient lesson in that regard.

All of these things need to be borne in mind.

The shortest part of the book, but in many ways the most important, looks to the future. How could the government of the Nineties happen in BC? It was not because of a particularly bad group of men and women in government, though certainly a few of them were. Rather it was because our system holds too few checks and balances when ideologues quite unrepresentative of most British Columbians get their hands on the machinery of government.

The essential work now is democratic reform. Our system is a primitive one in a modern state, where the government is so deeply within all of our lives when what is needed is to live by cooperation and accommodation rather than by class warfare and contestation. That calls for reforms in parliamentary practice, above all the empowerment of the ordinary MLA and checks on the power of the Premier. It calls for consideration of electoral reform, and constraints on the overall power of government itself, such as more robust citizen initiative legislation. The author sets out his views on these things in a concise and constructive way. My views are different on some issues, but that matters not. Let the debate be engaged, that reform may ensue! This is an excellent start, and a first-class reference work.

Gordon Gibson

Author's Introduction

There are many compelling reasons to write a book on BC's New Democrats and their time in office. Personal reasons are probably the least relevant to the reader; nevertheless, if understanding the motivations of an author helps one navigate a book, here are mine.

Born and raised in British Columbia, I left the province in 1988 at a time when BC was the envy of Canada. Over the years, when Albertans asked where I was from, they expressed surprise that I moved to Edmonton from Kelowna. Most wanted to make the reverse move. By 1999 (when I returned to British Columbia), the province had become the village idiot of confederation and, over thc decade, a strange reversal of expectations had occurred. Now *British Columbians* asked why I left Alberta and my friends in the wild-rose province simply shook their heads about my move west.

But the clincher for *Barbarians in the Garden City* occurred to me on an airplane, flying back from New York City in May 2000. While there, I walked into a Barnes & Noble bookstore and picked up *The Case Against Hillary Clinton* by Peggy Noonan, a former speechwriter for Ronald Reagan and George Bush.

Intrigued by her argument that the election of Hillary Clinton as a New York senator would prolong the vapid, unprincipled, and self-absorbed age of Clintonism along with its occasional abuses of power, it occurred to me that many of the events down south were paralleled and trumped by BC's government.

Conspiracy theorists on the right in the United States have attributed all sorts of misdeeds to the Clintons and I think most of their charges are nutty. (Noonan's book does not fall into that category; on the contrary, it is an insightful indictment.) One hardly needs to muck around in the murky swamps of conspiracies; Bill Clinton's administration committed its share of visible abuses of power.

Abuse of power is the central theme of this book. A surprise though it might be to some, my early experiences should have turned me into a fervent recycler of other people's money - a virtue to BC's rulers in the 1990s. When I was sixteen, the Royal Bank forced my father, a house builder in Kelowna, into receivership. He had too many unsold houses on the market when the 1981 recession hit and three years later the bank took those as well as the family home.

An eastern bank and tough family economic times should, perhaps by default, have led me to believe in massive government intervention in the economy. But I have never believed that my individual hardship (or anyone else's) is an excuse for adopting state-led economic policies of envy, for coveting the wealth or success of others, or redistribution for redistribution's sake.

Compassionate people and societies should share with those less fortunate, both through personal charity and out of their taxes where appropriate, and where helpful and not harmful to the long-term initiative and self-respect of the poor. (There is, for example, a vast difference between a single mother who cannot work and an able-bodied 20-year-old male who can.) But that ethical imperative does not also necessitate tearing down the average Canadian or even the wealthy. Nor does it mean, for example, that everything advanced by those who claim to represent the poor is smart public policy. Good intentions are easy to find; effective policies that deliver what is promised are much more rare.

This chronicle is necessary in part to provide an historical record of the past decade. No doubt there will be others. Almost a decade after the Social Credit party left office, its reputation for financial competence severely weakened and its ethical robe tattered, it is difficult to recall what all the fuss was about. That the view of the time was mostly correct is beside the point. By comparison, the government of the 1990s made the 1980s rap sheet short by any fair measure.

Some mistake criticism of certain political decisions as criticism of the institution itself. Governments are necessary and desirable, providing they are limited in scope and modest in aim. Few would wish to live in a world that is nasty, brutish and short; but unlike some, I do not believe that a large nanny-state is necessary to prevent such. Nor is government the primary creator of a civil society. In fact, a state can damage civility if, by excessive size and scope, it weakens the culture of independence and voluntary interdependence of its citizens. A civil society requires, among other foundational elements, the rule of law, the protection of property, and the ability to provide for one's family and to give to one's friends. Left alone, most people, families, and friendships will bloom quite well with those minimums. (And as there will likely always be those who need help, one should be neither romantic nor callous about that.) When political states interfere overmuch and attempt to "create" that which only flowers naturally, a rose is torn open before it is ready, and the result is neither attractive nor natural.

Today Canadians value political public service perhaps less than in any time in the last 100 years. And that corrodes public life in a number of ways: the talent pool for politics becomes smaller and citizens in a democracy hold their own freedom and responsibility more lightly than they ought. Neither is positive for the future.

Those who interpret my criticism of those that ruled BC in the last decade as corrosive cynicism could not be more mistaken. Democracy requires vigilance, and to ignore that duty is to show the greatest possible contempt for democracy itself. I do not sit in the crowd of cynics that believes all or even most politicians are corrupt, or that a better Canada is impossible. The art of politics is a noble calling and ought to be seen that way again.

But I would argue that the public's contempt for many of their political representatives exists, in part, because politicians promise and attempt too much and citizens expect miracles. For many in the 20th century, politics (and by extension, politicians and government) replaced God – as if every human desire and need could be organized through a bureaucracy. Thus, disappointment was inevitable. Our fellow human beings are not deities.

Politicians, though they are critiqued at times (not least from the organization I work for), come in all varieties and deserve neither general disdain nor hero-worship. Some who serve are excellent in conviction, character and purpose; some that rule are anything but. Power can affect all and none are perfect.

I have my own favourites, and they include Winston Churchill, whose victories need no reciting; Margaret Thatcher, who rescued a country about to descend into squalor; Ronald Reagan, who turned the tide of assumptions as it concerned international politics; and Lee Kuan Yew, who, despite authoritarian tendencies, took Singaporeans from shantytowns to prosperity in one generation. In so doing, he prevented another disastrous experiment of envy in the non-Western world. And there are the figures of history that also rank high, such as the 19th-century English politician, William Wilberforce, the English Member of Parliament who fought for decades for the end of slavery. There are admirable public servants closer to our own time and locale; W.A.C. Bennett comes to mind as one who set a high ethical bar for leaders in provincial politics. Pierre Trudeau's initial philosophical and constitutional liberalism are praiseworthy, though his later political decisions in that area left much to be desired. As for his economic policies and international politics, Trudeau should have befriended Lee Kuan Yew, not Fidel Castro.

In the case of British Columbia, many have supported BC New Democrats because they did, at least in the past, successfully talk the language of compassion and justice, wrong and incorrect though they were about the means to such noble ends. To those supporters, I would argue they at least deserved better than the government they received.

Of course, the problem for adherents of the NDP yet remains. It is precisely that the means to such ends, and the assumptions behind them, always include such a large dose of government intervention that makes them so problematic. The names could have been different this past decade; the results would largely have been the same, and mostly because of the philosophy of the NDP and their proximity to power. Of those still convinced of the virtuous power of large states in and of themselves, I doubt my book will change their minds. If anything, it may well enrage them. So be it. I think those who hold such ideas should rethink their basic assumptions and ask themselves if virtuous ends require the intervention of the state as often as some still believe to be the case.

The final reason for this book, perhaps the most important one, is my growing unease about the concentration of power in Canadian politics, demonstrated most disastrously this past decade in British Columbia. Power politics in East Asia was a personal fascination when I lived in Japan for two years, and was later the subject of my Master's thesis. Simply put – I dislike bullies.

A word on the focus and on the chronology of the book: this is not a book about politics in BC in general; it is specific to the NDP government. Government parties have the levers of power and as a result, little the opposition says or does matters. That is just one more argument for some reform of the political system.

I should also mention that this book and the views expressed in it are solely my own, and are not to be mistaken as a representation of the views of the Canadian Taxpayers Federation or its members. The Federation employs me, but this book was written on personal time and is not sponsored by the CTF.

While the subject matter of each chapter itself (mostly) flows in general chronological order, the chapters do not. I tend to think, and write, in themes. Thus, those who want to read up on a certain topic can dip into the relevant section without fearing they have somehow missed the context provided by an earlier chapter.

The title, for those not from these parts, refers to Victoria - the physical and symbolic seat of power in British Columbia. Lastly, this book is an attempt to sketch out alternatives to the status quo. The proposals are not meant to satisfy every academic argument on the subject. They are meant to prod British Columbians to ask whether there is anything they can do to improve the institutions of power so that they are less subject to abuse. My answer to that question is "yes."

Mark Milke
Victoria, British Columbia
November 2000

IF MICROSOFT MOVED TO BRITISH COLUMBIA:
NEWS
TODAY MARKS THE 50th DAY OF PICKET LINES AT THE MICROSOFT COMPLEX. MEANWHILE, ANOTHER THIRTY SOFTWARE DEVELOPERS DEFECTED TO THE ORACLE PLANT IN ALBERTA. BILL GATES COULDN'T BE REACHED FOR COMMENT, AS HE IS STILL STRANDED ON THE PACIFICAT FERRY THAT BROKE DOWN AND HAS BEEN DRIFTING FOR TWO DAYS.
RAESIDE
Victoria Times Colonist - Dist. by Koko Press Inc. www.raesidecartoon.com

1

Pride & Prejudice, *and* Power

"Don't forget that government can do anything."[1]
- NDP Cabinet Minister David Zirnhelt

Why did New Democrats do it?

Their disastrous decade in British Columbia was not preordained. In the late 1980s, an over-budget Coquihalla highway and the return of deficits punctured the Social Credit reputation for fiscal competence. And when the New Democrats came to power in 1991, neighbouring Conservative-led Alberta ran multi-billion dollar deficits, and Albertans saw one government-financed business venture after another implode, a disastrous corporate welfare experiment that added $2.6 billion to that province's total debt.[2]

Both examples of small-c conservative incompetence provided the perfect excuse (if needed) for cleaner, sober, and more honest government. By the time the NDP took control of British Columbia, the stage was set and all the props were in their favour.

Revising history: what might have been

Thus, the NDP could have trashed right-wingers for their hypocrisy and cleaned up the accounting and spending debacles. Public construction projects might have been properly planned, accounted for, and bid on; the contrast would have been obvious. In addition, BC's social democrats could yet have berated corporate "fat cats" and killed business subsidies. The party held that position since the days of David Lewis anyway, and that action would have kept anti-business types in the party cheery for a time without doing any real damage to the province's economy.

Given the state of that economy in the early 1990s, buoyed by Asian and interprovincial immigration, New Democrats might have even rewarded union allies (as they did anyway) with favours in the name of balance. To appear moderate, all the NDP had to do was not wholly share power with big labour and to drop the anti-business rhetoric. On the environment, the party could have preserved more parkland and tightened environmental controls; for moderation's sake, the NDP could have ensured the rules of resource development were clear in advance and not later reneged upon.

Unwise as it might be, New Democrats could have even raised taxes (as they did) and argued such increases were temporary (which they did not) to fight Socred deficits. Had the NDP controlled or – heaven forbid, cut spending in the early 1990s, they could, by mid-decade, have produced actual balanced budgets as opposed to fake ones. Lower debt interest charges, more program spending choices, and substantial tax cuts later in the decade would have been the result.

And in fact, the early signals from the NDP and the new Finance Minister, Glen Clark, pointed in that direction; at the time, *Vancouver Sun* columnist Vaughn Palmer labelled Clark "the most right-wing finance minister in Canada."[3]

The Jonestown Kool-Aid Gang

But the much-vaunted moderation promoted by the party in the 1991 election and periodically sighted by media pundits afterward never materialized. The decisions of Mike Harcourt, Glen Clark, and Ujjal Dosanjh and their colleagues weakened British Columbia at a time when it should have been a strong partner in confederation.

In retrospect, the 1991 moderation was largely show. Whether that was intentional on Mike Harcourt's part, or whether his underlings ran the palace is up for debate. Some of his more disloyal staffers certainly treated the first NDP premier as a figurehead, a face of moderation that would make their left-wing ideas more palatable to the general public. Presumptuous as it was, the advisers thought all they needed to do was ensure that the face did not take the election promise about moderation seriously. Sharon Prescott, a political aide to Mike Harcourt's Principal Secretary Linda Baker, once told an aide to NDP MLA Bill Barlee, "I don't envy you – you're going to have the same problems with Bill that we're going to have with Mike [Harcourt]. Watch that he doesn't go off and say something stupid."[4] The aide, Mike Geoghegan, understood it quite clearly to mean that the two men must be muzzled as they were prone to moderation, and too much of that in caucus would undercut the agenda. The comment itself was revealing; Prescott simply assumed Geoghegan was as ideological as she was.

Bill Barlee and Mike Geoghegan later mocked the ideological political staff behind their back and referred to them as *apparatchiks*. And whenever their loyalty was questioned, the MLA and his aide would roll their eyes and tell each other they should just "drink the Kool-Aid." The NDP senior political staff – the "Jonestown Kool-Aid Gang" as Barlee and Geoghegan called them, "were always busy formulating strategies to kill us all."[5] The apparatchiks, of course, never quite saw it that way.

The British Columbia disease

The Jonestown Kool-Aid Gang did force some dangerous drinks on British Columbia in the early 1990s. Higher and new taxes and reams of regulation hobbled business, the engine of wealth creation, jobs, and higher wages; those same tax hikes eroded already-stagnant family incomes. As a result, the public was left with the correct impression that the NDP loved more and higher taxes for taxes' sake and wallowed in them. In that context, later tax reductions looked forced, in direct response to moves by Ottawa and competition from other provinces.

The NDP's biases, either ones overly sympathetic to the more purist environmentalists over moderates, or their reversal of BC's traditional position on native land claims, threw the province's main wealth creators into a weightless universe. For forestry and mining, property and resource rights meant nothing in practical terms. The result was the painful and unnecessary decline of the mining industry and uncertain, tentative, and weak investment in forestry.

By the end of the 1990s, the books were not yet balanced,[i] and – despite a later court judgment that found the government was not guilty of fraud in any narrow, legal sense – the 1996 "fudge-it" budget correctly symbolized anything but plain public dealing as regards provincial finances. That, along with wasted tax dollars, was a charge often repeated by the province's Auditor General in the 1990s. The rot was infectious: the public service in British Columbia was never so contaminated by partisan patronage and direct interference; Crown corporations were badly run when political appointees with no business or boardroom experience were placed at the helm. And business bashing was regular, sometimes purposely for electoral reasons and occasionally the result of an unplanned verbal slip that revealed a deep bias. Moreover, despite anti-business rhetoric, the NDP sent out confused signals: the environmental review of the proposed Windy Craggy mine (a project worth eight billion dollars) was sacrificed in haste while taxpayer subsidies to corporations were dished out in an effort to soften the NDP's anti-busi-

---

i. In August 2000, the government, with the Auditor General's backing, announced that the budget year that ended in March 2000 was balanced. But that claim only applied to the Summary Accounts. The overall debt of the province still climbed.

ness reputation.

Even on labour relations, the NDP was not destined to overdose on their own rhetoric. Despite the occasional staged pillow-fight for the TV cameras between labour and the NDP government, big labour's demands were rarely turned down. Public and private sector unions suffered losses only when their demands were badly stage-managed by the Premier's office. Labour code changes could have been made without giving the BC Federation of Labour a virtual seat at the cabinet table: where else would labour go in the next election anyway? And occasionally, the NDP's attempt to artificially boost wages was simply silly; in 1995, their attempt to compel parents of young children to ante up the $6.50 hourly minimum wage for babysitters, was swiftly dumped as soon as the public mocking began.[6]

Worse than the NDP's labour and economic policy in the 1990s was their treatment of individuals who defied them. When ministry of Finance official Brenda Eaton protested the "fiscal optimism" pumped into the 1996 budget by Elizabeth Cull just prior to an election, her warnings were ignored. After the vote, Eaton was transferred out of Finance. A biologist in the ministry of Environment was suspended for two weeks after he wrote a report critical of the government's position on grizzly bear hunts. Witch-hunts were conducted in the bureaucracy to find the source of embarrassing leaks to the media, and a private detective was once hired to root out the same.[7] Retired union members who returned to work for non-union firms found their pensions were suspended, and even the party faithful were not immune from sacrifice when necessary: former NDP president John Laxton was fired from BC Hydro as a victim to Glen Clark's re-election plans.

If individuals received little respect from the NDP, neither did their rights. An election gag law to restrict free speech by citizens' groups and opinion polls by the media was passed in 1995. That same year, pro-life demonstrators faced restrictions on their speech and association in a manner unthinkable if applied to native, environmentalist, or labour protestors. Human rights laws were written to make dissent from government orthodoxy an offence.

If new laws could not silence critics (as they were often thrown out by the courts) legal intimidation might; touchy government politicians and political aides regularly targeted the press with taxpayer-financed lawsuits. In the 1990s, all of the province's major media outlets and columnists faced either a lawsuit or the threat of one.

Even the rule of law was sacrificed to the NDP's political agenda. In 1992, Prince George-based Carrier Lumber faced a government that willingly ripped up its legal contract to log timber. Seven years later, a judge shredded the ministry of Forests for deliberately withholding evidence, concealing the truth, and fabricating a cover story. And the judge put NDP cabinet minister Dan Miller at the centre of the illegal decision to revoke

Carrier's licence.

A weakened partner

If individuals and business suffered in British Columbia in the 1990s, so too did BC's position within confederation. As one of the three "have" provinces along with Ontario and Alberta, the province once had a stronger national punch. In the constitutional debates of the early 1980s, British Columbia chaired and led the provinces in their tête-à-tête with Pierre Trudeau. By the late 1990s, BC's rank fell dramatically. Even in BC proper, muscle-flexing vis-à-vis Ottawa and the United States (which once rallied British Columbians to the provincial government's side) was ignored. After an initial burst of such rhetoric in 1996 over American fishing in Canadian waters, then Premier Glen Clark overplayed his hand and his antics damaged provincial interests; by 1999, Ottawa could and did deliberately snub the premier. In salmon preservation talks with the United States that year, the province was barred from sensitive discussions given that Clark embarrassed federal negotiators in previous sessions.

When, also in 1999, the federal government declined BC's request for money for an expanded Vancouver convention centre, Ottawa hinted that given the NDP's fiscal bungling, sending money to BC was akin to burning it. The project was shelved and BC wrote off $71 million in already incurred costs. Blustering from the provincial government over possible U.S. weapons testing (at Vancouver Island's Nanoose Bay testing range) was seen for what it was: crude anti-American rhetoric from a desperate government that ignored its own constitutional limits. (Defence policy is within the federal government's jurisdiction.) The federal government, which needed to renew the Nanoose lease with British Columbia, instead expropriated the property after provincial intransigence led to stalled negotiations. As a result, BC sacrificed at least $100 million in federal lease payments.

Despite the fact that a significant portion of British Columbia's electorate did not vote for federal Liberals, the NDP's anti-Ottawa, anti-American rhetoric fell flat and most British Columbians yawned over Ottawa's snubs. After all, many *British Columbians* were embarrassed by Glen Clark and his caucus, angry, and wanted them out. Who could blame Liberals in Ottawa, even ones perceived as arrogant central Canadians, for feeling the same way?

Hypocrisy

And then there was the hypocrisy. In early 1992, Speaker-designate NDP MLA Joan Sawicki fired Virginia Jessop from her clerical job because her husband had been press secretary to Bill Vander Zalm and Bill Bennett. Ian

Jessop was a political hire, Mrs. Jessop was not, and the NDP, which professed a dedication to women's rights, fired a woman because of her husband's political past.[8]

While the NDP railed against American tax levels and health care, Washington D.C.-based adviser Karl Struble helped New Democrats in the 1991 election campaign and throughout their first term: the tally exceeded 900 phone calls and 100 faxes over a three-year period. Some calls lasted as long as ten hours. The American advice, apparently valuable for the NDP, was costly for taxpayers at $500 a day.[9]

There was the personal hypocrisy: cabinet minister Moe Sihota enrolled his children in a private school all the while touting the province's public school system as one of the world's finest.[10] He also used non-union labour to build himself a new home.

The double standard was especially evident when it came to ministerial resignations. The NDP were sharp opposition critics – perhaps the best in the country. And it had results; whenever a whiff of a Socred ethical lapse was detected, the NDP quickly demanded a sacrifice: Jack Kempf, Cliff Michael, Bill Reid, Bud Smith and Peter Dueck all resigned from cabinet when they were accused of misconduct and Stan Hagen was briefly relieved of his duties.

In contrast, in the first few years of the NDP government, Robin Blencoe, David Zirnhelt, and Colin Gablemann were all under investigation for either conflict of interest and/or alleged perjury. All stayed in cabinet.[ii] Only Dan Miller was removed temporarily for three months but only after he was found guilty of conflict of interest.[11]

Later in the decade, resignations did occur but never as quickly as New Democrats called for when they were in opposition. Chronic bad-boy Moe Sihota resigned several times only to be welcomed back into cabinet after a brief time-out. In the most damning case, Sihota was found guilty of professional misconduct and stripped of his right to practise law for 18 months; this, after he neglected to tell clients to seek independent legal advice over an investment in his father's company.[12] Sihota resigned, but only *after*, not during, the Law Society's investigation. The Moe Sihota of the Eighties would have railed against any Socred minister who remained in cabinet under such a cloud. His suspension lasted all of four months.[13] Sihota was again suspended later in the decade after he lobbied the Motor Carrier Commission on a friend's behalf, a no-no for a cabinet minister. That time, he was out of cabinet for 22 months.[14]

In perhaps the prime example of NDP hypocrisy on the ethics issue, the

---

ii. Later, in the mid-1990s, Robin Blencoe was fired from cabinet over alleged sexual harassment.

July 1999 judicial comments against Dan Miller in the Carrier case not only did not lead to a resignation, but Miller was chosen by his colleagues as interim premier one month later. There was never a danger that the NDP would imitate Japanese politicians in the art of contrition.

By 2000, with poll numbers below Brian Mulroney and Bill Vander Zalm in *their* last political days, few would describe the BC NDP as a moderate social democratic government a la Roy Romanow. Comparisons were more often made to Bob Rae's four-year flameout in Ontario and BC's early 1970s NDP government of Dave Barrett: re-election was impossible. The only question left to answer was how badly the party would fare at election time. And as a final indictment of just how badly the province had been run, the size of Alberta's economy surpassed BC's in the year 2000 – and Alberta had one million fewer people than British Columbia.[15]

Pride...

But hypocrisy and overzealous political aides do not explain the disaster of the 1990s. More dangerous flaws, desires, and assumptions were at play beneath the surface. A cursory look at comments from NDP MLAs in the early 1990s points to the pride, the unshakeable belief that government MLAs just knew what needed to be done. There was certainly a belief that the new MLAs were superior to those who came before. In 1993, interior MLA Harry Lali argued that an NDP government listened to the people "unlike the dictatorship of the Vander Zalm era."[16] Glen Clark also thought the former government was morally inferior in comparison to the new tenants in the Legislature. "Clearly, the previous administration, combined with the Mulroney administration, has done more to discredit politicians, political life, and those who serve in this very difficult environment than anybody else that's gone before."[17]

Their unshakable faith in their knowledge and solutions usually involved money, and this added to the disaster that became British Columbia in the Nineties. And for this they have company. Intellectuals, and there were some on the government benches, never err so often as when they think that smart people combined with enough public money can solve any private problem.

That belief is folly. And it was odd when it came from those on the Left who often argued that money is not everything in life. The assertion is correct. Money is certainly not the sum total of life; it is but a tool and nothing more. Some on the right err when they argue the free market can solve most everything, though that is more a characterization than an actual claim, based more often on a misunderstanding of what is asserted by free market proponents.[iii] But those on the Left argue hypocritically when they pronounce that money cannot solve every problem, only to then use the levers of state to extract as much wealth as possible from citizens. Thus, in a vain and contradictory effort, the Left attempts to demonstrate that when governments spend money, that money *can* solve every problem.

... and prejudice

Another part of the NDP's menace to themselves and by extension to those that they ruled, was their prejudice. Not the racial kind, but prejudice in the sense of an over-reliance on one's own history, ideas, and beliefs to the practical exclusion of all others. And their bias is an almost paranoid fear of buying and selling with minimal government interference, an activity constant since the beginning of time and one now simply called the free market. The NDP's prejudice includes a fear of people, in that citizens free to make their own decisions may not create what the NDP envisions as a "good" and "fair" society.

New Democrats had a history and were unwilling to let go of it. Just as the city of Victoria could be considered more English than England, as is often the case with immigrant communities, the NDP was heavily influenced in its early CCF days from the radical union wing of the British Labour party.

Unlike Labour, who gradually expunged the more radical elements and direct union ties from the party over the course of the Thatcher years, British Columbia's New Democrats learned no similar lessons during their time in the electoral wilderness. And as behind the times, over-taxed, and reliant on inefficient Crown corporations as Saskatchewan was, even that NDP government was more pragmatic than the one in BC.

BC's social democrats should have learned the lesson of accommodation before any other New Democrat government in the country. After all, they were in the wilderness for sixteen years after their last shellacking by voters. Then again, given that the NDP was on the political upswing in the late 1980s against a declining and scandal-ridden Social Credit government, it appears their lust for power blinded them to developments around the world.

---

iii. The argument is that free markets allow people to use their creativity and ingenuity to solve problems, while preserving diverse choices - nothing less and nothing more. Those who read into that process a claim that it will "solve" a particular problem, never mind all societal ills, miss the central point: Markets allow more individual choice than in more restricted economies, and in that choice-based environment, ingenuity and creativity (and wealth) flourish and may solve *some* problems. The free market expands choices in goods, services, jobs, and thus ultimately in lifestyles. What people *do* with such choices is up to them.

The NDP entered office in 1991 rhetorically committed to moderation and some acceptance of the free market. But apparently at heart, and as they demonstrated since, they were yet firm in the belief that government could direct as much of the economy as possible.

New Democrat MLAs, their policy advisers, and whoever they drew meagre intellectual nourishment from these past years, thought the nod to the free market was all so much talk. Sure, rhetorically acknowledge that it "has a role," but organize government and policy in such a way that revealed if anything, that life on the Left would continue as normal. Any claim to accept the market's role was betrayed by the policy decisions that pointed away from markets, not to them.

On a practical level, that belief meant it was inevitable the government would attempt to jumpstart (or restart) a shipbuilding industry from scratch. A more moderate government, one that wanted public transportation but not direct involvement on every matter, would obtain the best ships at the best price, period. But a party that believed it could ignite a major industry set sail on a collision course with three, untested, unproven, and disastrous fast ferries. That, combined with the political impulse – to make sure the jobs from such shipbuilding would happen *here* – ensured a debacle.

And it was as true with fast ferries as with Forest Renewal British Columbia (and will be with SkyTrain) and any number of other projects that were more costly, less effective, and less what people wanted but what the NDP knew they needed.

Occasionally, the NDP's prejudice revealed itself in ways that would have been fatal for a politician on the right. In a 1998 speech to Simon Fraser University, NDP cabinet minister Corky Evans argued that the defunct Soviet Union's prime mistake was not its ideas, but how it implemented them:

> *In the Soviet experiment, we can all point to the abuses of power. In the Soviet experiment we can all point to the Gulag and the secret police etc., and say that these acts and institutions of dictatorship were abuses of power. But the antecedent of that abuse was, in large part, the decision in the Soviet Union that organizing around the world and making coalition (sic) was too slow and dangerous and bothersome, so they would build and defend "Socialism in one country" instead.*[18]

> *My thesis here is that the environmental movement has, like a sort of reincarnated Achilles, inherited both the vitality and the weakness of the last great human experiment and, even at the moment of capturing the world's attention, given up on organizing the world in favour of trying to impose and defend sustainability in one cul-*

> *ture, one province, one community, and it won't work this time either, pretty much for the same reasons.... Perhaps there are some things we can do to reverse our losses, but first let me tell you a story to explain why I think "sustainability in one province" won't work, and a broader objective might.*[19]

Ever the optimist, Corky Evans went on to explain the need for more regulation and higher taxes in all the world if command and control economies are to ever succeed.

The comments were remarkable. The Soviet Union spilled more blood than perhaps any other power in history except communist China, and a BC cabinet minister blamed it "in large part" on a strategic mistake (in his opinion) to build socialism in one country.[iv]

His reference to the "last great human experiment," obviously communism given the Soviet Union context of his remarks, was also telling. If a conservative politician ever blamed Nazi Germany's crimes "in large measure" on bad Third Reich strategy, or referred to the twentieth century's other mass murdering ideology as the "last great human experiment," the reaction would be justifiable outrage; the politician would be rightly hounded from office. Nothing of the sort occurred when Corky Evans gave such forgiving, forlorn remarks about a bloody dictatorship of the Left.[v]

The missing link: power

But pride and the particular prejudice of the NDP do not alone explain the 1990s in British Columbia. Power is what gave New Democrats the ability to initiate and carry out their mega-projects, to ram through the Nisga'a deal without a referendum on treaty principles, and to restrict free speech (successfully in some cases, unsuccessfully in others). It was power that allowed them to disregard the rule of law time and again until the courts

---

iv. Besides the kid-glove treatment of the Soviet Union's crimes, Evans was also deficient in history. What were the East bloc alliances and exported advisers to Cuba et al. if not an attempt to make coalition partners around the world?

v. The double-standards in the West as regards the crimes of the Soviet Union versus those in Nazi Germany are legion, and it is no mark of sympathy for either to note that oddity. In another related but little-noted example of the same hypocrisy, Premier Glen Clark hired Geoff Meggs as his communications chief. Meggs belonged to Canada's Communist party until 1989. It does not require much imagination to conceive of what the reaction would be if a former Nazi had been hired as a spokesperson for a conservative politician. A book could be written on the West's double standard on the last century's most destructive ideologies.

reined them in. And it was virtually unchecked power that allowed the NDP to commission three fast ferries and to ignore inside and outside critics, to spend Forest Renewal British Columbia tax dollars without proper accounting, and to thwart the wishes of 80 percent of British Columbians for workable referendum and recall laws.

That power, a result of our parliamentary system that provides few checks on the decisions of majority governments, was always available to past British Columbia governments. But none, at least not modern and recent ones, abused it to the extent that New Democrats did in the 1990s. Like a vial of nitroglycerine, power in concentrated form is perilous. As such, it is only a matter of time until some government, left, right or centre, once again mishandles it to the degree that New Democrats did in the 1990s.

For that reason, institutional change that separates BC's politicians from a portion of their power must take place. Those who believe a change of government will "solve" what ails BC learn nothing from the past. While the NDP committed more than their share of political sin this past decade, the temptation of power should not be so rich to begin with. Cosmetic changes and a switch on Legislature nameplates will temporarily mask, not fix, the underlying weaknesses in British Columbia's system of government. The power available to future governments must, for the sake of British Columbians, be diluted.

But to understand why and how that can be accomplished, one must first understand the pride and prejudice of the past. And as almost everyone expected in the early 1990s, those early prejudices revealed themselves first in the NDP's economic policies.

A B.C. BALANCED BUDGET:
DEBT
TAXES
BC
RAESIDE
Victoria Times Colonist - Dist. By Koko Press Inc. www.raesidecartoon.com

2

Debt & Taxes

"It's not fun to tax the rich; it is only fair."[1]
- The Honourable Corky Evans, NDP Minister of Agriculture

Welcome to the 1990s

In 1991, as perhaps their last act of hara-kiri before they drifted off into obscurity, the Social Credit government introduced two high-income surtaxes which, along with other changes, amounted to a $247-million tax hike.[2]

After the election and before the 1992 budget, the new NDP government hired Peat Marwick to scour the government books and report on any Socred accounting oddities. Peat Marwick's Ron Hikel, the former adviser and deputy minister to Allan Blakeney's Saskatchewan NDP government, reported back that the deficit was larger than expected and that British Columbians were "under-taxed" by $500 million a year.[3]

To rectify such a problem, the New Democrats – who disliked most of what Social Credit did – matched the 1991 tax increase and then some. Giddy with the levers of Finance, Glen Clark hiked the basic rate,[4] raised the surtax,[5] applied the sales tax more widely,[6] raised business taxes,[7] upped the jet fuel tax,[8] hiked education taxes,[9] increased fines and user fees,[10] and – for those who wanted a stiff drink to forget it all – upped government-owned Liquor Distribution Branch prices by 9.5 percent.[11] The higher taxes were over and above 22-percent auto insurance hikes at the government-owned Insurance Corporation of British Columbia, and six-per-cent fare jumps at BC Ferries.[12] As a top-up, the government kept the Coquihalla highway tolls they once railed against in opposition.

That was just 1992.

In 1993, the architect of redistribution upped surtaxes again,[13] eliminated the renter's tax deduction,[14] hiked business taxes,[15] increased the sales tax,[16] expanded the sales tax,[17] hiked the sales tax on automobiles over $34,000 to

10 percent,[18] introduced a property surtax,[19] increased Medicare taxes,[20] and raised taxes on natural gas.[21] For those who wanted a brandy and a cigar to get through that round, well, tobacco taxes and liquor store prices were (again) raised.[22]

Thus, in the space of three years, British Columbians endured tax hikes of $1.8 billion,[23] an annual tax take that expanded as the population grew. Moe Sihota stoutly defended the increases, calling them "tough, but fair."[24] Corky Evans, the quirky MLA from Nelson whose "aw-shucks" routine endeared him to the NDP grassroots and the media, argued that "taxing the rich wasn't fun, just fair."[25] Ujjal Dosanjh argued that "a great budget is for ensuring that the top 8 percent of all income earners in B.C. pay their fair share of taxes for a change."[26]

Lost in the "fairness" claim was any understanding of what effect higher taxes and more regulation might have on the economy, wages, and jobs. But this was the early 1990s; British Columbia experienced net immigration inflows from Hong Kong, Taiwan and Canadian provinces. That helped mask the effect early budget and policy decisions had on the province's economic health. NDP politicians were in an Alfred E. Neuman mood – "what, us worry?"

Also lost in the fairness defence was a 1991 election promise about taxes. Mike Harcourt mentioned only two: one on high-income earners and another on "large profitable corporations." Together, the two new taxes were to cost no more than $250 million. Instead, the first two NDP budgets walloped taxpayers for more than $1.5 billion.[27] This was a tad more than the $500 million Ron Hikel recommended for "under-taxed" British Columbians, to say nothing of the election promise.

The taxes were not exactly welcome. In addition to their punitive effect upon entrepreneurs and anyone with the slightest ambition, there was also the regional insensitivity. Some environmentalists might love the higher 10-percent sales tax on cars and trucks over $34,000, on the grounds that gas-guzzling sport utility vehicles used by urbanites should be discouraged. But the social engineers – who imposed the tax from Victoria – forgot that half the province lived outside the lower mainland, many in areas and jobs where trucks and SUVs came in quite handy, especially on logging roads and during heavy snowfall on interior highways. And those vehicles often carried a hefty price tag without the additional tax hit. Thus, the *Prince George Citizen* later complained that "unlike our Lower Mainland cousins, we generally can't get away with driving a little four-cylinder vehicle all year. We get snow, and lots of it. This tax was obviously designed with Vancouver people in mind, a typical manoeuvre for the provincial government."[28]

It did not take long for the poison pill of higher 1991 and 1992 taxes to take effect. By late 1993, personal income tax revenues for the 1992 budget year were $270 million less than forecast – and this in the midst of a growing economy. Since the 1950s, the only other time the government's personal tax take declined was during the early 1980s recession.[29]

Years later, Glen Clark complained to the leftist *Canadian Forum* magazine that he "never received any letters of support" for giving BC the highest marginal tax rate in North America.[30] This was the new moderate NDP promised during the 1991 election.

Eat the rich: the case for wealth taxation

In truth, the moderation lasted as long as the election campaign. Early in their mandate, the new government reorganized Treasury Board[i] and hired Tom Gunton as deputy minister. Gunton was Glen Clark's thesis adviser at Simon Fraser University and on the far left of the party. He had long argued for higher stumpage fees, more mining taxes and regulation. Gunton also wanted a new business tax that could "collect the income left after deducting all costs of production as well as a normal profit allowance for capital."[31] One observer likened his hiring to letting a fox loose in a henhouse.[32]

Another key left-wing academic adviser to the government was Maureen Maloney. In a 1991 academic article, Maloney wrote that luck and inheritance were the main reasons for the fortunes of Canada's wealthy.[33]

Oddly, while she thought luck or inheritance were the chief reasons for riches, she also argued that there was a WASP conspiracy against everyone else. It was not, Maloney argued, "a mere historical accident that the distribution of wealth and income is also patterned on race and gender grounds."[34] Since conspiracies are, by definition, intentional, this seemed to contradict her first argument that riches were the result of luck.

In any case, Maloney thought it unfair that wealth could be built up over generations; the government needed to intervene (beyond what it already did) to redistribute money to those whose ancestors had not been so prudent or fortunate. She suggested "three viable options," including a new death tax (levied directly upon the deceased's estate itself), an inheritance tax (where government could tax the inheritance distributed to children), or an annual wealth tax.[35]

The academic-turned-budget-adviser argued that any of the three new taxes would be a good start: "Any type of wealth tax will aid progressivity and, to a lesser extent, impede excessive accumulations of wealth,"[36] she wrote. But forced to choose, she preferred the annual wealth tax. After all, it would redistribute money more often (a positive in her mind), and it taxed

---

[i] Treasury Board is the government's top committee on taxation and spending priorities and is usually composed of senior cabinet ministers.

"home ownership and expensive consumer durables which otherwise eludes the tax system."[37]

For those who already owned homes and paid hefty property taxes, Maloney's suggestion that home ownership somehow helped one elude the tax system might come as a surprise. But then, academics did have a reputation for detached, ivory tower thinking. Maloney suggested a rate of two to three percent, levied annually, and calculated on total net worth. That meant a 60-year-old teacher with a paid-off home, money stashed in RRSPs, and other investments that (after a lifetime of work) together equalled, say, half a million dollars, would face an annual wealth tax; $10,000 every year at a rate of two percent, or $15,000 at three percent.

The new property surtax

While Maloney's ideas were unpalatable to any British Columbian save those who advised the Finance Minister, a watered-down version of one idea did crawl into the 1993 budget.

The "school property tax surtax" as it was called, hit homeowners with an extra tax on properties worth half a million dollars or more.[ii] A $700,000 home would pay another $1,000 in property tax every year; the owner of a million-dollar home would fork over another $3,500.

Presumably, Finance Minister Glen Clark, who grew up in east Vancouver, thought most people could care less if west Vancouverites paid higher property taxes. What he overlooked was that some property owners, now elderly, bought their (now) $600,000 homes in the 1950s or 1960s, back when Vancouver was still considered a mid-sized, resource-dependent city, one not much more expensive than Edmonton. Since property values shot up since the 1970s, some homeowners became asset rich while they remained cash poor.

Even some New Democrats thought the 1993 budget overdid it on the class warfare, including the former mayor of Vancouver and now Premier, Mike Harcourt. The NDP was elected on a 1991 platform of moderation, not on one of new property taxes on retired school principals who bought their homes in the 1950s and got lucky. TV, talk-radio, letters to the editor, front-page stories, and columnists all chronicled the growing opposition (which included street protests) to the new property/wealth tax. Within a month, and hours before a rally in downtown Vancouver drew several thousand protestors, Clark dropped the $37 million tax.[38]

[ii] The amount over $500,000 was subject to a half-percent tax (in addition to regular property taxes,) while another percent and a half was levied on any value that exceeded $900,000.

The NDP and Fiscal Conservatism

Throughout their time in office, and despite increased taxes, doubled debt, new Crown corporations, and mega-projects without business plans, NDP premiers and ministers, especially finance ministers, claimed to be fiscally conservative.

"If the money's not there, we won't spend it."
Mike Harcourt: Premier 1991-1996
From a 1991 television election campaign ad

"The fact is that we're a fiscally conservative government."[1]
Tom Perry: Minister of Advanced Education 1991-1995

"I'm a fiscal conservative."[2]
Glen Clark: Premier 1996-1999, and Finance Minister 1992 -1993

"I'm actually fairly fiscally conservative."[3]
Andrew Petter: Finance Minister 1996-1998

"I tend to be a fiscal conservative."[4]
Gordon Wilson: Finance Minister 1999

"Personally, I'm a fiscal conservative."[5]
Paul Ramsey: Finance Minister 1999 – 2001

"The choice comes down to fiscally conservative New Democrats..."[6]
Ujjal Dosanjh: Premier 2000-2001

---

[1] *Hansard,* 1 June 1992.
[2] *BC Report,* 22 January 1996.
[3] *Vancouver Province,* 18 June 1996.
[4] *Vancouver Province,* 27 July 1999.
[5] *Vancouver Province,* 22 December 1999.
[6] *Vancouver Sun*, 7 August 2000.

Glen Clark was shifted out of Finance later that year, but Maloney's tax views lingered on in government. In 1997, Attorney General Ujjal Dosanjh hiked probate fees (the tax levied by courts to process a will) by 133 percent. The family of the deceased now faced a court tax of $1,400 – up from $600.[39] The deputy attorney general at the time was none other than Maureen Maloney; apparently there was more than one way to introduce taxes on wealth and death. Dosanjh denied Maloney made the decision and instead took responsibility. "The buck stops here," he said.[40]

Dosanjh also denied the probate fees were a tax. That excuse lasted until 1999 when the Supreme Court of Canada struck down excessive Ontario probate fees because they had no relation to the cost of the service. The court said, in effect, that if it walked and quacked like a tax, it was a tax and politicians must vote on it. Ujjal Dosanjh, with Maloney still at his side, retroactively legalized the 1997 jump in probate fees through an act of the Legislature.

U-turn?

The NDP reversed course later in the decade, slightly, and some token tax cuts were introduced. They could hardly do otherwise given competition from other provinces and the public mood, but even then one had to look closely at the actual tax cuts offered and interpret the spin.[iii]

If the government hit a taxpayer wall in 1993, they found a way around it: by stealth. Revenues were extracted in ever-growing amounts from Crown corporations and user fees. Thus, in a year where a Crown might be exceptionally profitable and able to cut rates, individuals and companies still paid higher than necessary bills simply because the government wanted more cash.[41] In 2000, the government received $1 billion more from Crown corporations and user fees than it did in 1991.[42]

By 1999, real per capita after-tax income was under $16,000, down from $17,753 in 1992.[43] By October 2000, the effects of nine years worth of NDP policy showed up in another way: Alberta – with a million fewer people –

[iii] For example, in the March 2000 budget, taxes dropped by $227 million. But at least $175 million would have occurred anyway because of decisions made in Ottawa about tax rates. BC "de-linked" its taxes from Ottawa precisely because the federal government had announced multi-year tax cuts, which would automatically reduce provincial taxes – the exact opposite of what occurred for two decades when provincial taxes also rose because of Ottawa. As a bonus – for the government – they could take credit for tax cuts that would have occurred anyway. So in reality in 2000, only $52 million could really be claimed as a "made in BC" tax cut.

had a larger economy than British Columbia.[44] And the gap threatened to grow: Alberta planned to cut business taxes in half over four years and already low personal taxes by 20 percent.

Debt follies

Probably nothing is so deadly boring as debt and as irritating to pay for either personally or collectively. But running up debt can be quite fun, especially for politicians. Milton Friedman once argued that deficits allow our representatives to vote for spending without having to vote for taxes to pay for it, and that creates irresponsibility.

As it applied to the BC government, that accusation was half-true. Early on, they tried to tax their way into balanced budgets but backed off any more visible tax increases after the 1993 property tax revolt. After that, the government followed Friedman's accusation to the letter. And they paved the way for that increase in debt when (in 1992) they scrapped the Socreds' Taxpayer Protection Act, a weak law but one that set targets for balanced government books. The legislation was the first of its kind in the country and the NDP voted for it while in opposition. Once in office, the Taxpayer Protection Act was dumped.

But then, New Democrats never paid much attention to Friedman's views anyway – except at election-time. In 1991, the NDP were the deficit hawks and the Social Credit government the drunken fiscal sailors. In his critique of their last budget, Glen Clark said the Socreds "pretend the debt is associated with other people: the hospital financing authority, the education financing authority, or the B.C. Transit authority. The reason that's unfair and doesn't tell the truth … is that every year the government has to pay interest on that debt."[45] In a famous television election ad in 1991, Mike Harcourt dropped pennies into a piggy bank and promised that if the money wasn't there "we won't spend it."

In his 1993 budget speech, Glen Clark argued unchecked deficit spending was imprudent. "Allowing the deficit to rise unchecked during the upturn in the business cycle is not sound economic policy. More and more of British Columbians' tax dollars would go to banks to pay interest on debt instead of providing services to people."[46]

And as late as 1994, Mike Harcourt still argued that chronic deficits were indefensible. In a Legislature debate, Social Credit MLA Cliff Serwa ripped into the NDP about more red ink; in return, Harcourt launched a blistering attack on the 1991 Socred deficit that the NDP had inherited. He compared the previous Socred rulers to the Ontario Liberal government, which (before their ouster by voters) was well known for budget-busting spending and debt.

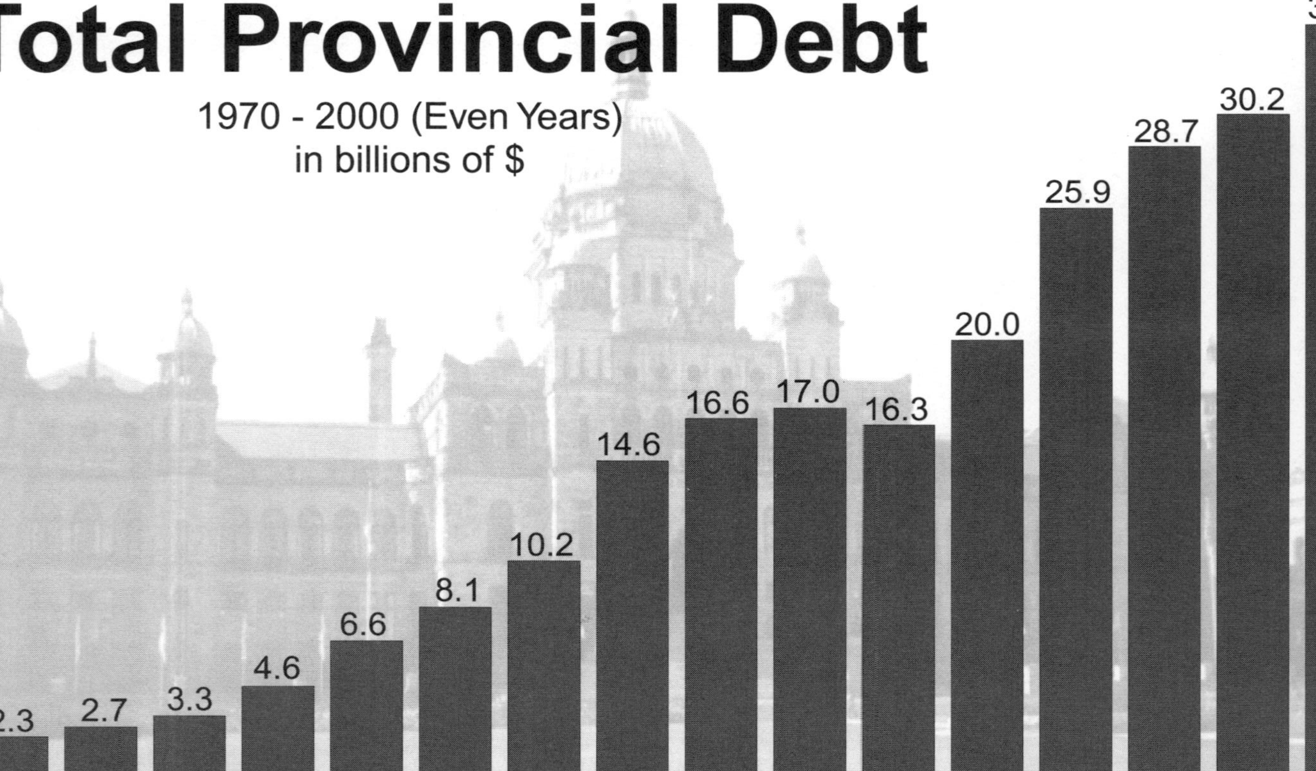

Total Provincial Debt
1970 - 2000 (Even Years)
in billions of $
2.3
2.7
3.3
4.6
6.6
8.1
10.2
14.6
16.6
17.0
16.3
20.0
25.9
28.7
30.2
34.2
1970
1972
1974
1976
1978
1980
1982
1984
1986
1988
1990
1992
1994
1996
1998
2000

> *It was a question of whether you were as bad as or worse than the David Peterson Liberals. I want to see that debate. I want to see the debate here in this Legislature as to which was the most spendthrift government in this country in the 1980s, the Ontario Liberals or the BC Socreds. That would make a very interesting debate — to see which was the worst in terms of overspending and living in a fool's paradise.*[47]

But about the same time as Harcourt blasted the fool's paradise of overspending, the government began to change their tune on the deficit. It moved from a statement of the obvious – more debt equals more interest equals fewer policy choices – to a defence that BC's growing debt was small relative to other provinces. Thus at budget time in 1994, Clark's replacement as finance minister, Elizabeth Cull, bragged the province's debt was "the lowest, in relation to the size of our economy, of any province."[48] That was a half-truth, since she meant the much smaller direct debt, not the province's overall debt. And the province's total red ink tally was not lower than Alberta's. Not when a straight comparison was made, or when that province's $10-billion nest egg (the Heritage Trust Fund) was put against its debt.

Achilles heel

In early 1995, the credibility gap widened with the leak of a Treasury Board memo that described the province's debt load as the "Achilles Heel of the government's fiscal record."[49] The memo, written by Chris Trumpy, a respected civil servant within Finance, concluded that ten years of surplus budgets wouldn't be enough to turn it around (in reference to new NDP debt). The leak occurred hours before Premier Mike Harcourt held a televised town hall meeting in Vancouver. That night, the audience and telephone callers ripped into the Premier and his government over the red ink.

The government's credibility was also shredded due to its massive spending binge. Compared to its pre-election promises, actual expenditures in the first three NDP years were higher by $500 million, $900 million, and $900 million respectively – a $2.3-billion overrun compared to pre-election promises.[50] Despite the public relations disaster, Elizabeth Cull crowed that "any other government in Canada would be delighted to have such a low debt load."[51]

The spin continued into 1996, when yet another new finance minister, Andrew Petter, argued the deficit was the fault of the Social Credit government. In his budget speech – five and a half years after the NDP took over from the Socreds – Petter argued that the NDP inherited a $2.5-billion deficit from the previous government in 1991.[52] That much was true, but Ralph

Klein inherited deficits of a similar size from his predecessor Don Getty in 1992. After the 1993 election, the Klein government went to work, cut the size of government, and by 1995 produced a surplus.

The NDP, who thought every civil service job and government program was sacred, never embarked on a similar budget-cutting exercise, at least nothing that could be described as anything more than cosmetic. Instead, they jacked taxes up, borrowed more money, and then spent all of it and more. The contrast was clear: Alberta's Conservatives did more with less and the BC NDP did less with more, and yet blamed the Socreds five years after voters tossed them from office.

Besides the latent blame-it-on-the-Socreds tack, the government found other ways to deal with real and potential debt: they dumped it elsewhere. The best example was the transfer of road and transit spending to greater Vancouver in 1998. That shift allowed the province to make the region responsible for roads and transit in the Vancouver area, a $2-billion to $3-billion transfer of spending over a decade,[53] never mind new spending desired by the new transit authority.

The debt excuses continued with each successive finance minister: in 1998, Joy MacPhail claimed BC's per capita debt was the lowest in the country.[54] Wrong. British Columbians owed over $7,500 per person in total debt in 1998, compared to $5,900 per Albertan. And if Alberta's Heritage Trust Fund were ever cashed in, each Albertan would owe only $2,300.[55]

A "fool's paradise" revisited

By 1998, in a revealing article in the NDP party newspaper, *The Democrat*, Mike Harcourt argued deficit hawks were wrong, that they never paid attention to what debt "bought" in the way of infrastructure.[56] Apparently then, his 1991 promise was all show, as were his later 1994 comments. If that was the case, Harcourt's latent defence of borrowed money brought to two the number of elections in which a central NDP campaign plank – balanced budgets – was discarded once the election was over.

More to the point, Harcourt's flip-flop did not change the math: a politician could charge the public up front with the necessary taxes to pay for a government's spending. Alternately, they could give it to them for "free," only to have voters and their children pay for it later, with interest. The NDP taxed the young to buy the votes of their elders, a sort of taxation without representation. It was unethical vote buying, but hardly new in Canadian politics.

By 1999 Joy MacPhail dropped all reference to debt in her budget speech, and instead argued that "deficits mean little to patients on waiting lists."[57] MacPhail's clever sound bite was designed to justify drowning fiscal prudence in the same waters soon to be traversed by over-budget ferries. It was also mathematical nonsense: in 1999, $750 million less was available to healthcare and education, since that was how much extra interest the province paid out annually on debt compared to 1992. The NDP, which once argued debt arithmetic was simple, now claimed the math didn't matter.

Post-script: the backhanded Bennett compliment

Throughout the 1990s, NDP MLAs regularly claimed that BC was not as indebted as some other provinces. That was true, but the attempt to take credit for a relatively low debt was the equivalent of grand theft; the credit was not theirs to take.

When BC was walloped by the early 1980s recession, then Social Credit Premier Bill Bennett enacted a restraint program that slowed government spending. At the time, New Democrats and their labour allies went berserk; a province-wide strike was called, and the anti-restraint coalition went so far as to appropriate the Solidarity moniker - the name of the early 1980s anti-Communist resistance movement in Poland. The restraint program became the central issue in a hard-fought 1983 election which Bennett went on to (narrowly) win.

BC slowly crawled out of stagnation and by the mid-1980s, provincial finances improved. The province's total debt hit a peak of $17.1 billion in early 1987 and then declined to $16.2 billion by 1990. Bennett's spending restraints set the stage for that debt reduction, though it flowered in the reign of his post-1986 successor, Bill Vander Zalm. Though the debt did shrink, Vander Zalm's government began to spend more freely and by early 1991, the debt climbed back past the previous high-water mark and hit $17.2 billion. By the NDP's first spring budget in 1992, the debt was $20 billion, most of it arguably the fault of the Socreds.[58]

Although Social Credit departed from the more fiscally cautious course Bennett set in the early 1980s, the budget was up to New Democrats after 1992. By 2000, annual interest on BC's debt was over $2.55 billion[59] up from $1.75 billion in 1992.[60] The total debt rose to $34.2 billion and BC's debt per person hit $8,300, up from just under $3,000 in 1991.

When the NDP claimed BC's debt was smaller than some other provinces, they stated a factual truth. But the credit was hardly theirs. Instead, they should have sent Bill Bennett a late thank-you note for his 1983 restraint program.

RAESIDE
Victoria Times Colonist - Dist. by Koko Press Inc.
www.raesidecartoon.com
NDP TIES TO ORGANISED LABOUR
...JUST PRETEND HE ISN'T THERE.
B.C. BUSINESS

3

Labour of Love

"It was something unions felt they were entitled to."
- Then Labour Minister John Cashore, on where proposed 1997 changes to the labour code originated.[1]

The love affair between organized labour in British Columbia and the political Left is a long and not very complicated one. From Scottish immigrant miners and imported labour politics to the early days of the Co-operative Commonwealth Federation, on through to the BC Federation of Labour and New Democrats, rare is the lover's quarrel that did not end in mutual admiration, labour code changes, and pay increases all around.

Occasionally, such as during the self-immolation of BC's first NDP government, labour and the NDP could hold a grudge. But in the 1990s, governments and unions staged the occasional pillow fight for the cameras before elections; during and after a campaign for votes they acted like long-lost friends.

Some of this was inevitable; BC's main left-wing party and unions were tied at the hip. In the 1991 provincial election, 71 percent of union households voted for New Democrats. In addition, the Provincial Council of the party, which served as its unofficial advisory board and representative of the party's grassroots, was heavily labour-dominated. A leaked 1996 list of the Council showed, not surprisingly, that most members were union representatives.[2]

The importance of labour to the BC NDP easily exceeded that of unions to Britain's Labour Party or to the Saskatchewan NDP. In Britain, chronic defeat squeezed the more radical labour influence out of the Labour party, most dramatically under Neil Kinnock. And in power, Tony Blair has mostly ignored any radical ideas from that wing of the party. Margaret Thatcher's corrective medicine was tough, necessary, and *worked*, so there was no need to pander to the far left and once again make England the sick man of Europe. In Saskatchewan, Roy Romanow believed in big government, but owed few favours to organized labour itself. Romanow understood that helping union members and helping union bosses was not always one and the same. In comparison to BC, Saskatchewan unions were regarded as just one more interest group in the public square.

But as much as labour had a tight grip on the BC NDP this past decade, a province without some union influence is equally undesirable. Unions are useful allies in the fight against concentrated power, both in the workplace and in politics; the question, as in most things in life, is one of balance.

Two for the price of one

In British Columbia, moderation from labour was doubtful right from the start. Less than a month after the 1991 election, then British Columbia Federation of Labour president Ken Georgetti made it known he wanted to be an "equal partner" with the new Premier Mike Harcourt.[3]

That demand might be bold elsewhere in Canada, but not in British Columbia. The BC Fed boss, a former Trail steelworker, led a labour coalition that represented 275,000 union members, just over half the unionized employees in the province in 1991. And the statement was less a request than a demand from Georgetti, later referred to as the nineteenth member of the NDP cabinet (when it numbered eighteen). It also didn't hurt that the BC Fed president had a romantic liaison with Joy MacPhail, one of the senior cabinet ministers in both the Harcourt and Clark governments.

The ear of government

But if labour had any doubts about their place in the NDP's orbit, Mike Harcourt quickly dispelled them. In an address to a BC Federation of Labour convention shortly after the 1991 election, the new premier assured them that as long as he and Labour Minister Moe Sihota were around, "you'll always have a friendly ear in government."[4]

As it was, labour hardly needed a hearing given they were so well represented *within* the new regime: The more powerful ministers had strong union ties. To name a few, Glen Clark once organized for the Ironworker's union, Colin Gablemann was a former director for the BC Federation of Labour, and Dan Miller a one-time union officer at his pulp mill in Prince Rupert.

What was true of links with private sector labour was even more obvious when it came to the public service. In Mike Harcourt's first cabinet, eighteen of nineteen cabinet ministers were either on the public payroll in some capacity in the past, or had spouses then employed by government or a taxpayer-funded agency.[5] Harcourt's first cabinet was probably the most unrepresentative of the province's citizens in BC's history; the ship of state listed heavily to organized labour, and even further to the left.

Forget the bone - have the sirloin. The NDP and the public sector

Initially New Democrats preached moderation when it came to the public sector, especially due to the enormous Socred deficit the new government inherited. But that talk was quickly undone by the government's actions. The first sign was the death of the Compensation Fairness Act.[6] That Social Credit law allowed the government to roll back public-sector wage increases considered excessive. After that, it was open season on the taxpayer wallet. Negotiators in talks with the BC Government Employees Union in mid-1992 tried to hold annual increases to two percent but that idea hit the brick wall of Ken Georgetti. "Two percent," declared the BC Fed boss, "was not in the area of settlement. Whoever is in charge of this bargaining... should start to pay a little more attention."[7] Someone did. A month later, the government tripled its offer to six percent and the union settled.

After that, the floodgates opened. Within the first year, the new government gave in to support staff demands at the BC Institute of Technology, then rolled over for striking University of British Columbia employees. BC teachers were awarded a seven-percent pay raise.[8] The Hospital Employees' Union, who gave the NDP $34,180 in 1990,[9] garnered a fifteen-percent wage hike over three years.

The bonbons to the public sector did not stop there. British Columbia Government Employees Union president John Shields exulted that more than 100 contract provisions were renegotiated in the union's favour.[10] In another sop to the BCGEU and against small business, the government halted new licences for private beer and wine stores, natural competitors for union-staffed and government-run liquor stores.[11]

None of this was a coincidence, especially not the success of the provincial government's largest union. In 1992, then Principal Secretary to Premier Mike Harcourt, Linda Baker, herself a former organizer with the BCGEU, personally intervened in government-BCGEU negotiations to enrich its contract.[i] "There is not a shred of neutrality there," commented one-time Harcourt speechwriter Marcus Davies in a later interview.[12]

During the first year of the Harcourt government, public sector wage increases averaged 5.4 percent compared with 1.7 percent in the private

---

i. Baker would later go on to head the Public Sector Employees Council, a new bargaining unit representing government.

sector.[13] The pay hikes might have been justified had inflation run at late 1970s levels, or if the previous government kept a tight reign on expenditures. But as new Finance Minister Glen Clark pointed out in his maiden budget speech, the Socreds hiked spending by an average of twelve percent annually in the previous three years. This, Clark said, was "far in excess of revenue, inflation, or growth."[14]

The 1992 scenarios were repeated in 1993 when other healthcare workers secured three-year deals ranging from ten percent to 13.7 percent while the workweek was cut by an hour and a half. The Opposition pegged the deal at half a billion dollars over three years.[15] Despite the new wealth, it was apparently not helping the health of public sector workers. According to the government negotiator in 1994, long-term disability rates ran 250 percent higher than the industry average. That cost taxpayers an extra $50 million every year.[16]

Everybody into the pool

Other public sector unions joined in the free-for-all during the NDP's first term. In November 1992 and without warning, ferry workers staged a wildcat strike and stranded motorists. While that did not endear ferry unions to the public – one trucker blocked the employee parking lot at the Tsawwassen ferry terminal and told striking workers they could leave just as soon as he did – the illegal strike had the desired effect. Ferry workers gained increases of close to seven percent between 1992 and 1995.

While the pay hikes were reasonable, the same could not be said of all wage scales, even when extra certification for on-ship duties was accounted for. By November 1995, a snack-bar cashier made $20.17 per hour, almost $37,000 a year. Ticket agents, *on shore,* also garnered $37,000.[17] That was on par with nurses who had two to four years worth of university. Public sector monopolies were on a roll.

The first two years of the NDP government were prosperous for public unions; the main government union, the BCGEU, saw its membership rise by over nine percent.[18] While private sector wages stalled or declined in the early nineties, the average BCGEU member took home an extra $4,476 in 1994 compared to 1991, not including benefits.[19] Over those three years, wages and benefits for government workers jumped by 26 percent.[20]

Bill Clinton's adviser, James Carville, once joked that if reincarnated, he wanted to return as the bond market, referring to the money market's power to influence governments. In BC, public sector unions would be the reincarnated body of choice: they were quite adept at carving up the government who, in theory, was supposed to look out for the general welfare of taxpayers on occasion. The reality was quite different.

The WWF in Victoria

By the mid-1990s, relations between the public service and the NDP soured, at least publicly. This, despite the fact that the government implemented measures from a 1993 report that recommended re-hiring many contract employees – an action that substantially boosted membership in government unions, unions that - not coincidentally - contributed massive amounts of money to the NDP.[21] The move might have been publicly defensible if the government's budget for contracting services declined. Instead, it remained at $500 million a year.[22] Taxpayers paid for additional government employees *and* funded as much contract work as ever – a case of paying for government cake and then, well, paying for it again.

Fake wrestling and meat cleavers

The occasional stage-managed spat between NDP politicians and the public sector took place with all the suspense of a World Wrestling Federation match, but both parties played their respective roles with dramatic flourish. During an NDP convention in 1995, an anti-Harcourt leaflet proclaimed that "Bill Vander Zalm makes appearance at BC NDP Convention 1995!" The author was apparently upset with proposals to hold public sector wage increases to between one and six percent that year.[23]

The alleged rift between the NDP and labour was more unbelievable nearer to the election. In early 1996, on the first day of his campaign for the party leader, Clark announced he was a "fiscal conservative."[24] To prove it, he held the sword of Damocles over the entire public service: "There's no question we have to cut the size of government. If necessary, we may have to eliminate ministries. We may have to literally take a meat cleaver to management layers in the bureaucracy."[25]

This was Glen Clark in his finest, brashest hour: if Clark had remotely resembled a fiscal conservative, the party would have ripped him to shreds in the campaign gauntlet for leader. His ascension despite such a comment was a measure of how well labour knew its candidate: his "fiscal conservative" comments were never taken seriously by the rank and file; it was pre-election propaganda for the general public.

As for its role in the run-up to the 1996 election, public sector unions regularly held rallies in Vancouver and Victoria and professed shock, *shock*, at Glen Clark's supposed radical turn to the right. After all, didn't taxpayers owe lifetime employment to public servants? Public sector unions pouted and staged demonstrations for the cameras, all the better to let the public know the NDP turned into Klein/Harris slashers. (Never mind that Harris never actually cut overall spending and that Klein's restraint program had ended; the facts were inconvenient.) Then, behind the scenes, wage increases were granted, the threatened cuts never happened, and life continued as normal.

Glen's dull knife

"Exhibit A" on this one was the 1996 promise by Glen Clark to cut civil service jobs. That promise came in response to the "discovery" by the NDP after the 1996 election that the provincial budget was not balanced. This was somewhat different than the NDP's *pre*-election claim. The public's discovery of more red ink left Clark with another conundrum: an angry public that believed the NDP deliberately lied about the budget.

Glen Clark was in a bind; he owed the Premier's chair to organized labour. BC Fed chief Ken Georgetti made Mike Harcourt walk the resignation plank in November 1995 which set the stage for Clark's ascension. In addition, unions played the key role in his leadership campaign in which 64 union locals donated $1,500 apiece.[26]

Glen Clark's entire campaign team looked like a meeting of the union brotherhood. His campaign manager was the former president of the BC Teacher's Federation. The chairman was a former official with the BC Government Employees Union, and media relations were handled by communications staff from the BC Federation of Labour and the Hospital Employees Union.[27] As one-time NDP cabinet minister Robin Blencoe pointed out, Clark was "owned politically, lock, stock and barrel by the high echelons of organized labour."[28]

In particular, Clark and the party owed favours to the public sector. In pre-election donations in 1996, the BC Government Employees' Union donated $135,000 to the NDP, while the Hospital Employees Union handed over $67,000. Ken Georgetti, who pulled strings on behalf of both private and public unions, personally cut a cheque for $3,350.[29]

Given the union support for Glen Clark, the elimination of public sector jobs was seen as a betrayal. This was not, after all, before the election where such talk could be written off as public posturing. Alternately, the province's debt continued to climb. And as the dreaded Clark knife loomed closer, Ken Georgetti once again fired across the government's bow: "The government is accepting the right-wing prescription that has repeatedly been proven wrong."[30] But unlike 1992 where the government gave in after a Georgetti ultimatum, Clark summoned up the courage to cut spending and promised 5,500 job cuts in order to staunch the flow of red ink.

There was only one problem: it turned out the announcement was more Clark b.s.: bravado and spin. The job cuts never happened. As *Vancouver Sun* columnist Vaughn Palmer discovered in 1997, the numbers moved depending on who he talked to. BCGEU president John Shields admitted only fourteen people ever faced the dreaded Clark knife.[31] The Ministry of Finance thought perhaps as many as 50 positions had been axed.[32] After more investigation, it turned out they were both wrong; the correct number was 1,400 – hired, that is.[33] The job cuts were as illusory as any claim to two balanced budgets.

At the end of it all, by 1998, the BCGEU and the government signed a contract that prevented any layoffs at all for three years.[34] Of course, the government could lay off *private* contractors, since they were not part of the union, and anyway disdained by New Democrats.

Zero, zero, and $1.3 billion

Exhibit "B" in the ongoing love affair between the government and the public service was the late 1990s stage production of Zero, Zero, and Two – wage restraints supposedly in effect for three years between 1998 and 2001. This Ebenezer Scrooge approach came after the NDP realized the public was tired of promised balanced budgets, only to find a note on the pillow after budget day, professing complete love, devotion, and another IOU.

The union agreed to zero, zero and two guidelines in exchange for the 1998 no lay-off clause. This, presumably, to avoid the bloodletting that occurred when 1,400 extra people were hired during Clark's last public claim to restraint.

As it turned out, while Glen Clark and Co. again publicly played Scrooge in the front office, the old fellow slipped lots of spiked eggnog and expensive treats out the back door as employees left for the evening. It was classic public opinion manipulation worthy of Bill Clinton: say whatever you think the public wants to hear but proceed with the original agenda; in this case, dishing out favours to public sector allies.

In 2000, after Finance officials told the new premier Ujjal Dosanjh that the 0-0-2 policy would still cost hundreds of millions of dollars,[35] he ordered the cost of the bogus policy revealed. Dosanjh, with the fewest ties to labour of any NDP leader, could afford to distance himself from his predecessor. While it took Finance a while to crunch the numbers – two NDP appointees from Saskatchewan and the Yukon negotiated the contracts and did not keep tallies – Treasury staff calculated the tab at $1.3 billion.

By the end of nine years worth of NDP love affairs with the public service, those same BCGEU Government Liquor Store employees granted a reprieve from private competitors at the beginning of the decade once again found themselves the object of government affection. The Liquor Distribution Branch offered incentives such as television sets just for regularly showing up to work.[36]

Whatever happened to a conflict of interest?

When in opposition, the NDP burned its collective hair over a whiff of conflict of interest by the Social Credit government. Once in power, massive multi-million dollar conflicts of interests popped up regularly. Former activist union employees turned politicians or senior bureaucrats oversaw contracts with their former employers, some whose spouses were members. It was akin to Jimmy Pattison becoming premier and then doling out government contracts to his former companies now owned by his wife.

All the favours certainly helped. In just the last three years of the 1990s, public sector union coffers and membership swelled: in BC, the Canadian Union of Public Employees (CUPE) increased its rolls by nineteen percent. The BCGEU's membership shot up by ten percent.[37]

The NDP and private sector labour

Given that the public sector was so lavishly courted by the NDP, one might think private sector unions would be jealous. Lucky for both the government and public unions, private labour had not a jealous bone in its body. Besides, Ken Georgetti's influence on government was big enough to haul in favours for both sides of the labour spectrum. Georgetti even tried his hand at economics in the early NDP years, and demanded that employers pay their "fair share" in taxes and for workers to get their "fair share" in profits.[38]

That the first demand might hamper the second, and thus squeeze his own membership out of wage hikes, never occurred to Georgetti. Regardless, Finance Minister Glen Clark obliged soon enough. Greedy capitalists and other British Columbians (including union members) were hit with $1.5 billion in tax increases in the first two NDP budgets.

The labour code changes: how high, Ken?

But more important than Georgetti's requested tax hikes were labour code changes. By late 1992, the wrapping was off planned changes to the code, most of which ended up in the final version. Dead and buried was Bill 19, the previous government's labour law. Bill 84, the new labour code, banned replacement ("scab") hiring, grounds for opting out of unions on religious grounds were narrowed, and secondary picketing was allowed – which knee-capped a business that had nothing to do with an actual dispute. Management could not be transferred to a struck site, and the definition of a bargaining unit was expanded: a small business with one employee could find itself unionized if that employee signed a union card.

The death of the secret ballot

Also served up in 1992 was the death of the secret ballot. If 55 percent of a company's employees signed union cards, certification was automatic; no questions asked, no vote needed. The government spin on this bear hug into union brotherhood was that it protected employees from intimidation during recruitment drives.

Perhaps. But it was a weak excuse for removing the franchise. As it was, other provisions in the code prevented employers from offering wage increases, promotions, or improved conditions if a certification drive was underway. In addition, Bill 84 gave the Labour Relations Board the power to impose a union if management intimidated employees in any way. Of course, getting *out* of a union was not so easy. In that case, a sign-up of 55 percent of fellow employees would not cut it; to fire a union, a vote was required even if 100 percent of the employees signed a de-certification card.

But if employees thought their secret ballot rights were dumped because the NDP came up with the idea first, they underestimated how cozy behind-closed-door talks could get, even in British Columbia and between two polar opposites. In discussions in early 1992, the BC Federation of Labour and the BC Business Council bartered on a number of issues, including the secret ballot. And it was the BC Business Council (which represented some of the province's largest employers) that first horse-traded away that right. Naturally, after big labour and big business agreed on this point, big government happily obliged.

The reaction to the Old Boys Club from small business was *not* so positive; they were furious. Small business expected significant hikes in the minimum wage, more regulation, and red tape courtesy of the NDP, but not a sell-out to organized labour's wish list by business allies. As it was, they were the ones most affected by this new provision - not large-scale employers mostly unionized already. It took a *mea culpa* and several months of patch-up meetings to smooth things over.

Post-1992, that blunder by the BC Business Council did force changes to how business played chess with the NDP government. Kathy Sanderson, provincial head of the Canadian Federation of Independent Business, spearheaded the creation of a larger business umbrella coalition, which grew to include not only her own association and large employers but also 50 other groups. Years later, employer associations in other jurisdictions called the Coalition of BC Business (as it became known) to ask how they stayed united, given conflicting interests and large egos: "Get an NDP government" was the stock reply. The Coalition would prove to be quite effective later in the decade when the government tried to pass more radical labour code changes, but other NDP experiments on business came first.

Prosperity by decree

If NDP MLAs ever thought the economy could not be directed by government, their actions rarely revealed such doubts. In March 1992, not six months after the government was elected, and in the middle of a multi-billion dollar deficit, the NDP introduced a "fair" wage policy, which alternately, could be called a soak-the-taxpayer policy depending on one's vantage point.

It was a blatant attempt to cut non-union contractors out of as much work as possible and make union firms more competitive via government intervention. So, a company that might win a contract and pay $20 an hour was instead forced to pay $27 and up. In one move, the government turned competitive bidding on its head: any attempt to strike a balance between decent but market-driven wages and the most effective use of taxpayer money was replaced with a policy that made highway, hospital and school projects as expensive as possible. Within the first year, the policy cost taxpayers as much as an extra $35 million.[39] As it happened, the unionized share of government projects declined anyway. One year after the policy was enacted, 79 percent of contracts were still awarded to non-union companies, albeit at a higher cost to taxpayers.

If at first government intervention does not succeed, one could always legislate again. In 1994, then Employment and Investment Minister Glen Clark announced that the Island Highway project (planned for years but re-announced in 1993) was henceforth a "closed-shop." To manoeuvre around the law that required a project to go to the lowest bidder, union or no, the government announced *it* was the "employer." That allowed it to sign a master collective agreement with the Building Trades Council, a collective of eight labour unions fanatically loyal to New Democrats. It was another blatant payoff to government friendly unions at the expense of both non-union firms and labour not closely aligned with the NDP.[ii] Those few workers allowed on the project and not members of the Building Trades were forced to join up temporarily.[iii] Clark's move also forced additional contributions to the government-friendly unions.The $1-billion-plus project was thus safely delivered to friends of the government.

---

ii. Companies that won a contract and did not already hire exclusively from the Building Trades list could only bring five of their own employees, even if all their employees belonged to another union.

Critics argued the fair wage policy would lead to fewer capital projects overall, given that the increased wage bill would force each development to be more expensive. The other likelihood was that projects would be scaled back. Either way, citizens would receive less bang for their public buck. As it turned out, both scenarios unfolded in short succession on the Island Highway. To halt escalating costs, the government cut planned four-lane sections to two and dropped overpasses. In a further short-term face-saving measure for the public accounts, the government postponed completion dates for some sections by several years.[40] The entire project looked like a repeat of the interior Coquihalla freeway built by the Social Credit government in the 1980s. That project was budgeted at $500 million, but by the time the bills came in with the corners cut on later sections, the cost hit $1 billion.

In 1994 the Vancouver Board of Trade estimated that labour costs on the Island Highway project would be 37 percent higher than necessary, or $72 million. Turns out they were conservative.[41] A year later, Clark admitted the project was already over budget by $150 million.[42] That was never as bad as the over-budget Socred freeway, but it also reminded the public that pork barrelling and over-budget blacktop was not restricted to one political party.

In 1997, Glen Clark broke the taxpayer piggy bank once again with more economic intervention. The government upped the premium for workers on the Island project yet again. The new top-up meant taxpayers paid $12 more per hour than might be paid by a non-union firm in the private sector.[43] In 1996 the Island Highway project was pegged at just over $1.3 billion. A straight numbers comparison meant it looked similar to the government's 1993 estimate; the difference was that major sections were delayed for years or chopped from the original plans.[iv]

Fair wages in the courts

The Island Highway project illustrated the cozy relationship between government-friendly unions and New Democrats in another way: integral to

---

iii. The government-friendly unions later returned the favour. 27 unions in construction or road building donated $45,000 to Glen Clark's 1996 campaign for NDP leader, a third of all the money raised. (Vaughn Palmer, *Vancouver Sun*, 3 April 1996.)

iv. In a similar action in 1997, Clark promised that the hundreds of millions of dollars spent through Forest Renewal British Columbia would go to a mainly unionized workforce. Once again the optics of government-created forestry jobs, even union ones, was more myth than reality; the union jobs to replant forests via FRBC simply displaced existing workers, some unionized, some not. It was a shell game of jobs, but one that helped Clark's relations with labour.

the project was a provision that paid unions up to 25 cents per worker, per hour, extra, for "advancement funds" that added up to over $2 million.[44]

The opposition charged that some of the money might make its way back to the NDP. Ironworkers Local 97 sued Opposition leader Gordon Campbell and *Vancouver Province* columnist Brian Kieran. The judge wrote that Campbell defamed the union in his press release. Despite that, the justice found that because some of the extra money was not specifically directed (to training for example), the union left itself open to the Campbell and Kieran allegation.[45]

In 2000, a federal judge ruled that the federal government, which by law must pay the prevailing market rate, wrongly followed the BC fair wage guidelines. The court found that wages differed widely across the province and that federal tax dollars were overspent as a result. The BC government ignored the verdict and continued its policy, one that cost at least an extra $310 million over six years.[46]

The missing links: economics and patronage

In its patronage to allies, the government missed the central economic point: most people desire higher salaries but extra tax dollars for inflated wage scales could not build the highway to prosperity for all. In a hot economy where unemployment is low, workers are in the driver's seat vis-à-vis their employers. That's why 24-year-old computer programmers today demand salaries their parents had to wait until 45, if ever, to get.

The government had it backwards: it punished all British Columbians with high tax rates, user fees, and higher than necessary Crown corporation bills to boost select wages for a few workers in some industries (or in the civil service itself). And even those who might directly benefit from the policy - a tradesman on a government construction project, might just as likely find himself unemployed. Two billion dollars spread between ten school construction projects created fewer jobs than the same money spread over twelve. A temporary wage boost for some at the expense of fewer projects and less work for all was the trade-off.

The New Democrats, who regularly mocked the idea that the free market could create wealth, jobs, and wage increases without their help, thought they had a better way: by fiat. So they passed laws that mandated higher wages, as if government-directed salary levitation would somehow create prosperity. In reality, the decision had nothing to do with economics and everything to do with politics: wealth was transferred from taxpayers to politically connected unions.

Détente or deterrence?

Later in the decade, and especially after the 1996 election, some business heads tired of explaining economics to New Democrats. Others thought the new Premier's pre-election corporate bashing was so much talk and that reason might prevail after the ballots were cast.

Those that viewed Glen Clark in such a generous light soon changed their mind. Accompanied by Business Council of BC president Jerry Lampert to a meeting with Clark shortly after the 1996 election, business leaders were told by the premier how the universe would unfold. Over the next four years, he (Clark) would routinely announce loans and bailouts with individual businesses, the cameras would click and the photo-ops would let the public know Glen Clark was in charge and that *some* businesses could work with his government. If corporate British Columbia felt snubbed, well, that was life. This would proceed until the next election when Clark and his government would be re-elected.

Given the attitude, employers had little to lose from an open confrontation with the NDP. Until then, business was often co-opted anyway. Despite the death of the secret ballot in 1992 – albeit at their own hands, the shutout of non-union companies on the Island Highway, or Clark's relentless business-bashing, employers were reluctant to engage in public duels with New Democrats. It was partly understandable; severe public criticism might lose contracts and invite petty bureaucratic and political harassment. But mild criticism from business throughout the 1990s only encouraged the NDP and their labour allies to extract more concessions, especially if Clark was anywhere near the levers of power. It also meant the average citizen had no idea just how badly the government undermined business confidence, jobs, and investment.

In terms of strategy, it was a question of détente versus deterrence. Business tried the first strategy ever since 1991 and its success was mixed; 1997 provided the opportunity for a more muscular response.

Difficult labour: Bill 44

In early June 1997, Suromitra Sanatani, head of the Coalition of BC Business, along with other select business leaders, was due to be briefed by key Ministry of Labour officials on proposed labour code changes. In contrast to 1992, where labour and business both gave substantial input, the 1997 legislation was drafted without so much as a postcard to the province's employers.

Fifteen minutes before the meeting was to begin, business heads were informed the meeting was cancelled. A Labour Ministry session with top union officials earlier that day meant some proposals had to be re-worked. When details of the legislation leaked out,[47] it was clear why business was kept in the dark; among the labour-friendly proposals was sectoral bargaining. This allowed master contracts in an industry that then applied to any firm subsequently unionized. Bill 44 was aimed at the construction industry but business feared it would soon land in other mostly non-union sectors such as retail and restaurants.

As it was, construction unions could negotiate separate contracts with various businesses; the assumption was that location, profitability, and other factors made that flexibility crucial. Employers could reasonably be asked to pay more in an area with a high cost of living such as Vancouver, less in Penticton. The same logic applied to profitable companies versus ones that teetered on the verge of bankruptcy.

But the draft legislation lumped every company into a one-size-fits-all straitjacket. And the sectoral provisions – the first contract negotiated applied to all businesses in that sector – meant a union organizer could walk up to a tradesman on a non-union site, show him a copy of the union agreement signed next door, and "guarantee" higher wages. All he would have to do was sign a certification card.

The immediate attraction for workers was obvious. What was not so attractive or apparent was that it could also mean unemployment. An independent contractor with five employees would be forced to pay the same salary as a contractor with 100 tradesmen and a flexible line of credit at the bank.

More likely, the smaller contractor might just go out of business or leave the province. And with higher prices for construction (and thus the customer), the industry, union or non-union, was not likely to be on a hiring spree. Once again, the NDP had the economics backwards; a rising economic tide lifts all boats. New Democrats shot at successful ships with one-sided labour legislation and punitive taxes and then wondered why business fled to safer waters.

To top it all off, business leaders saw Bill 44 as another broken Clark promise: twelve months earlier Clark wrote that "sectoral certification was not the most appropriate way to solve the problems of those people not traditionally represented by labour unions."[48]

Labour's back pocket

The proposed 1997 changes to the labour code were cooked up entirely in the Premier's office. Rumour had it that NDP lawyer Jeffrey Haskins vetted proposed labour code amendments to ensure they were to big labour's liking. Labour minister John Cashore fumbled the official launch at a press

He's going too far.

Glen Clark's new labour bill goes too far.

Unbalanced and undemocratic changes to BC's Labour Code will drive badly-needed new jobs and new investment away from BC. They will take British Columbians further down the road to economic uncertainty and instability. And they could drive up prices for consumers ... everything from a cup of coffee to a new home.

Among the changes are "one size fits all" union agreements. They will take away the democratic right of each individual business and its workers to bargain their own collective agreement. First it will be the construction industry, then it could be yours.

BC's economic growth has fallen to 10th place in Canada under Glen Clark's existing labour policies. Now, with no consultation, he is imposing even further job-killing labour law changes. He's ignoring the advice of the government's own independent advisors. They said: "one size won't fit all."

What's worse, he's ignored the advice of small and medium-sized businesses – the people who create the majority of BC's new jobs. It's time their voices were heard. It's time to put the brakes on Glen Clark's flawed and one-sided legislation.

CALL THE PREMIER AT 660-2701 – TELL HIM WHAT YOU THINK.

Support the

Coalition of BC Businesses.

Over 50,000 small and medium-sized businesses creating jobs and investment in BC.

BC Restaurant and Foodservices Association • BC Chamber of Commerce
BC and Yukon Hotels' Association • Canadian Restaurant and Foodservices Association
BC Automobile Dealers Association • BC Shake and Shingle Association
BC Motels Campgrounds Resorts Association • BC Horticultural Coalition
British Columbia Trucking Association • Building Owners and Managers Association of BC
Building Supply Dealers Association • Canadian Federation of Independent Business
Canadian Home Builders' Association • Canadian Steel Service Centre Institute
Council of Tourism Associations of BC • Canadian Retail Hardware Association
Greenhouse and Nursery Trades Association • Recreation Vehicle Dealers Association
Independent Contractors and Businesses Association of BC • Insurance Brokers Association of BC
Retail Merchants Association of BC • Roofing Contractors Association of BC
Urban Development Institute • BC Technology Industries Association • Vancouver Board of Trade
Association of Canadian Travel Agents BC/Yukon

THE COALITION OF BC BUSINESSES, CALL 682-8366.

From the Coalition of BC Business: A 1997 ad against proposed Bill 44 changes to the province's labour code.

conference – he admitted the draft changes came about because "it was something labour felt entitled to."[49] "Labour" in this case meant Ken Georgetti and the BC Federation of Labour, but Cashore could just as easily have held up a list of past contributors to Glen Clark's leadership campaign, or the NDP before the last election. As the *Victoria Times Colonist*'s Les Leyne pointed out, trade unions donated over $1.6 million to New Democrats in the pre-election period.[50]

As John Cashore admitted, since the 1992 labour code changes, BC lost fewer days to strikes and lockouts than at any time since World War Two. Despite the smooth hum of the labour relations engine, the government threw the Bill 44 wrench into the machine anyway. Cashore, when questioned as to why business was not consulted, once again aimed his career for the government back-bench: "There are some things where, no matter how much consultation you do, you're never going to achieve consensus."[51] This sort of ignored the small but important fact that business was *never* consulted on the new changes.

Divide and conquer?

Initially, some NDP MLAs thought business might roll over. As in 1992, when corporate BC gave away the right to a secret ballot, the NDP strategy included a calculation that business would divide. Given that large companies were already unionized, those firms might gain back some business from smaller non-union firms. Smaller companies might not like Bill 44, but since it only provided for sectoral bargaining in construction, not other areas, the NDP chanced that small business might let it pass given that they were not yet a direct target.[52]

The NDP's logic was Machiavellian and, as regards big business, not without foundation given their actions in 1992. But that screw-up provided the impetus for the larger Coalition of BC Business. The result was that whatever separate interests were at play in 1997, the business community was more united, and – always helpful – had a common foe: Glen Clark. Besides, Bill 44 was a sharp reminder of what business could expect from détente with New Democrats when Clark was in charge.

Business to Clark: drop dead

After the introduction of Bill 44 in the Legislature, the government finally made overtures to business for its input: "Thanks but no thanks," was the response. Suromitra Sanatani, the Coalition of BC Business chair, wrote the government a "drop-dead" letter. Given that the NDP already introduced the proposed labour changes in the Legislature, business was not now interested in fake consultations. Sanatani also accused the premier's deputy, Doug McArthur, of bullying business leaders. McArthur, a former Saskatchewan NDP cabinet minister under Allan Blakeney, replied that "if it's a fight you want, it's a fight you'll get."[53]

That was a mistake. For one thing, business spoiled for a fight with the NDP and Bill 44 provided a choice opportunity. The government geared up for battle anyway. Labour leaders were trooped out to argue that the bill was no big deal, only about "unionized workers and unionized employees,"[54] said Ken Georgetti, ignoring the main feature of Bill 44, *his* bill, was to certify large sectors of the construction industry.

Business fought back with full-page anti-Bill 44 ads in newspapers, one with a cartoon of Glen Clark driving over the cliff in a car labelled "the economy." Another more hard-hitting ad pictured a construction worker from Delta, along with his wife, kids and requisite beer belly. Joe Six-Pack held out a handful of nails and the caption read "Mr. Clark should try hammering these instead of us." The housing industry put the word out that home costs could increase by ten percent[55] – not an attractive mental picture in an already expensive province.

In addition to business reaction, the media was generally critical, not least because of NDP-labour back scratching. The *Vancouver Sun* accused the Premier of paying back "his construction-union cronies for their loyal support with taxpayers' money, with the office tower builders' money, with the residential home buyers' money."[56] The *Kamloops Daily News* argued that while sops to labour were expected from the NDP, the surprise was "the totally cavalier manner in which the government is bringing in changes for which there appears to be no need."[57]

The *Victoria Times Colonist* argued Bill 44 "effectively delivers the entire construction industry into the maw of big labour."[58] For good measure, the capital city paper sarcastically wrote that "now we know why the New Democrats made their recall law so ineffective. If it was even remotely workable, Premier Glen Clark and many of his province-wrecking minions would be yanked from office."[59] Freelance columnist Hubert Beyer, generally quite sympathetic to a more union-friendly labour code, argued sectoral certification was one step too far.[60]

The *Vancouver Province*, with a heavy concentration of blue-collar readers, ran a front-page picture of a jean-clad, hard-hatted, middle-aged house builder. Emblazoned across the page was the headline "Should I leave B.C.?"[61] The message was clear: the bill cooked up by labour and the Premier's advisers did not go over well in the real world.

The death of Bill 44

In late July 1997, three weeks after the introduction of Bill 44 and one day before a planned protest at the Legislature, the Premier called business leaders and offered to pull the bill if they cancelled their planned rally. Clark could not have known it at the time, but organizers were not sure of a successful turnout anyway. Rent-a-mobs were always available to some of BC's wackier demonstrations, and plentiful public sector employees always ensured a large turnout for labour protests. But business demonstrations in Victoria were tough to arrange; protestors were often the employers themselves who had wealth to create, most of which was not formed anywhere near Victoria. Spending an afternoon on the Legislature lawn was something students and career protestors did, not small business owners. After a late night conference call between Jerry Lampert, Suromitra Sanatani, Phil Hochstein and other members of the Coalition, the rally was off and Bill 44 was spiked the next day; Glen Clark blinked first.

The defeat marked the first time New Democrats and their labour allies suffered a knockout blow from business. It was all the more remarkable given that labour legislation was central to the NDP's core constituency and given all his labour IOUs - Glen Clark.

Back scratching

While Bill 44 went down in flames, the plums to labour allies over the 1990s did not go unheeded, not by unions in the public or private sector. While it may be the thought that counts, cash buys political advertisements. In the 1996 election, which saw the NDP squeak back into power with 39 percent of the vote compared to 42 percent for the Liberals, organized labour provided both cash and muscle to the governing party.

On the cash side, labour donated $1.6 million to the party and candidates.[62] On the list were the Canadian Union of Public Employees, the Hospital Employees Union, the United Food and Commercial Worker's Union, the Teamsters, as well as the Ironworkers Union that benefited from the Glen Clark decision to build the Island Highway with union-only companies.[63] Lucky for the NDP, labour was adept at getting union members to donate directly via pre-authorized cheques; $2.8 million came from individuals via that route.

However, the NDP-designed election disclosure law only made it necessary to disclose financial contributions, not volunteers loaned *from* labour. Also convenient was that the disclosure law did not take effect until *after* substantial donations were already made to the party. Glen Clark's riding association fund collected $61,000 before the law took effect in June 1995; party headquarters built a $1.5-million election war chest before the government proclaimed the new law.[64]

Friends in need: recall help

Beside election-time help, big labour also helped defeat two recall campaigns in northern British Columbia.[v] In November 1997, when the recall legislation could first be tested, citizens angry over the 1996 fudge-it budget began gathering signatures in two NDP ridings: the Prince George constituency of then Education Minister Paul Ramsey and Helmut Giesbrecht's Terrace riding.

Labour was there to help oppose the recall drive. The Canadian Autoworkers Union,[65] Teamsters Local 213,[66] and the Prince George and District Trades Council[67] all urged members not to sign recall petitions. A later 1998 *Vancouver Sun* investigation found that union allies flew in help from Vancouver and Toronto to help defeat the recall campaigns.[68] The NDP sued the newspaper but later dropped the case. An investigation by auditor Ron Parks (who scoured the books in the Nanaimo bingo scandal) later substantiated the *Sun* story.[69]

Long distance labour

The import of labour activists from Toronto was particularly hypocritical given that during the campaign the NDP criticized "outsiders" for helping recall proponents. That criticism was aimed squarely at Troy Lanigan of Victoria, then BC director for the Canadian Taxpayers Federation. Unlike labour help from Ontario and Vancouver, Lanigan never made a secret of the CTF's advice and legal help for pre-recall activities, a point acknowledged by the *Prince George Citizen*.[70] The Federation also withdrew before the recall campaigns began, unlike the NDP/labour help brought in during the actual fight.

The NDP survived the 1996 election and the 1998 recall campaigns. The

---

v. In the 1991 election, 80 percent of British Columbians voted for legislation that allowed them to recall their MLAs. Then backbench MLA Ujjal Dosanjh later constructed a diluted version of the proposal. As it was designed to never work, it was thought any effort would automatically fail; there were multiple legal tripwires built into the law that could invalidate most attempts. Dosanjh's masterful job of creating an almost unworkable recall law, as well as a watered-down referendum law, was one important reason he was later elevated to cabinet.

recall law required signatures equal to 40 percent of the names on the last voters' list: 8,908 in the case of Paul Ramsey's riding. Organizers scooped up 8,400, or 37 percent. The NDP was helped by an outdated list that neither they nor Elections BC cared to update. By one estimate, a proper voters' list would have required only 7,500 names to force a recall by-election.[71]

Futurewatch: the division of labour and the NDP

By the end of the 1990s, organized labour was as strong as at any time in the past two decades, though without the secret ballot, their members were individually weaker. Thirty-six percent of the workforce was unionized in 1999, less than the 55-percent plurality it enjoyed in the 1950s, but up consistently on a numbers basis for the eleventh straight year.

In 1999, union membership hit record numbers in British Columbia – 592,000 in all and half of those in the public sector.[72] The 1990s were rough on private incomes, business, and the economic health of the province in general, but New Democrats ensured that government workers were better paid than ever before: public sector wages ballooned by 43 percent since 1990.[73]

But that apparent union strength masked underlying divisions more likely to become evident after an NDP election loss. A British Columbia without labour influence would be a mistake, but concentrated power was as disastrous when wielded by powerful union chiefs as when handled solo by a politician or a robber baron. And some of what labour leaders advocated in the 1990s – the anti-wealth creation rhetoric and the bizarre opposition to free trade given Canada's dependence on such – was harmful to union and non-union British Columbians alike.[vi] In addition, some labour leaders never met a loopy political cause they didn't like, or fund.

While some union leaders divert union dues to their favorite political causes that they would describe as progressive, and bash tax relief and balanced budgets as a conspiracy of the rich, it is not clear that all, or even a

---

vi. Opposition to free trade, especially by organized labour, is a mystery. Free trade is nothing more than a gentleman's agreement about the rules of trade. Those who argue free trade is a net loss to our sovereignty have it precisely backwards: Without free trade agreements, Canada, a trade-dependent nation, and British Columbia in particular, would be at the mercy of American protectionist sentiment whenever it arose. And union members are more dependent on NAFTA then they may realize. Without it, the U.S. or Mexico could shut out BC products overnight and keep the doors closed for as long as they wished. Agreements, even imperfect and fought-over ones, prevent arbitrary disruptions in trade.

majority of their members, share those passions and opinions. And not every union member is created equal; after all, what does a union logger in Prince George have in common with a public sector bureaucrat in Victoria who touts affirmative action? Nor should it be assumed that private sector labour automatically identifies with the public sector and their large appetite for ever-more tax dollars.

This divide will be more apparent in the future, especially after an NDP loss; the glue of power masks many a division. For a look at labour's future, look east to Ontario. Mike Harris won ridings in the automotive belt among blue-collar rank-and-file labour, despite opposition from their leaders. He went over their heads and directly appealed to overtime workers on the assembly line. It turned out that punitive tax rates irritated them as much as any stockbroker in red suspenders. Joe SixPack liked the Harris tax cuts as much as any small business owner, maybe more, given that wages are often a worker's only source of income.

Closer to home, the provincial NDP stronghold of Nanaimo voted Reform in national elections in 1993 and 1997. The core constituency of New Democrats is not with them lock, stock, and barrel on every issue and this will be more true in the future. Another development yet to unfold is the greening of the New Democratic Party. A shift further in that direction could alienate those in their ranks that rely on forestry and mining for their livelihood. If that happens, look for some labour unions in the private sector to split off to become more politically neutral though not necessarily less active.

Labour and the NDP had quite the torrid love affair over the past decade; it may have been their last.

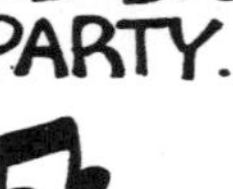

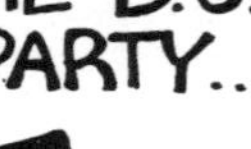

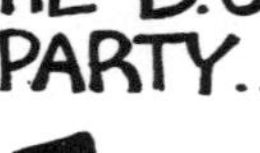

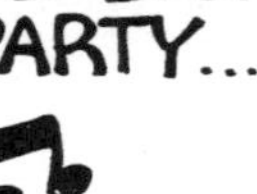

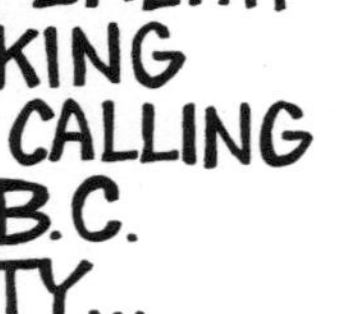
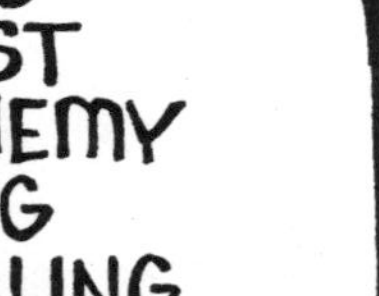
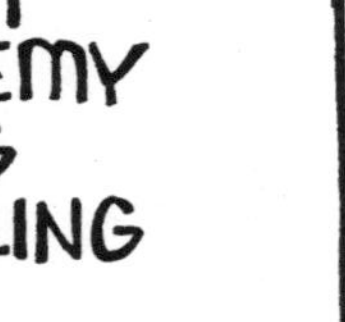

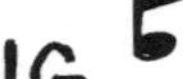

NDP FUNDRAISING
BIG BUSINESS DIVISION
PROCEDURES 1 BEG 2 WHINE 3 PLEAD 4 DONT MENTION THE BUDGET 5 CRY
GOOD MORNING FILTHY CAPITALIST RUNNING DOG ENEMY OF THE WORKING PEOPLE ... I'M CALLING FROM THE B.C. NDP PARTY...
RAESIDE
Victoria Times Colonist.

4

¿Habla Espanol?

How the NDP Sent BC's Mining Industry to Chile

(and made –40 Alberta attractive to everyone else)

"If you define business in terms of huge profits, those days are gone."[1]
- NDP Cabinet Minister David Zirnhelt

The NDP was never a tremendous fan of business and it showed. In the 1990s, the government hiked business taxes, vastly expanded the much-hated profit-insensitive corporate capital tax, yanked the labour code as far in the direction of big labour as it could, increased regulations, and bashed free enterprise rhetorically and repeatedly. Some remarks even thumped business immediately: in 1998, an anti-private health care rant by Health Minister Penny Priddy wiped out $110 million worth of stock market capitalization from MDS Metro Laboratories, a Vancouver company with government contracts.[2]

Initially, New Democrats thought none of this would matter. In the early 1990s, money and immigrants poured into the province as the rest of Canada suffered through a recession. At the same time, the initial influx of Hong Kong capital due to political uncertainty in the British colony also lulled the NDP into a false sense of confidence. But that flow soon dried up, in part because Premier Mike Harcourt reneged on a 1994 promise to kill a much-hated corporate capital tax. $500 million in planned Asian investment walked away after the Harcourt flip-flop.[3] Vincent Lee, a private banker who helped investors set up in the province, commented to a reporter: "You try explaining to people you have to pay tax even if you're losing money."[4]

The NDP vs. entrepreneurs

One reason for New Democrat disdain for free enterprise was their philosophy, which saw the economy in "fixed-pie" terms. If a business turned a large profit, "huge" to use David Zirnhelt's term, it meant the company was not taxed enough or workers were underpaid, or both. The idea that a business could grow, employ more people, pay higher wages a la Microsoft (without government intervention), and one day be a cash cow for all (even the public treasury), was a foreign concept.

Environmental justifications also proved to be a barrier to investment. The ruling view, especially in the first term, was that business would just have to adjust if new red tape delayed a project or, as in the case of one high-profile mine proposal, ended such plans entirely. A more purist environmental view took prior consideration over development, jobs, and tax revenues.

But even that approach would have been less economically damaging if the rules were clear. California had more stringent environmental regulations than did British Columbia; the difference was that business projects in California had a clear checklist that, once complete, ensured approval. In BC, there were often no fixed criteria and no predictable hurdles. The result was that the rules were never clear in advance. Thus, companies were reluctant to spend money given that projects might be approved or, then again, they might not. What was true of California was also true of Alberta. Mike Geoghegan, a one-time aide to an early 1990s NDP cabinet minister, characterized the difference both within government and the bureaucracy as one of attitude: Alberta civil servants possessed a "How can we help you?" attitude to business. In BC, the more common reaction was: "Why do you want do that and why should we let you?"[5] The political bias of those in charge only added to the bureaucracy's bent.

The land claims issue was a third reason business confidence declined, a direct result of early NDP policy on this issue and its subsequent tremors.[i] Business became increasingly unsure whether plans for resource extraction or tourism development would actually come to fruition. After a mid-1990s native blockade at Apex Alpine ski resort bankrupted the owner, business was on notice that the rules had changed. Problem was, no one knew what the new rules were or what they would cost. In another example, when Princeton Mining wanted a new copper mine in west-central British Columbia, the 200-member Chelsatta Carrier Indian band demanded that Princeton

---

i. For example, one month before a key case on native land claims was to be heard before the BC Court of Appeal in 1992, the NDP dismissed the legal team that successfully argued that original case in the Supreme Court of British Columbia. The new government and their legal team were much more sympathetic to the case put forward by the native plaintiffs than to the original position argued by the previous BC government. Thus, the original decision was somewhat weakened at the Appeals level and completely gutted at the Supreme Court of Canada. For more on this case, see Chapter 10.

pay its legal bills and give an annual retainer, equal to an executive's salary, to a band elder. But that was nothing compared to the demand that Princeton hand over a royalty share from the mine. Princeton agreed to quotas for native hiring but refused to ante up on other demands.[6]

A fourth catalyst for the rough ride of business was the NDP's own arrogance. Cabinet minister Dan Miller, in the middle of a $300-million taxpayer-financed bailout of the pulp mill he once worked at, bragged that he "understood business." This was in comparison to bankers who were "very bad business people."[7] In fact, the bailout revealed the NDP's lack of understanding about how their actions reminded potential investors to stay clear of BC.

Favouritism in the forest

Skeena Cellulose, a pulp mill located within Dan Miller's north coast riding, was on a mid-1990s deathwatch. Pulp prices were depressed, and the mill was in miserable shape: inefficient, polluting, and unable to survive in the marketplace, its life cycle was about to expire as newer, cleaner and more efficient mills eclipsed it.

That the mill was important to not only its workers but to Prince Rupert was obvious. And the politics of it were clear, as was the value of the photo-op: heroic former employee, now cabinet minister and local MLA, saves jobs. So the government made $300 million in loans and guarantees available for the mill.

Miller's concern for his former fellow employees was understandable but wrongheaded. In actual fact, the economics of the bailout including the "jobs saved" claim were illusory. Since the government did not alter its stumpage revenue targets overall, the bailout meant fees went up elsewhere, a policy known as "waterbedding." So when the government cut stumpage fees at Skeena Cellulose to head off financial ruin, other mills paid the extra money instead.[8]

Moreover, the bailout merely displaced workers at other mills that also faced depressed world prices for lumber. One year before the rescue, University of British Columbia professor Les Reed predicted that at least two BC mills would shut down.[9] As it turned out, government subsidies meant neither of those was Skeena Cellulose. But the warning was prophetic and the first one down was a more efficient and less polluting mill: Castlegar's Celgar, which already poured $800 million worth of *private* money into modernization. And the second closure occurred soon after in Gold River, a forestry-dependent community on western Vancouver Island. The message to investors was clear: don't invest private money to rescue a weak business; the government might later help your competitor with your tax dollars.

Two years later, after the Skeena Cellulose mill turned the economic corner, New Democrat MLAs bragged that the bailout worked. The claim itself was suspicious; there was, as of yet, no third-party analysis of the books. Such audits were generally less than complimentary to government claims. Even if the numbers could stand up to scrutiny, it actually pointed to something very different: yet more evidence that the government did not think beyond one riding or region at a time. At best, their action came from a mistaken belief, based on a narrow and provincial view of economics that did not take in the larger picture. At worst, the mill bailout was cronyism under a loftier justification. By late 2000, the mill was once again on the verge of bankruptcy. Taxpayers would have been better off if a large cheque were cut to workers on the condition they move somewhere else, tragic as that would be in the short-term.

Mining for nothing and your parks for free

If government MLAs did not understand how bailouts dragged down healthier, subsidy-free enterprises, their grasp on the need for predictable government resource policy was even less sure.

British Columbians treasure their province and its natural beauty. Given its multiple vistas and almost unmatched beauty anywhere in the world, it is no surprise that environmental and preservationist movements in Canada have been strongest in its westernmost province. Greenpeace started in Vancouver in 1971, and although some of its later campaigns cost it sympathy in North America, environmental awareness in BC is as strong as ever.

Given the sympathy, Mike Harcourt's early 1990s announcement of a plan to preserve twelve percent of the province as parkland was generally well-received. The unanswered questions concerned what land would be off-limits to forestry and mining and what the compensation would be for expropriated resource rights.

History lessons

As it concerned mining, New Democrats had to be careful not to repeat history. In 1972, BC's first NDP government came to power along with an election manifesto that targeted BC's resource industries. The platform stated that forestry and mining would be nationalized if they were not managed to the NDP's liking.[10] Two years later, Dave Barrett's government passed legislation that imposed exorbitant new royalties on the mining industry; profit was effectively killed.

Opposition parties went justifiably nuts and accused the government of trying to devalue the sector in preparation for a government takeover. The industry, which knew of the government's intentions since at least 1972, already cut back investment in BC, while development in the Yukon and elsewhere climbed. By late 1975 the NDP was out of power and the attack on the mining industry was a key reason.

Sixteen years later, the NDP had no specific promises to nationalize much of anything, much less the province's mining sector. Still, memories were long and mining companies were wary. To add a few nervous ticks to mining executive's uneasiness, Harcourt even had some old Barrett warhorses running for Legislature seats, including Colin Gablemann. Back in the 1970s, Gablemann (later an Attorney General under Harcourt), argued that "maybe we have to say that land can no longer be owned privately. No one ever suggested air should be owned privately."[11]

Given party history, Harcourt promised voters that he would not repeat the mistakes of Dave Barrett's government and specifically singled out mining policy as an example. In 1991, the NDP campaigned on ending valley by valley resource fights and promised certainty through the environmental and regulatory review process.

There was trouble from the start though it's not likely Harcourt was aware of it. "Problem One" was the new deputy chair of Treasury Board, Tom Gunton. In a 1981 paper for a leftist think-tank, Gunton proposed new taxes on the resource industry, which he thought paid too little and received too much in road and rail services. Gunton also argued for new Crown corporations (similar to Petro-Canada) that could compete with private companies.

Tom Gunton versus the mining industry

Under that system, Gunton argued that private firms wouldn't "extract unjustified profit"[12] because the Crown corporations could respond "by either taking over the private firm or undertaking new public investments."[13] *Vancouver Sun* columnist Vaughn Palmer wrote that Gunton was "sympathetic to bona fide socialists who want to use the power of government to break the private sector resource companies once and for all."[14] Gunton claimed Palmer's characterization misrepresented his views. Hardly. Palmer's only error was that he was too generous: Gunton was not merely sympathetic to bona fide socialists; he was one. Political appointees that suggest direct or stealth nationalization can hardly be described in any other way.

Moreover, Tom Gunton's views were in perfect alignment with not only party history, but as later demonstrated, some NDP actions in the 1990s. Gunton and several other senior policy advisers were fans of ever more Crown corporations, and during the 1990s several more were added to the government's stable. It was nationalization by stealth but nationalization all the same.

In the early stages of his government though, it is unlikely Mike Harcourt paid much attention to an eleven-year old academic paper from a Glen Clark adviser. The political reality was that mining was a policy disaster for the NDP in the 1970s and Harcourt was probably sincere about avoiding the same mistake.

¿Habla Español? Lessons from Tatshenshini

The first major test of the new NDP and its mining policy was tucked away in the northwest corner of British Columbia. The Tatshenshini-Alsek region was a pristine and spectacular wilderness, so remote that one either had to be rich enough to fly into it, or capable of a very long hike.

Geologist James McDougall began exploratory work in 1957 and concentrated on 20-million-year-old Triassic sulphide deposits. A year later, McDougall and a pilot prospector flew to a nearby lake and glacier. Further work by prospectors led to an eventual claim on Windy Craggy mountain.[15]

By 1988, Geddes Resources, which then possessed the claim, entered the permit process and if successful, intended to ship out ore and truck it to port in nearby Alaska. Initial capital investment would be $550 million, with another $150 million spent annually in extraction. Well-paying jobs that averaged $70,000[16] annually were in store: 500 direct jobs annually plus another 1,500 in spin-off. The company estimated a mine life of 50 years and direct taxes to governments at $1.3 billion. The provincial ministry responsible gave an even higher estimate: $1.6 billion.[17]

All in all, Windy Craggy contained drill-proven reserves of $8.7 billion in copper, silver, and gold, confirmed in 1992 by a government geologist. Another four anomalies in the area meant reserves might be worth $40 billion.[18]

Rich as the area was in mining potential, not everyone was eager to see it developed. Ric Careless, director of Tatshenshini Wild, argued the area was the finest wilderness in North America, included the largest grizzly bear population on earth, and said the mine project would have enormous technical environmental problems with acid-rock drainage. He wanted the project stopped.[19]

Other environmentalists sought far less, and few ever demanded the entire region be fully closed off to mining. As recently as 1988, the Sierra Club, Western Canada Wilderness Committee, and Canadian Parks and Wilderness drew a "wish-list" map with just two strips of land along the Tatshenshini and Alsek rivers; the area represented half of what later became a protected park.[20]

American cousins

By 1991, the plan for the mine found its way into *Life* magazine. It highlighted the area with a photo essay, and alleged Geddes was hell-bent on removing copper, cobalt, and gold out of the ground "never mind the ecological devastation."[21]

About the same time the proposed mine was undergoing a substantial environmental and regulatory review, a confidential May 1993 White House memorandum stated that the U.S. president and vice-president "have great interest" in the Tatshenshini. The memo revealed that "the British Columbia cabinet has decided to ban mining in the Tatshenshini region."[22]

Thus, in the midst of a process designed to reassure the mining industry that regulation and environmental approvals could be fair and predictable (if not somewhat laborious), it was all abruptly scrapped. The government pulled the plug on a company that spent over a decade and tens of millions of dollars in pursuit of an $8.7-billion claim and thousands of jobs.

In addition to the damage done to the government's stated intent to bring more predictability to resource development, the fact that the American government knew before British Columbians was itself a surprise: BC's New Democrats were often anti-American. Harcourt's Tourism Minister Bill Barlee once said he was "tired of the Americans. They call me anti-American and that's probably true."[23] From cabinet minister salvos about how Americanized health-care left people dead on the street, or how tax cuts would create U.S.-style slums, the United States was always a convenient bogeyman to shut down a policy debate.

Not so when it came to the environment. When federal Environment minister Sheila Copps and U.S. vice-president Al Gore endorsed the creation of a massive World Heritage Site in the Tatshenshini,[24] NDP MLAs might as well have saluted the Stars and Stripes.

How much influence the White House exerted on the final decision is hard to say. Northwest BC was not likely high on the priority list for U.S. presidents, even one with a vice-president that took an active interest in environmental issues. But an American vice-president joined with easterner Sheila Copps (whose home riding was the polluted steel-mill town of Hamilton) to tell BC how to run its affairs. The environment was a provincial matter, not under federal jurisdiction, and was certainly not the responsibility of the White House. Any BC politician with half horse-sense would, in the past, have jumped at the opportunity to tell both parties to keep their opinions out of British Columbia.

Instead, British Columbians found out the mine was a dead prospect in late June, two months after the White House was informed. Mike Harcourt held a press conference and declared 9,600 square kilometres of remote northwest BC off limits to development: mining executives around the world took notes and then scaled back any investment intentions in British Columbia.

Mine tailings

To put the size of the park and the proposed mine in perspective, the new preserve was 958,000 hectares. The proposed mine would have disturbed only 1,100 hectares – barely more than one-tenth of one percent.[25] Mary Webster, who first studied the area as a budding geologist, later argued it was one of the most important mineral finds in North America.[26] British Columbia itself was 95 million hectares, and all the mines ever developed equaled one tenth of one percent of the total land mass of the province. As Webster put it: "You could tuck all thc land disturbcd by mining into a corner of the greater Vancouver area."[27]

The Tatshenshini park was twice the size of Canada's smallest province, Prince Edward Island. Unlike PEI, actually accessible to the public, Tatshenshini was available mainly to the very wealthy or the very hardy. So American vice-presidents, members of the Kennedy clan, or Hollywood celebrities up north to protest on issues about which they generally knew little, could always charter a helicopter or float-plane to see the new preserve. Unlike other areas of the province that were opened up for general tourism after loggers and miners first built roads, the Tatshenshini was available only to a select few.

As for the claim that tourism might one day replace the potential wealth and employment the mine would have created, the suggestion was laughable. Annual tourism in the region was worth $1.5 million annually,[28] or $30 million over 20 years. That hardly measured against the guaranteed $8.7 billion the mine would have contributed to British Columbia's prosperity, a commodity the province lacked in the 1990s.

In 1995, shortly before an expected election (later delayed due to the Nanaimo bingo scandal), the government compensated Windy Craggy investors for $29 million in direct investment. Given the government's now-tattered reputation in the mining community, the NDP offered up $138 million in incentives for another proposed mine in northern BC, just to ensure that mine still came on stream.

Learning Spanish

Windy Craggy and the government's approach to mining became a poster-child for the NDP's erratic approach to resource development. The debacle was the worst kind of ad hoc exception and by the late 1990s, the mining industry was in a near-fatal tailspin. In a 1998 Fraser Institute survey of 280 mining companies, British Columbia was third last in investment attractiveness; it barely beat out Prince Edward Island, which had no mining industry to speak of, and Wisconsin, where a moratorium was in place. BC topped the list on concerns about unclear regulations, too-stringent environmental policy, uncertainty about where future park and wilderness protection would occur, taxation, labour issues, and native land claims.[29]

Put another way, mining companies needed consistency. If the government promised that any new mine would have half its wealth confiscated, and the companies knew the NDP would never come back for more, they could at least plan their budgets. But instability, whether war or policy flip-flops, kills investment.

To no one's surprise, the government ignored the Fraser Institute report, at least publicly. But the numbers from the mining industry revealed the same story. Exploration investment sunk from $220 million in 1990[30] to $83.5 million in 1995[31] and just $22 million[32] in 1998. Meanwhile, mining investment in the rest of Canada climbed.[33] As $150 million must be invested annually in BC just to sustain the current number of mines, the future was not bright. By 1999, for every mine that opened in BC since 1990, two had closed.[34] In comparison, by the mid-1990s, Canadian companies in Chile had long-range investment plans worth $2.2 billion.[35]

Mining policy in the 1970s and the 1990s: Can you spot the difference?

Late in the decade the government made some laudable attempts to improve its mining policy; Mining minister Dan Miller attempted to streamline mine approval policies, and a refundable exploration credit was introduced. But there were still conflicts: the mining industry pulled out of the government's land-use management process in early 1999. It argued the government dragged its feet on compensation and broke their promise on restricting official parkland to twelve percent of the province (a charge borne out one year later with the leak of an NDP pre-election strategy document that proposed more fenced-off parkland).

In response Miller appointed a former mining executive as a mining advocate to cut red tape and recommend legal improvements to secure tenure. But by this time, 225 special management zones such as park study areas, native reserves, military land, and urban areas were all off the mining map. The BC and Yukon Chamber of Commerce of Mines estimated that 50 percent of the province would soon be off-limits for the industry.[36]

The NDP approach to resource development in the 1990s was potentially more dangerous to the prosperity of the province than even their 1970s economic jihad. In 1972, Dave Barrett justified his assault upon mining with the argument that minerals were better left in the ground if mines were not developed the NDP way,[37] i.e. – with excessively high tax rates or nationalization.

Mistaken as that policy was, it at least presumed *some* resource extraction. In the 1990s, and especially in the case of Windy Craggy, the NDP swung to an extreme where environmental purity won out over reasoned compromise. That approach was somewhat moderated later in the decade, but in the long run, a repeat of that hard-line view under any government poses a unique threat to British Columbia's prosperity. Eco-purism, as separate from reasonable environmental safeguards and some preservation, is utopian. But it has a growing following, and it may well be the next dividing line for BC politics in the 21st century, just as left and right economic debates were in the twentieth.

Speak no evil

Confused and contradictory government policies were not the sole cause of the mining industry's ills in BC in the 1990s. Price weakness for metals was also there – though it should be noted that investment elsewhere in Canada and in other countries often increased at the same time it declined in BC.[38] In 1998 when Mining minister Dan Miller blamed BC's poor showing on a worldwide slump, he was promptly corrected by the industry itself.[39] But mining companies were also partly to blame. The Fraser Institute began its anonymous survey precisely because mining CEOs were reluctant to speak publicly about how disastrous NDP policies had been.

Away from a public microphone, mining executives excoriated the NDP for their pureed Marxist economic views which drove mining companies south to Chile. Publicly, they professed a desire to co-operate, which allayed the public's concern as to just how ill conceived government policy really was. After all, if a mining company president could get along with Glen Clark and Moe Sihota, how bad could it be?

After nine years of NDP rule, the mining industry hollowed out and could not be restored overnight: from planning to mine startup takes five to ten years. Thus, like other NDP policy disasters, the mining decline would outlast the government that helped create it.

Blaming the victim

When it came to blame, what was true of mining in specific also applied to business in general. If the NDP government had been a child and the electorate the parents, child-rearing would have been an exhausting task.

This admittedly over-the-top cover, from now-defunct Equity magazine, raised a few eyebrows when published in 1993.

Whenever New Democrats were caught with their hands in the cookie jar, it was always someone else's fault: Ever-elusive balanced budgets were blamed on Socreds (true in 1992 but not after). In the mid-1990s, red ink was due to Ottawa, even though other governments, including the NDP in Saskatchewan, also suffered through cutbacks and yet produced surpluses. When the Asian economic flu hit, *that* was the reason for BC's unbalanced books (despite the fact that provincial own-source revenues in balanced budget Alberta dropped by *five* times the decline in BC[ii]). When fast ferries were over budget, an NDP-appointed board was at fault. When, in the 1996 election, the NDP claimed the numbers were in the black – and despite warnings from their own economists that such claims were nonsense – private sector forecasters were later blamed.

Likewise, when the private sector was suspicious of New Democrat policies, it was not the government's fault: business *itself* was to blame. Shortly after his elevation to the Finance portfolio in 1999, Paul Ramsey warned that negative discussion about the economy hurts everyone and lamented that "the rhetoric splits us apart."[40] Shortly after, Dan Miller scolded the mining industry for focusing on its problems, and said he was "concerned about self-fulfilling prophecies."[41] It was as if the government was in another world: in their view, economic realities were not the problem, but the broadcasting of such facts. The politicians lived on sound bites and inch-deep economic assumptions and thought business should do the same.

Given that New Democrats rode to re-election in 1996 on their ideological anti-corporate hobbyhorse, the lectures were a bit much. It was also a stretch coming from a government that had little respect for due process (Windy Craggy) or the rule of law (Carrier Lumber).

On the policy side, the government's attitude was schizophrenic. In general, they punished enterprise with high taxes, red tape and reversals of policy decisions, and then favoured specific businesses with government loans, grants, and bailouts. One day the NDP berated corporations but then professed their love for dot-coms. In the late 1990s the small business tax rate was cut but the minimum wage was hiked.

None of it made sense from a wider perspective. Where was the magic size at which the favoured *small* business became the mythical and hated "corporation," the supposed fount of all that was evil in NDP mythology? Of course, there was no easily identifiable dividing line and any silly attempt to define one only further revealed the economic and intellectual bankruptcy of

---

ii. In the first full budget year that immediately followed the Asian economic flu –1998-99 – Alberta's own-source revenues dropped by 6.5 percent (almost $1.1 billion) due to low oil prices in 1997 and part of 1998. In BC, affected by the Asian flu, own-source revenues dropped by 1.2 percent ($222 million).

the governing party. At various points, some New Democrats referred to the idea of British Columbians being "owners of their economy and not merely tenants in it,"[42] an idea that meant precisely nothing.

Unless the NDP was prepared to embark on nationalizing the entire province, something the NDP had not seriously contemplated since the 1970s Waffle declaration, such blather meant little in the way of concrete policy. British Columbians already *were* owners of the economy, through shares, union pension funds, and individual RRSPs. They also owned other parts of Canada and other countries. That is how widely dispersed share ownership works. And of course, billionaires such as Jimmy Pattison also owned a good chunk of the BC economy, though that was probably not the kind of ownership some NDP MLAs meant to endorse.

Because of their prejudice against business and free markets, New Democrats tilted at windmills. The only sure way to help British Columbians own BC was to allow for general wealth creation. To do that meant the NDP had to create a stable regulatory regime, reduce personal and business taxes significantly, and forsake cherry-picking individual companies with $5-million loans, as if such tinkering made any economic difference when the government killed $8.7-billion projects.

Out of business

The decade was not a complete writeoff. Forestry expert and *Vancouver Sun* columnist Ken Drushka noted that New Democrats did deserve credit for tackling some overdue issues left from Socred days, forest practices, cut levels, and environmental conflicts. He argued though that their worst forestry blunder was their refusal to set up a royal commission to consolidate some policies they did act on and add some ones they avoided.[43]

But by the end of the 1990s government policy bit into business and into real wages. Productivity actually *declined* by 0.6 percent over the period from 1992 to 1998, while it shot up by over 12 percent in Alberta and by 18 percent in NDP-led Saskatchewan. In fact, BC was the only province that recorded a decline in productivity. Even Atlantic provinces trumped BC. [44] Not surprisingly, BC ranked ninth among the provinces in attracting investment.

Watch your asset base

By the end, business leaders publicly attacked the government. In August 2000, new BC Business Council chief Jeff Mooney roasted the NDP in a late-summer speech.[45] One month later David Emerson, the president of forestry giant Canfor, also broke what he called the unwritten rules of forest executives: "You keep your mouth shut because the government controls your asset base." In a speech before the Vancouver Board of Trade, he argued that industry "had been used as a social engineering tool because it was politically vulnerable.[46]

The speeches were direct but late. The NDP was stuck at 20 percent in the polls and thoroughly discredited. The public should have heard from business heads much earlier, especially before the 1996 election. Instead, most sat on their hands or cut deals behind closed doors with the government for their particular industry; all British Columbians suffered as a result.

If business did not make much money in BC in the 1990s, their employees were even worse off. In 1992, per person disposable income[iii] was $500 higher than the national average; by 1999, it was $700 *lower* and $2,400 less than Alberta.[47]

By 2000, the new premier, Ujjal Dosanjh, was more careful about public anti-business rhetoric, but the reflex was still there. In an election-style speech before the Hospital Employees Union convention in October 2000, Dosanjh went on the attack against private medical clinics. Such facilities include doctor's offices and were long part of the Canadian health care system, but the Premier charged ahead with a 1970s-style NDP approach to the private sector: nationalize where politically possible. "I want to tell you," he roared to a cheering crowd, "as soon as we can afford to outlaw private clinics, we will do so!"[48] Similar to Penny Priddy's remarks several years earlier, some NDP reflexes just twitched uncontrollably.

iii. Per capita income in current dollars, after subtracting for personal taxes.

(Not to scale...)

5

Three 'F's and You're Out

The Fudge-It Budget
Forest Renewal British Columbia
Fast Ferries

"But what I think would be a travesty is if people were to say, 'we don't know what you stand for. We don't really think you guys know what you're doing. We think you're just throwing away money, therefore we're not going to vote for you.' I would find that hard to take."[1]

- Glen Clark, in a 1994 *Vancouver Sun* interview

The Fudge-it Budget

In September 1996, after a province-wide address by Premier Glen Clark on the 1996 "fudge-it" budget, *Victoria Times Colonist* cartoonist Adrian Raeside drew a variation on the Pinocchio metaphor; the Premier's nose stretched out from the cartoon frame right across the five columns on the other page. A *Vancouver Province* cartoon portrayed a nervous Glen Clark with the caption: "Uh, um, the dog ate my election promise."

Cartoonists were not the only ones who made the comparisons. A UTV viewer poll after Clark's talk revealed that 81 percent of the audience trusted their government *less* after the speech than before it.[2] In a MarkTrend poll later that autumn, 68 percent of British Columbians believed the NDP was aware (before the election) that the budget was not balanced.[3]

Budgets, trials, economists and accountants

The 1996 provincial budget set off a chain reaction of political landmines that, even though not immediately fatal, continually bled the party during its second term in office. The collateral damage began almost as soon as the election was over. In June, the new Finance minister let it slip that the budget was, well, not exactly balanced. Leaked Finance ministry documents revealed that senior Treasury officials repeatedly warned that pumped-up revenue estimates were not credible; the government became the target of a high profile lawsuit that alleged electoral fraud; late 1997 recall campaigns were fuelled by anger over the bogus estimates; an Auditor General's report added more fuel to public anger; and the fraud allegation itself, though unsuccessful, dragged the NDP through court and forced the party to spend hundreds of thousands of dollars – all for the very thin gruel of satisfaction that no *legal* proof existed to prove that NDP MLAs lied.

And throughout the second term, the government's claim on any topic connected to numbers was met with instant scepticism from the media, the Opposition, and the public. The view was that the NDP fudged an entire budget – why would anyone believe anything else?

Public pre-election scepticism

After the 1996 budget was revealed as red ink, much was made of behind-the-scenes scepticism about the budget forecasts – forecasts pumped full of "fiscal optimism" by Finance Minister Elizabeth Cull. But even before those red flags were revealed publicly (after the election), there was plenty of doubt before the vote.[i]

On the last day of April in 1996, Cull tabled the annual budget and claimed that the 1995 budget (which ended on March 30, 1996) was balanced, and forecast another surplus for the new 1996 budget. Hours later, the election writ was dropped. The balanced budget claim gave the NDP pretty good cover against the charge they could not manage a six-year-old's popsicle stand, never mind Canada's third-largest province. Given that the NDP ran hard against the Social Credit government in 1991 over the issue of budget deficits, it was crucial to reassure voters that New Democrats were indeed moderates who knew the value of a balanced buck. Thus, the claim

---

i. For a detailed chronology of the important dates surrounding the 1996 budget, see Appendix B.

was a key plank in their 1996 re-election strategy.

But post-budget reaction was sceptical. BC Business Council economist Jock Finlayson criticized the rosy revenue forecasts as risky, and pointed to weakening commodity prices and financial losses in the forest industry.[4] BCTV reporter Clem Chapple dismissed Cull's budget as "an elaborate election pamphlet full of pie in the sky."[5] The *Vancouver Sun* dismissed it as rife with "tricks, fancy footwork," and called it "hopelessly optimistic."[6] Their main political columnist Vaughn Palmer wrote that the Cull/Clark forecasts were way out of line with reality: "As a result, the books are cooked."[7]

NDP MLAs later claimed that the budget forecasts were within the margin of error historically, if a little on the optimistic side. Elizabeth Cull argued that ministry forecasts were conservative in the past, thus she had every right to bump up revenue projections.

The claim was half-true but the devil was in the details: revenues were indeed understated in 1994 and in 1993. But in 1992, revenues were equal to the forecast and in the year before that, actual revenues were half a billion dollars *less* than hoped for. The crucial point was the direction of the economy, and when Elizabeth Cull injected "budget optimism" into the books, economic signs pointed down, not up.

Inside warnings and $800 million in spare change

As far back as February 1995, Treasury predicted a 1996 budget deficit as high as $800 million. By September 1995, the figure was $1.15 billion. In January 1996, the shortfall was still pegged at $725 million.[8]

Suddenly, one day after Glen Clark was sworn in as Premier after his NDP leadership win, Treasury Board had two sets of forecasts, one with revenue estimates of $19.9 billion and another one with predictions as high as $20.7 billion. Apparently, $800 million in spare change had been found after Glen Clark became Premier.[9]

It helped that revenue forecasts were suddenly bumped up. Sales tax revenues, which grew at an average of three percent annually for half a decade were changed and forecast to grow by six percent. The personal income tax take was expected to climb at twice the rate it had the year before. Oil and gas revenues were targeted to grow at triple the rate forecast by the energy ministry itself. BC lottery revenues were expected to grow by seven percent even though BC Lotteries itself predicted zero growth. On corporate taxes, collected by the federal government, federal Finance officials predicted a five-percent revenue increase; BC's new estimate was a *twenty*-percent jump.[10]

A March 8, 1996 memo from Treasury Board said BC had gone into the "tank."[11] The paper, entitled "Economy Tanks in Fourth Quarter," referred to

MINISTER OF FINANCE AND CORPORATE RELATIONS
95Ch479
RECEIVED DEC 2 2 1995

File: 10765-30/QUAR
280-30/SBP

DEC 20 1995

To: The Honourable Elizabeth Cull
Chair, Treasury Board
Minister of Finance and Corporate Relations

From: The Honourable Andrew Petter
Minister of Forests

Re: Small Business Enterprise Program

Attached is the first quarter report for 1995/96.

You should be aware that information obtained in recent days indicates a significant shortfall in revenue from the 1995/96 forecast due to less harvesting and billed volumes than forecast. This trend is attributable to a rapid decline in markets from last year and less volumes sold than forecast. I will be providing further information on this at the earliest opportunity.

Andrew Petter
Minister of Forests

Attachment: Small Business Forest Enterprise Program 1st Quarter Report
April 1, 1995 through June 30, 1995.

This letter, sent from then Forests Minister Andrew Petter in December 1995 warns of declining forest revenues. Despite the warning, Finance Minister Elizabeth Cull bumped up revenue projections for that year and the next budget year. In June 1996, Andrew Petter, then the new Finance minister after Elizabeth Cull's defeat in the election, proceeded to re-introduce Cull's two "balanced" budgets despite what he wrote six months earlier.

the final three months of the 1995 budget year, a budget that would end only three weeks later. The report stated: "Now that most of the data has become available, it is evident that the provincial economy suffered a sharp decline."[12]

Plausible denial?

Elizabeth Cull was later asked if she was informed that revenues were collapsing in early 1996. She replied: "No, of course not."[13] But besides the flurry of memorandums and personal briefings from senior Treasury Board staff, Forests Minister Andrew Petter also informed Cull of plummeting forestry revenue (in December 1995). His letter to her warned of a "significant drop" in revenue from Forestry, and in particular, the Small Business Forest Enterprise Program. Given the existence of that warning, Cull's later reply appeared less than frank. Just as curious was Petter's introduction of Cull's balanced budgets after the 1996 election (when he became Finance minister to replace the defeated Cull) given the memo he wrote just six months previous.

Despite the multiple warnings from senior Finance officials that the optimistic numbers were baseless, the staff were instructed to deliver two surplus budgets come hell or red ink. Treasury staff later told *Vancouver Sun* columnist Vaughn Palmer that the order was never given in writing, just verbally.[14] As to who delivered it, speculation centered on senior Glen Clark adviser Tom Gunton, who met with Finance officials in February 1996. Deputy Finance Minister Brenda Eaton, a career civil servant, later told the Auditor General that she assumed Gunton provided her with the views of the Premier on budget matters.[15] Tom Gunton later claimed that the February meeting was the last contact he had with Finance officials about the budget. He denied ever giving any orders to fudge budget numbers.

The David Stockell lawsuit

After the 1995 and 1996 budgets were revealed as woefully optimistic at best or, at worst, intentionally fake, Kelowna printer David Stockell decided to take the NDP government to court using the BC Election Act clause that prohibited election-time fraud.

Stockell approached both the Canadian Taxpayers Federation and the National Citizens' Coalition for help with legal costs. Then CTF British Columbia director Troy Lanigan declined the request. While morally supportive, he refused participation on the grounds that the recall law was a more effective tool of accountability than the courts: the recall process ensured required widespread citizen involvement; court judgments did not.

The National Citizens' Coalition helped fund the lawsuit, and lawyers argued that the NDP committed fraud in introducing, advertising, and trumpeting two balanced budgets which were later revealed to contain deficits of $355 million and $337 million.[ii]

The Clark government first tried to block the case. Lawyers argued that the Election Act section on fraud only applied to tricking a person about where an individual should vote, not to statements that might be made during an election.[16] The NDP lawyer argued that political disagreements with the government could be settled via use of the recall law, not the Election Act.[iii]

The same lawyer also argued that a broken election promise was not fraud. It was not, stated Robert McDiarmid, "the same thing as pointing a gun at their [the voter's] heads. Election promises can be, uh, unkept after the campaign is over."[17]

The court allowed the suit to proceed anyway, though it ultimately met defeat in 2000. In that judgment, Madame Justice Humphries wrote that: "I am unable to conclude, based on the evidence, that there was any such conspiracy, and that Ms. Cull's beliefs in the projections contained in Budget '96 were anything other than her best judgment in the circumstances."[18]

> *If the petitioners could actually prove that there was a conspiracy between Mr. Clark and/or his advisors and/or Ms. Cull to insert grossly exaggerated numbers into this budget, ones which they knew would never materialize, they might overcome the hurdle placed in their way by the Court of Appeal – that is, that statements of intention or belief cannot constitute fraudulent means.*[19]

Given the judge's verdict, what should British Columbians make of the two budgets the NDP were accused of fudging? Was it all, as does occasionally happen, a whipped-up media-driven non-scandal that took on a life of its own? For the more conspiratorially-minded, was it a plot by nefarious Conrad Black-owned newspapers to blacken the name of the well-meaning but occasionally error-prone NDP aides who wanted to try their hand at detailed fiscal forecasting?

---

ii. Or $1.7 billion and $535 million if one looked at the total increase in public debt, and not just the more limited consolidated accounts.

iii. This support of recall to further one's complaints was curious in that the NDP later argued recall proponents in two northern campaigns "abused recall" when they used the provision to try and force two by-elections over the fudge-it budget. Apparently, in the view of some New Democrats, the Election Act was not a proper tool for anyone to pursue their complaints, nor was the recall law, both of which were designed and passed by the NDP.

In the age of Clinton now ended, almost any embarrassing political scandal could be seemingly spun away. A dash of denial, a touch of feigned innocence, the occasional spicy verbal offensive, all baked in the oven of a judgment that found no legal evidence of electoral fraud. The result, New Democrats claimed, was an undisputed win.

But Humphries, like any justice, ruled on the evidence introduced in court, not that which never appeared. And as she pointed to in her judgment, a conviction of fraud cannot occur when the only evidence offered is a statement of belief or intent. But besides the court trial, there is an existing record of events that led to the balanced budget claims. Some were recorded in the 1999 Auditor General's report; others were in the 1,000 documents released in 1996 after the *Vancouver Sun* used freedom of information laws to dig through the government's Maginot line of political spin.

Those documents and reports revealed that Elizabeth Cull and her fellow MLAs campaigned on a budget that had no visible means of support. Its revenue projections were, as the judge noted, within the range of error, but when her top Finance officials warned the economy tanked, Cull's estimates should have been grounded in reality and caution. Instead, they were inflated by her own baseless "optimism." Her Norman Vincent Peale approach to budget forecasting was convenient given the looming election. And despite her later defence that Forest Renewal BC funds were always an option, that possibility was, also conveniently, never shared with the public before the 1996 vote.[iv]

The NDP risked its re-election on budget numbers that were based in myth-making, not concrete economic conditions pointed to by Finance staff both within the provincial government and by federal government economists. The injection of "optimism" into the 1996 budget was a risky strategy that succeeded temporarily, but one that undercut the party's long-term credibility.

---

iv. Elizabeth Cull lost her seat in 1996 but did come back occasionally to work for the government for $1,000 a day and, in late 2000, was appointed Chief of Staff for Premier Ujjal Dosanjh.

BC's Auditor General on the 1995 and 1996 Budgets

On the 1995 budget:

Minister Cull's decision to include in the revised forecast a revenue projection of $156 million over and above the Secretariat's optimistic forecast seems inappropriate.[1]

On introducing "fiscal optimism" into the 1995 budget in January 1996:

(Given that the budget year ended on March 31, the January action allowed the government to project a balanced budget for the year then ending, even though most revenues and expenditures were already complete.)

Minister Cull's decision to introduce optimism in the revised revenue forecast, so late in the fiscal year, seems inappropriate.[2]

On risk and proper disclosure:

I concluded that the estimates of revenue for the 1996-97 fiscal year carried with them a disproportionate risk.[3]

Was the suggested alternate revenue forecast free of disproportionate risks of either over- or under-estimating the revenue for 1996/97? We believe it was not.[4]

In our opinion, information provided by government when these budgets were presented did not make full and fair disclosure of the extent of the business risk being assumed and the government's plan to address it. In that sense, crucial information was missing...[5]

On plans to divert money from Forest Renewal British Columbia, a Crown corporation set up to spend stumpage fees exclusively for forestry.

The Estimates reflected revenue estimates that were some $450 million beyond the comfort level of the Minister of Finance and Corporate Relations.... The Minister's approval of the revenue estimates was based on her knowledge that she could tap into additional revenue sources to compensate for any expected shortfall. However, these plans were not transparent in either Ms. Cull's Budget '96 or the Estimates for the Fiscal Year Ending March 31, 1997.[6]

On whether Finance Minister Elizabeth Cull was informed of Treasury Board's warnings on inflated budget figures:

Ms. Eaton wrote to staff that government had been repeatedly told of these factors, but that the time had come to produce the Estimates for 1996/97.[7]

On Glen Clark aide Tom Gunton

Ms. Eaton told us in her testimony that she was under the impression that Mr. Gunton was providing her with the views of the Premier's Office when discussing matters in the fiscal steering committee.[8]

On Elizabeth Cull's famed "budget optimism"

For all these reasons, prescribing arbitrary optimism to improve the accuracy of revenue forecasting had no merit.[9]

---

1 A Review of the Estimates Process, Office of the Auditor General, February 1999, p.140.
2 Ibid, p.165.
3 Ibid, p.5.
4 Ibid, p.185.
5 Ibid, p.139.
6 Ibid, p.142.
7 Ibid, p.176.
8 Ibid, p.189.
9 Ibid, p.151.

Forest Renewal British Columbia

"The money will not go into general revenue and no greedy ministers will be able to dip their fingers into that pot."[29]
- NDP MLA Harry Lali, in 1994, when FRBC was first established.

Under New Democrats, Crown corporations became a favoured way to sneak through unpopular measures that would be near to impossible if done via ministries. Thus, after visible tax increases became publicly unpopular in the early 1990s, Crown corporations could be milked for transfers to the provincial treasury instead. This prevented rate reductions at BC Hydro, for example. As a consequence, it also undercut the stated reason for Crowns in the first place: cut out profit and supposedly the public paid less for electricity and auto insurance.[v] But as Crowns turned over increasing amounts of cash to the government ($600 million more in 2000 than in 1991), that justification for public monopolies was shot.

Besides stealth tax grabs, Crown corporations were useful dumping grounds for political hacks. (The NDP dumped old friends in ICBC, BC Ferries, Catamaran Ferries International, and BC Hydro to name but a few.) And Crowns could also be used to offload social engineering objectives that might ruffle more feathers if done visibly by central government.

The stumpage sinkhole

Forest Renewal British Columbia, created in 1994, was used by the Harcourt and Clark governments for all of the above and more, though in fairness, the original intent of the agency was positive.

The new Crown was an attempt to deal with longstanding forestry issues, especially reforestation and environmental concerns. As part of its mandate, FRBC was directed to spend money in equal measure around the province, and was to be focused on the long term so that forestry jobs would still exist in the next century; no one wanted to see the decimation of Eastern cod stocks and the loss of jobs repeated in British Columbia's woods.

To accomplish the multiple goals, industry would have to cough up extra cash – $2 billion in extra stumpage fees over five years. Forest companies were willing to pay the new taxes, so long as the high prices for lumber

---

v. This is the theory. In reality, it is debatable that public sector monopolies are any more efficient than private sector monopolies. Without competition, staff and payroll levels tend to become bloated and as taxpayers/consumers have no choice but to pay, higher fees and charges result. Private sector monopolies are at least accountable to one or more shareholders; the accountability link between public monopolies and taxpayers is never that direct.

continued. The government promised it would never touch the Forest Renewal money; all of it would replenish the province's forests and retrain laid-off workers. "The money will not go into general revenue and no greedy minister – it doesn't matter what party or government they represent – will be able to dip their fingers into that pot," stated interior NDP MLA Harry Lali.[30] Dan Miller warned that "there won't be a politician next week, next month, next year or 20 years from now who will dare put their hands into that pocket of money."[31]

And to those concerned that perhaps the new Crown corporation would be an unaccountable bureaucracy, the government promised that employment at the agency would be, at maximum, 25 people.[32]

Post-election blues

It was not long before the promises were on life-support. Two years after the solemn assurances, the NDP eyed the forestry fund for a potential raid. That possibility was revealed after the election, not before, which would have spiked the possibility of a second-term New Democrat government. When the planned hijacking of the money was exposed, the Opposition claimed that Glen Clark's deputy minister, Doug McArthur, instructed the FRBC board before the election to prepare to hand over cash. McArthur and Clark denied that event ever took place and instead stated that the board had, "from day one, discussed [what to do with] the surplus."[33]

The surplus occurred because the new stumpage fees had not been spent as quickly as they poured in, a curious oddity for spendthrift New Democrats who figured, hey, if the money was there, use it or lose it. To the NDP, surplus money was a problem, a nuisance to be dispensed with as quickly as possible. As one New Democrat put it, "I think they [FRBC] got the message. If they don't fix the problem, we will."[34]

To justify the raid, New Democrats were helped by their appointed chair of the FRBC board, Roger Stanyer. Stanyer came to his job straight from the NDP-friendly International Woodworkers of America, and claimed that FRBC's proposed gift of cash was actually Forest Renewal BC's idea. "There will always be those people who believe government came to us in the dark of night and said 'we are going to take the money away so give it to us.' Well, it never happened."[35]

It never had to. The government and its labour appointees were as close as lovesick honeymooners; words were hardly necessary. A look of desire or a wink would accomplish the task and by September 1996 the government was ready to pull $500 million from the fund. This was about eighteen years earlier than Dan Miller had guaranteed as even an outside hypothetical possibility.

The government immediately ran into a firestorm of criticism. Canfor chair Peter Bentley said he wouldn't call it "theft," but "it is a complete double-cross of the intent of Forest Renewal BC."[36] At a Union of British Columbia Municipalities convention, an almost unanimous vote opposed the provincial government's action.[37] In response to the accusation that the government broke its word, Forests Minister David Zirnhelt uttered his now-famous line: "Government can change the law. Don't forget that government can do anything."[38]

Well, government could not, actually. The public and the courts regularly stopped wild-eyed New Democrats in the 1990s, and Zirnhelt's statement was viewed as just another sign that the government paid little heed to its promises; moreover, it was arrogant about its power. Even allies of the government took a swipe at the planned raid. The IWA opposed it because it meant less work for members; environmental groups hated the idea because it meant fewer cleanups in the forest.[39]

After the government took numerous lumps, the raid was cancelled in early 1997. But that left the question of what to do with the $500 million.

Who wants a million bucks?

"My number one goal is jobs,"[40] said Premier Glen Clark, after the raid was spiked. Instead, FRBC was to spend its surplus money on "job creation." Over the next several years, just about anything fell under that category. Forest Renewal BC shovelled out grants of up to $27,000 for career paths that included dog grooming, music and golf.[41] One tree planter was paid to learn the saxophone.[42] An FRBC subsidiary built a new office at a cost of almost $1 million on a native reserve – a building that critics argued was unnecessary.[43]

Much of what governments do in the name of job creation is often a combination of pork-barrel politics, questionable economics, spurious statistics, and boondoggles; FRBC excelled in all four categories. In one absurd example, thousands of logging roads were deactivated. The justification was watershed restoration but forestry expert Ken Drushka argued the reality was that most roads were probably harmless. Besides, they would be needed in several decades when tree stands were mature enough to be cut once again.[44] In the meantime, the forests would be inaccessible for other uses including backcountry tourism.

As for job creation, a 1999 *Vancouver Sun* investigation found that in some cases, employment lasted only as long as the FRBC cheques were cut; the jobs vanished as soon as the money ran out.[45] The former head of FRBC's Forest Jobs Transition fund, argued that the public should take job creation numbers from Forest Renewal BC with a grain of salt. Don Cochrane argued that "when you hire spin doctors, they are charged with giving you the information they want you to have."[46]

In an internal FRBC report authored by Cochrane and later obtained by the *Sun*, it turned out that the tight political-union ties common in the Clark government also cropped up in FRBC. Cochrane accused Forest Renewal BC and IWA-Canada of subverting a $100-million aid program intended for workers. The former head of the fund wrote that politics, greed, and bad management crippled the program; it was supposed to help all laid-off workers in the industry, including non-union tree planters. But this clashed with the IWA's goal to use the money for its own workers as much as possible.[47]

In the lower mainland, the Transition fund was run from union halls, and the local director was also the business agent for a local IWA branch. Vancouver-area offices were union-dominated and bypassed the program's chain of command to deal directly with the FRBC head (a former IWA local president) and Glen Clark.[48] After Don Cochrane was dismissed and the program folded into another FRBC job creation scheme, the woodworkers' union got its way as scores of coastal tree planters were forced into IWA ranks.[49]

The Auditor General's check-up

By late 1999, the Auditor General stopped in on the party and examined the wreckage. Employment in forestry dropped from 88,000 in 1995 to 76,000 three years later.[vi] Costs for reforestation were higher in FRBC than in the ministry of Forests, in part because of loose financial controls and in part because of the additional social engineering aspects in the Crown's mandate.

Moreover, Forest Renewal BC also took over many responsibilities formerly under the Forests ministry. So instead of funding more silviculture – one justification for the $2-billion stumpage increase – the government dumped more duties into Forest Renewal BC and reduced ministry spending. In 1992, the ministry of Forests spent $190 million on reforestation. By 1999, that budget was only $38 million while FRBC cut cheques for $140 million. This allowed the government's main set of books to look that much more prudent. But in effect, the government slipped through a 1994 tax increase via a new Crown corporation and channelled as much "old" government spending through its new arm.

And then there was the bureaucracy: In 1994, government MLAs reas-

---

vi. This, despite the much vaunted "Jobs and Timber Accord" promoted by Glen Clark in 1997 where he promised that 20,000 new jobs would be created in forestry. Like most other projects, the New Democrats and Clark in particular thought jobs could be created by a combination of photo-ops and legislation.

sured critics and promised that at most 25 positions would be created by Forest Renewal British Columbia; most of FRBC's money would go to forestry workers, not a new bureaucracy. By 1999, the new Crown had offices in Williams Lake, Prince George, Kamloops, Smithers, Cranbrook, Campbell River, Victoria and Vancouver; at least 253 people were employed across the province.[50]

Young, stupid, and rich

In 1994, the government created a new bureaucracy with few financial controls. Once in place, the government raised stumpage fees by $2 billion, injected it into FRBC and, after 1996, instructed that it be spent as quickly as possible.

That mandate encouraged every interest group or individual to apply for money no matter how questionable the application, assuming one was even required. Social engineering plans included affirmative action and quotas, and the agency was instructed to dish out money equally across the province. As the Auditor General pointed out, money was thus spent in areas of the province that did not even require it. Mixed in it all was big labour's influence, which grabbed away as much money as possible and turned already questionable job creation programs into guaranteed job redistribution slush funds.

Given the loosely defined goals, the lousy accountability, and all the cash – the five-year binge was guaranteed: it was akin to supplying $10 million, a Porsche, and a year's stash of cocaine to a 17-year-old.

Beautiful but costly: Despite 1994 warnings from the ferry corporation not to build the ships (BC Ferries recommended leasing a test ferry), three fast ferries were constructed at a cost of $463 million, $253 million more than originally promised by Glen Clark in 1994. Over-budget, late, and much slower than expected, the ferries were put up for sale for only $40 million each in 2000. (UWC photo)

Fast Ferry Follies

How's that apportioned with respect to bookkeeping? I couldn't care less."[51]

- Dan Miller, minister responsible for BC Ferries, when asked if the $13 million in facility costs for the fast ferries were included in the overall project total, or whether the cost had been "buried" elsewhere in the government's budget.

"I wouldn't say they are lemons."[52]

- Glen Clark, in 1999, on the three fast ferries.

If the 1996 budget revealed an NDP talent for picking budget numbers out of thin air, three high-speed aluminum-hulled ferries displayed how spectacularly incompetent they were with public dollars above the surface. The fast ferry debacle resulted from a belief in politically driven mega-projects over and above legislative scrutiny and private sector advice. The bias for Crown corporations combined with potent ministerial power, and despite opposition to the project from BC Ferries, became the showcase indictment against the NDP in power.

Sailing in BC waters

BC's ferry system was a privately run affair until 1960, when Social Credit Premier W.A.C. Bennett edged out the operators and created what later became known as the BC Ferry Corporation. (Bennett blasted socialist hordes but like most successful politicians, borrowed an idea or two from the Opposition when necessary.) The new Crown agency grew to service both the frequently travelled routes from greater Vancouver to the Sunshine Coast, Victoria, Nanaimo, and as far north as Prince Rupert. As for political interference; it was assumed as a right of governing.

For most of its history, BC Ferries kept its head above fiscal water. In 1991, the year the NDP came to power, the corporation's debt was $60 million, in part because the Socreds kept it on a short financial leash. By then, new ferries were overdue but, as was routine throughout the 1990s, the new government chose the most expensive way to obtain them. The first warning sign occurred in June 1994 when Premier Mike Harcourt announced a ten-year $840-million shipbuilding plan. Bucking inter-provincial free trade, he decreed that any new ships must be built in BC and that the government would create a company for that very purpose.

Harcourt and his caucus could never accept that while some industries and jobs might decline in British Columbia, others would rise to take their place, or even that well-paying union jobs could be created elsewhere in Canada or even outside the country. Organized labour might be about brotherhood and solidarity, but for BC's politicians, it was simple: union welders who worked on ships in Halifax did not vote in British Columbia elections. Damn the torpedoes and the bean counters in the head office at BC Ferries; the ships would be built in BC.

$70 million and toilet paper

As part of the plan, three new aluminum-hulled ships were to be built to service the West Vancouver-Nanaimo crossing. At the June 1994 announcement, Mike Harcourt claimed the vessels would chop the two-hour voyage in half.[53] Intended to be sleek and speedy, the new vessels also came with a snappy name: Pacificats, later known informally as the "fast ferries." The West Vancouver to Nanaimo run was not exactly a lengthy New York-London voyage, but few thought to ask why a high-speed ferry on one of the world's shortest ocean ferry routes was such an urgent necessity.

Employment and Investment Minister Glen Clark promised that the three ferries would cost no more than $70 million each. "It's all in the price, right down to the toilet paper," he assured reporters.[54] The promise was worthless; Clark and his political aides picked the numbers out of thin air. The government had not yet specified the dimensions of the ship or even what type would be built (single hull or catamaran).[55] In fact, with only sketchy details, BC Ferries' own estimate was already in the range of $80 million each and that was $2 million higher than the estimated cost of an equivalent conventional ferry.[56] To solve that problem, Clark's political hacks at the NDP-created Crown Corporations Secretariat arbitrarily changed the number to $70 million before the public announcement.[57]

More ominously, the government barged ahead despite inside criticism. In a confidential 1994 report to BC Ferries, the author warned that "there is no clear proof that large, high-speed catamaran ferries can produce a faster marine transportation system which is more economical, has higher safety, or has less environmental pollution than existing, more traditional ferry systems on short-haul routes."[58]

But to the government, the issue was not what the public needed, i.e. – new transportation across the Georgia Strait, it was about the chance to shore up union support on the docks and jumpstart a new industry. Getting the best ferries at a competitive price was sacrificed to visions of a revitalized BC-based shipbuilding industry. At the June press conference, Harcourt boasted that "This new technology will bring new industry to our province."[59]

History repeats itself

Unfortunately for ferry passengers and taxpayers, that strategy had already been tried before with mixed results. As it was, two 470-car superferries, which operated on the southern Vancouver – Victoria run, were touted as the salvation of BC's shipbuilders at the time of their early 1990s construction. But by 1994, the *Vancouver Sun* reported that the superferries, while popular, were expensive. Moreover, the shipyard jobs created by the superferry program did not last.[60] So, just as the government commissioned new boats, newspapers warned that the last experiment did not work as planned. Never ones to let history or prudent budgeting interfere with a dream, New Democrats forged on ahead.

The early critics

Besides internal resistance from BC Ferries itself, there were also early public critics of the venture. In a late 1994 *BC Report* article, the magazine pointed to potentially costly annual operating expenses and questionable efficiency. Much more fuel would be required than needed by conventional ferries; even with a best-case scenario, the three fast ferries would still carry as many as 36 percent fewer cars and passengers than two superferries. For the new ships to be economically feasible, fares would have to be substantially higher. To top it off, the catamaran was likely the wrong vessel for the planned route.[61]

In June 1995, more predictions about the aluminum-hulled ships were ventured: the aluminum to be used weakened when exposed to welding temperatures, was susceptible to cracking under duress, required more than double the amount of time to cut per ton, and was more costly than steel. Also, the new ferries would never be able to travel as quickly as predicted. Moreover, it would cost as much as $15 million to overhaul Vancouver shipyards for the project. *BC Report*'s story pegged the ships at over $100 million each.[62]

That estimate turned out to be conservative compared to the eventual money-pump the ferries became. But once the project was underway, the government, BC Ferries and Catamaran Ferries International (the new Crown corporation set up to build the ships) dismissed the criticism.

The source for many early questions was Sidney-based marine consultant Bob Ward. In mid-1995, then BC Ferries vice-president Tom Ward (no relation to the marine consultant) waved off the doubts and said they were "mostly triggered by Bob Ward writing letters."[63] The executive dismissed the other Ward as a self-appointed critic, with "no experience in building, operating or designing fast ferries, who is sitting on the sidelines, reading about these things and setting himself up as an authority."[64]

In February 1996, the British shipping journal, *Fairplay*, also estimated the cost of the ferries at $100 million each. Those in charge still maintained all was well. Glen Clark said the $70-million price was "fixed."[65] Tom Ward claimed: "We haven't seen anything at this point that would make us believe we won't be on budget."[66]

Board games

In the summer of 1996, the government finally appointed a board to oversee Catamaran Ferries International. It was an empty gesture. Chief financial officers within BC Ferries itself could not even access financial information about CFI, and CFI board requests for cost estimates, timetables, and marketing progress plans (for ships beyond the government order) were regularly delayed or denied by their own company. This, despite the fact that Tom Ward, still BC Ferries vice-president and now also in charge of the fast ferry program, also sat on the CFI board.

If CFI's own board could not access the facts about their own project, the provincial civil service had even less luck. Lawrie McFarlane, head of Treasury Board, later told an inquiry that his attempts to get information from Tom Ward were unsuccessful. "I'm not used to being lied to face to face,"[67] is how McFarlane described his dealings with Tom Ward. In addition, McFarlane also notified then Finance Minister Andrew Petter of the bureaucracy's concern about CFI's unaccountable attitude. Petter, apparently, did nothing.[68]

The head of BC Ferries, NDP appointment Frank Rhodes, was also on the CFI board,[69] not that it helped anyone who wanted answers about the project. In fact, Rhodes turned out to be the chief obstacle. After construction delays and an internal report that showed the three ferries would cost at least $260 million, not $210 million, three CFI director heads rolled in the spring of 1997.

Lucille Johnstone, Kevin Murphy, and Michael Goldberg were all asked to submit their resignations. It turned out they were shown the door not for

vii. The Rhodes/Miller defence that Rhodes edged out the three critical board members was reminiscent of the 1992 Carrier Lumber decision. There, a senior civil servant claimed to have pulled the logging licence (illegally as it turned out) of Carrier Lumber. In the later trial, the judge refused to believe that story and instead put Miller at the centre of the decision. Apparently Dan Miller was often an absentee minister in major affairs under his watch. Unlike the Carrier Lumber case, in the fast ferry mess, there was no evidence that Miller or Clark pushed Rhodes to get rid of the critical directors, but the parallels were nonetheless intriguing.

incompetence but the opposite reason: for their persistent demands for accurate information about construction schedules and costs. Johnstone, the board's head until her resignation, was described as fiercely independent. She was also an expert about the shipping industry. Murphy was a businessman and Goldberg a university professor. All had performed their due diligence and were shown the door for their efforts.

And it was Frank Rhodes who pushed them out, at least officially. At one point shortly before their ejection, Rhodes informed them that they were not to concern themselves with "such issues,"[70] in reference to a remark by one director who asked what their purpose was if not to keep the project on budget and on time. The bumped directors, who knew something about ships and budgets, were replaced by NDP stalwarts like Jack Munro whose knowledge of the industry was rather weak as he himself admitted: "I don't pretend to understand the building of a ship."[71]

In later testimony before the public accounts committee, Frank Rhodes claimed that he, not the politicians above, moved directors aside because Auditor General reports on Crown corporations suggested they get a tighter grip on subsidiaries.[vii] Dan Miller backed up Rhodes' assertion.[72] Rhodes' excuse was ill timed; the Auditor General made it clear shortly before Rhodes' statements that his (the Auditor's) advice was the opposite: Crown corporations needed more independent advice, not less. Nevertheless, Frank Rhodes used the excuse anyway. Perhaps he hoped no one would notice.[73]

Miller vs. accountability

As late as November 1997, a full year and a half after the first ship was supposed to hit the water, the Crown corporation building them still claimed the ferries would be "mostly" on budget,[74] and in one case, blamed the extended launch delay on the tides.[75]

By January 1998 the first ferry cost escalated to $86 million, a 23-percent overrun.[76] But that was minor compared to what Miller and BC Ferries already knew. And despite that 1996 internal report that showed the project costs would hit at least $260 million and Dan Miller's knowledge of that fact in December 1996,[77] BC Ferries took until March 1998 to inform the public.[78]

After that tardy disclosure, Miller was his usual helpful self. When reporters asked for more details in a May 1998 press conference, the minister responsible tried the damn-the-questions approach to public service. Those who asked were merely critics and "a critic never built a damn thing."[79]

His next strategy was to go on offence and attack the doubter's patriotic pride in BC. Miller: "So, where are you going to be when these things hit the water? Are you going to say: 'We're proud of this.' Or are you going to look at a few dollars and say: 'Oh dear. We shouldn't have done this'?"[80]

Approach three was to attack the motives of the questioners: "Self-serving is a rather mild term when it comes to some of the claptrap that I've heard from the media relative to BC Ferries."[81]

Have a little faith

Finally, Miller appealed to a nobler impulse – faith: "Why," Miller asked, "is it that there are so many doubters?"[82]

Dan Miller's response to reporter's questions was typical of the personal style of both Miller and Clark when faced with rough questions: if forced, deal with the issue but insist the obvious facts don't matter; change the subject if possible; and, if all else fails, engage in personal attacks. Never mind that hundreds of millions of taxpayer dollars were at stake or that the public had every right to answers.

But then, New Democrats often treated taxpayer dollars, civil servants, and BC itself, as if it were all their own property. In their minds, they won the election; parliamentary niceties, rules, and accountability could take a holiday. Forget the distinctions between political party and the public service; stuff it with hacks. Ignore requests for detailed information; what right did anyone have to hold a minister to account? Public institutions were the property of the election's victors – in this case, the NDP MLAs and the partisans they appointed.

No surprise then when reporters asked about the $13 million spent on construction facilities for the fast ferries, that the response once again dripped with arrogance. Was that $13 million included in the overall fast ferry cost, or had the government buried that cost elsewhere in the BC Ferries budget in an attempt to make the new ferries appear less expensive? "How was it apportioned?" asked one reporter?

Miller's response: "How's that apportioned with respect to bookkeeping? I couldn't care less."[83]

Would the minister allow an independent audit of the books? "No. There are clearly issues that are clearly political in nature, as they ought to be."

When asked point-blank about whether there would be a public inquiry to find out the total cost of the fast ferry project, Miller replied: "No, that exercise will not take place."[84]

"That was then"

Miller's obstructionist attitude was distasteful for another reason: when in opposition, New Democrats were unforgiving critics of Socred cost overruns on the Coquihalla highway. In particular, Glen Clark and Dan Miller even went after then Highways Minister Alex Fraser about the overruns while he was terminally ill and unable to speak except through a device in his throat. And that had happened *after* a public inquiry into the project.[85]

Ten years later, Miller refused to answer any questions on the fast ferry debacle, attacked critics, and stonewalled his way through 1998. In a January 1999 legislative debate on the ferries, former Social Credit MLA Jack Weisgerber reminded Miller of his attack on Fraser ten years previous. Miller's response: "That was then."[86]

By early 1999, fast ferry costs hit $300 million,[87] $90 million higher than the original Glen Clark "fixed" estimate but about what critics estimated as early as 1995. And Clark had his excuse: he didn't know the ferries were built on a cost-plus basis.[88] That was odd; Dan Miller knew about that contract provision as far back as 1996 when he assumed responsibility for the ferries. It seemed unlikely the new minister knew but not the previous one who started it all.[89] Then again, with Clark, it was always a toss-up as to which personality was in play: the truth-challenged Minister/Premier or the hyperactive political spin-master who paid little attention to major components of a deal once the photo opportunity was over. Neither option was comforting; either it was another Glen Clark fib or a case of reckless disregard for public finances.[viii]

There was also the third Glen Clark, the one that blamed others: "The mistake I guess was that I trusted the people who were giving me the information. I was not given the correct information. I don't want to point fingers, but clearly there were real problems managing this, which I think is beyond the politicians' oversight."[90]

BC's Bre-X politicians

By 2000, the Auditor General reported on the mess and reported that the three fast ferries would cost $463 million – in essence, $154 million each. The fast ferries turned to be wildly over-budget; on the first Pacificat alone, the target of 410,000 man-hours was exceeded by 200,000 hours.[91] Each job

---

viii. Glen Clark's inattention to detail cost the province on more than one occasion. When the NDP took over from the Socreds, Clark was told by the outgoing government to hire sharp negotiators for discussions over providing power to Washington state's Bonneville Power Administration. The Socreds warned that the BPA possessed tough negotiators and that any agreement should be carefully scrutinized for legal language that might allow the Administration to jump out of a deal. Clark never heeded the warning and an open-ended contract was signed. In 1995, BPA pulled out of the deal, potentially worth $5 billion to $6 billion over 30 years. Worse, the BC government already spent the first $250 million it figured it would receive from BPA.

that the project created cost, on average, $110,000 annually.[92] The ships were forced to cut back their speed lest they swamp pleasure-craft in the Georgia Strait. They carried fewer cars than forecast, made less runs per day, dumped raw sewage into the ocean, could be plugged up by logs, and were once stopped dead by marine life – mussels – that lodged themselves in the ship's intake. On some holiday weekends in 1999, drivers sat in their cars for five to eight hours waiting to get across the Georgia Strait because of the breakdowns.

The three Pacificats were object lessons in what separates private sector projects and the politically inspired dreams occasionally offered up by a reckless governments such as the one in BC in the 1990s. In the private sector, grand projects are filtered with cost-benefit analyses, scrutinized by investors, vetted by financiers, managed by professionals, and ultimately subjected to the feedback of the buyers, i.e. consumers. Despite such rigorous checks and balances, many private sector projects yet fail.

Politically motivated projects are something else entirely. In specific to the fast ferry project, there was: no cost-benefit analysis, no venture capitalists with a tough checklist, and no feedback from the marketplace on a leased trial ship. There were professionals both at BC Ferries itself and on the board, but they were pushed aside by a government too interested in some futuristic press conference where they pictured themselves with a sleek ferry under the Lions Gate Bridge as a backdrop for the photo opportunity.

If the BC Ferry Corporation and Catamaran Ferries International were in the private sector, the ships never would have been built. Since CFI in particular had neither the market nor the expertise, financing would be impossible. If such a company could manage to build such ferries despite the obstacles, the company's share price would plummet, management would be fired, lawsuits would fly, and the entire debacle would have a Bre-X-like stain attached to the entire sordid affair. In BC though, it was mind and political power over economic matter.

Ships overboard

By spring 2000, with a new Premier in Victoria, the ships were a political liability. With every voyage, the ships cost taxpayers more money, the NDP more votes, and it was time for damage control; the ferries were put on the international market for $40 million each. The latest cabinet minister responsible for the orphaned ferries, Labour Minister Joy MacPhail, said critics who doubted the ships would sell were "fear mongering."[93] MacPhail could have saved her breath: the entire project was beyond any serious discussion by then. The fast ferries were now the objects of daily jokes around water coolers, government ones included. And one witty but anonymous wag even listed a fake fast ferry ad on the popular Internet auction site: E-Bay. The anonymous "seller" posted a picture of MacPhail beside a fast ferry: The bidding started at one dollar.

By late 2000, and despite a $4-million marketing campaign,[94] no ferries were yet sold and the third and final catamaran was in storage near Richmond, wrapped in white plastic to protect it from the elements.

If Kevin Costner hadn't already starred in a motion picture flop about life in a fictional sea colony that was chaotic and haphazard, the three fast ferries would have made perfect props for *Waterworld.*

NS B
the Legislatu

6

Jealousy in the Election Sandbox:

The NDP Gag Law

"Well, obviously the legislators in their wisdom passed the law."[1]

- Then NDP Attorney General Ujjal Dosanjh in 1997, on the election gag law

In the spring of 1995, NDP re-election hopes were perched just above the trash bin of history. Polls put the opposition far ahead, red-ink budgets were still the norm, MLA pensions (which almost toppled Alberta Conservatives in 1993) threatened as an election issue, and the Ontario NDP looked soon to be ousted, a nasty omen for west-coast social democrats.

Looming over those negatives was another, more explosive item due to be released that year: a long-awaited report on the Nanaimo charity scandal, which involved former long-time party stalwart Dave Stupich. All signs pointed to a one-term NDP government, the same fate that met New Democrats twenty years earlier under Dave Barrett. Given the rotten prospects, the government looked for an election advantage wherever it could find one.

Reaching for the tourniquet

The political impulse to control is never so strong as when the loss of power is at stake. Whether politicians give in to that temptation is one measure of their respect for free speech – a right often assumed by the public to be guaranteed, despite its rarity in history and in practice.

And in the mid-1990s, when re-election hopes were shaky at best, BC's New Democrats gambled and decided to chip away at that core political right with election-time restrictions on citizen groups and the media. At worst, the government could lose the election. At best and despite the likelihood that a court would strike down a gag law (as happened with a similar

1993 restriction passed by federal Conservatives)[2], the party would win a second term; the court case could be dealt with later.

Stay out of our sandbox: The new Election Act

It was in this context that the government introduced Bill 28 to amend the Election Act. Never ones to suffer from an overdose of humility ("Mirror, mirror on the wall, who's the most just, compassionate, and fairest of them all?"), NDP MLAs slapped a province-wide $5,000 spending limit on so-called third parties. The amendments were quickly christened the "gag" law, given the restriction on citizens to criticize parties or ideas during an election campaign.

The new limitations meant that if organizations wanted to advertise to increase the profile of an issue they thought was ignored, tough luck. So, Greenpeace and the Sierra Club would be forced to take a pass on the environment during a campaign, and the BC Fisheries Survival Coalition could forget about race-based double standards in the fisheries. Individuals such as Vancouver accountant Garry Nixon (who later challenged the law in court), were similarly restricted.

But then, hearing from the public was not exactly a priority. The $5,000 limit was a joke; it would pay for a one-time quarter-page ad in the *Vancouver Sun*. The limit was a tip-off that New Democrats didn't want competition in the election sandbox. Even the language of the bill was revealing. Citizen groups were "third parties," as if voters who felt their particular concerns were ignored were mere spectators.

In comparison, tax deductible political parties could spend $2.8 million throughout the province. Each candidate could also spend $50,000 per riding, almost $3.8 million in total if a party ran a full slate. That meant one political party might spend up to $6.6 million during an election, to say nothing of taxpayer-funded feel-good ads by government that coincidentally aired around elections.[i]

The new Act also included provisions to trip up the press every time they dared publish an opinion poll. Unless every "i" was dotted and "t" crossed, media outlets were subject to criminal prosecution. Polls about voter inten-

---

i. For example, the Auditor General reported that in 1996, the BC government spent $25 million on advertising. Some ads were necessary and routine; others were feel-good infomercials designed to bump up the government's popularity on certain issues. On forestry issues for example, the Crown Corporation Forest Renewal British Columbia spent $1 million. Other ads mixed a legitimate message with media exposure for politicians. Thus, ICBC spent $5.2 million on safe driving ads and featured NDP cabinet minister Andrew Petter.

tions were forbidden unless accompanied by reams of statistical data. They included: the name of the polling organization; the dates when the survey was conducted; the number of voters contacted; the proportion that refused to take part; the margin of error; the exact wording of each question; and the mailing address and telephone number of the sponsor.[3] Predictably, the poll restrictions did not go far enough for some free speech suppressors; Dan Miller wanted election-time opinion polls banned outright.[4]

The labour loophole

Thanks to the new law, there was also another election-time advantage helpful for New Democrats in particular. Draft amendments to the election bill required that help from organized labour (who donated paid organizers to work on NDP campaigns) be reported as a contribution. This was already required in some other provinces and in municipal campaigns in BC.

But the government ripped that section out of Bill 28 before it was publicly introduced. The inside attorney who reviewed the hollowed-out bill cautioned that "the failure to include some fairly tight provisions in this regard would be a large loophole in the effect of the legislation and considerable criticism on the introduction of the bill."[5] Simply put: the NDP bill was restrictive on every other interest except its own; the media would note the obvious bias.

Sure enough, the final version had a $5,000 limit on one side, a $6.6-million limit for parties on the other and no requirement to declare labour help. Along with regular media access and volunteers, political parties in general and New Democrats in particular had a lock on election-time ideas. This law, NDP lawyer Joe Arvay later argued in court, was "designed to ensure fairness in elections."[6]

Lies, damned lies, and factual information

As expected, New Democrat MLAs claimed the new legislation was *not* a gag law, but of help to voters who might become confused. Attorney General Colin Gablemann, the point man for the gagging, defended the onerous requirement that media outlets broadcast or publish reams of statistical data with every poll. In a heated exchange with reporters, Gablemann blustered that voters had "the right to vote without being fed lies and information that is not based on the facts. You simply have to demonstrate it's factual."[7]

Given that the NDP later claimed (in the midst of an election) that it balanced two budgets, the province's chief law enforcement official should have ensured his *own* party demonstrated the factual proof for such claims.

That of course would be difficult since there were none, as the Auditor General and others later revealed.[8]

Gablemann also defended the crackdown on citizen groups and argued they were still "free to notify their members of their positions."[9] Presumably, members already *knew* the position of organizations they belonged to; that's why they joined them in the first place. But should anyone preach outside the choir, at $5,000 for the entire province, they were limited to posting flyers on telephone poles. $6.6-million political parties could use radio, newspapers, television, the Internet, and billboards, i.e., modern communications, but everyone else was restricted to 19th-century technology.

Despite the obvious multi-million dollar imbalance, Premier Mike Harcourt claimed the law helped citizens see the really deep thoughts of would-be politicians: "You shouldn't be able to buy an election, it should be based on the quality of your ideas and your candidates, not who's got the deepest pockets."[10] And future Attorney General (and later Premier) Ujjal Dosanjh defended Bill 28 this way:

> *The issue is how much money can you spend in a particular campaign so that you can have a particular result. I think the issue is we don't want to be held hostage to large amounts of money, whether public or private, in terms of any campaign.*[11]

Given that political parties, and especially the government party with its labour allies and taxpayer-funded feel-good ads, possessed the home-field advantage as regards cash, the Dosanjh spin about "being held hostage" was brilliant symbolism, but inspired fiction.

Protecting the peasantry

When pressed, the Attorney General was remarkably candid about why the government didn't want citizen groups to mess up election campaigns; it was none of their business: "*Political parties* are in the business of contesting elections," he asserted.[12] The implication was that they didn't need competition. Speaking of so-called third parties, Colin Gablemann said "what they can't do is sneak in, around and under the limits by supporting or opposing political parties by spending money to achieve that purpose."[13]

That citizen groups might not give a damn about any political party seemed never to occur to Gablemann and his gag-happy colleagues. That citizens either individually or collectively might have a constitutional right to broadcast their views loud, far, and wide without government approval also didn't seem to matter. That the public might actually prefer a few *ideas* discussed, regardless of whether that upset the carefully planned election cart, simply never entered the minister's head. Then again, it probably did, which is why the critics were right to call the clampdown on free speech a gag law. The legislation forced people into political parties if they wanted to make any impact on the public debate during elections. Otherwise, zip the lip or tell it to the judge.

Another NDP cabinet minister also chirped in defence of citizen gagging. "Why," pleaded Dan Miller on the poor peasants' behalf, "do we allow the electorate to be pestered incessantly as though they have no mind of their own?"[14]

The answer was as simple as it was constitutionally important: because it is not within the government's scope to "allow" the electorate to be pestered or not. Pestering, otherwise known as free speech, was sanctioned by the Constitution, carved out of history, and available to all without prior consent by the state. One may not like a particular association's election ads or Saturday morning visits from Jehovah's Witnesses, but a free society is dependent on both being able to propagate their message as long as others can say "no." That's what the *off* button is for on televisions, and "no, thank you" is for, for door-to-door salesmen.

What Gablemann, Miller and Co. also missed was the contrary possibility: that maybe the electorate with their own mind might *like* to be pestered with views other than those that came from officially sanctioned political parties. After all, most Canadians liked vigorous competition when it came to sports, buying a car, and Chinese takeout. But with elections, the NDP assumed voters were shrinking violets, unable to see through various claims, ideas and philosophies and make up their own mind about it all. The pathetic citizens needed protection from too many ideas in the naked public square. And who better to do it than the BC NDP – a party that had a lot to lose if real ideas, as opposed to fluffy, recycled 1960s-era clichés, were openly debated.

See you in court: the 1996 election ads

The NDP gag law also forced anyone who wanted to spend any portion of their allowable 5,000 bucks to register with Elections BC, the provincial government agency charged with even-handed enforcement of the election law. Some, such as the BC Fisheries Survival Coalition, registered; others, such as Vancouver accountant Garry Nixon, did not.

Because the law also banned ads that promoted or opposed a position that might be associated with a particular party, commercials that attacked the Nisga'a treaty were thus off-limits since the NDP were solidly identified with it. Balanced budget ads were out of line since Liberal and Reform platforms endorsed the concept. In essence, anyone who spent money on election-time messages could advertise only on issues that, well, had nothing to do with the election.

Welcome to "Radio Free BC"

During the 1996 campaign, Elections BC quickly pounced on groups that appeared to flaunt the law, though some were beyond its reach. In a delicious high-profile snub of the gag law, and of the power of Elections BC to enforce it, the National Citizens' Coalition broadcast ads from Bellingham, Washington, dubbed the station "Radio Free BC," and aired commercials that accused the NDP of outlawing free speech. To attract Canadian listeners, the NCC bought pointer ads in BC that urged people to flip their dial to the American station.[15]

For those who advertised on the Canadian side and took a position that might contravene the new law, Elections BC wrote to station managers and ordered such commercials spiked. Victoria's CFAX radio station was accused of broadcasting "election advertising on behalf of the Canadian Taxpayers Federation.... This organization is in contravention of the Election Act."[16]

It was a curious letter, given that the organization was presumed guilty, not innocent. When the CTF[ii] asked for details, Elections BC head Robert Patterson wrote that the ads *appeared* to break the law; he did not cite an example as to why. The more neutral language communicated to the Federation was not what Elections BC wrote in its letter to CFAX. After the Federation's BC director, Troy Lanigan, requested a specific example, Patterson wrote back that the ad, which promoted balanced budget legislation, "indirectly opposes registered political parties by referring to debt incurred by 'successive governments since 1990.'"[17]

But if ads on balanced budgets by more conservative groups aroused the ire of Elections BC, it appeared that ads by labour unions on a variety of topics did not. For example, the BC Teacher's Federation never received a knock on the legal door from Elections BC for election-time ads it ran in 1996.[18] Also excused, apparently, were advertisements from the BC Nurses Union that featured Ralph Nader.[19] Those commercials criticized private health care, which was clearly the opposite of a publicly stated position by the BC Reform party. Elections BC responded that the BCNU ad did not "appear to be advertising used to directly or indirectly promote or oppose a candidate or registered political party."[20]

---

ii. The Federation does receive its share of mentions in this book. Given that it was involved in some high-profile political disputes in the 1990s, there is no way around that, immodest as it may seem to write about the organization for which I now work.

Elections BC head Robert Patterson later maintained he did not write the law, he only enforced it. Later, and on his own volition, the Elections BC head intervened in court over the David Stockell "fudge-it" budget lawsuit.[iii] There, observers argued Patterson defended the government and its contention that the case should not proceed.[21]

Regardless of Elections BC, it was pathetic that any media outlet complied with the law: the courts already cut down previous federal restrictions on citizen group spending, limits quite similar to the BC law. Pacific Press, which owned the *Vancouver Sun* and *Vancouver Province*, obeyed Elections BC, but promised to fight Bill 28 after the election.[22] Those who thought corporations ran the country (Pacific Press was owned by Southam) must have been pleasantly surprised. Faced with a law almost guaranteed to be unconstitutional, the country's biggest newspaper conglomerate meekly accepted the NDP's legal bluff.

Instead, it took a small chain to immediately oppose the law. Seventeen weekly newspapers published in the interior of BC, each owned by Cariboo Press, busted the $5,000 limit on purpose. Bob Grainger, the company president, argued that "if we allowed this to go unchecked, then it opens the door to more laws limiting more freedoms."[23]

The velvet hammer

After the vote, it was get-tough time with offenders. Elections BC sent files on all groups to the Criminal Justice Branch and asked for prosecutions.[24] It also sent a notice of fines to several groups that flouted the law.

For those who busted the limit, the penalty was severe: a fine ten times the money spent in excess of $5,000. The Fisheries Coalition spent $27,000 to criticize race-based fishing rights in the Nass Valley (part of the Nisga'a treaty). The $22,000 in "overspending" garnered them a $220,000 fine.[25]

---

iii. The NDP also appeared to benefit from another Elections BC decision in 1998. Halfway through the 1998 recall campaign, the Elections office declared that the names on the recall petition would be made public. This was akin to opening up the ballot box right after a ballot was inserted to find out how an individual marked it. It had the potential to cause people to shy away from signing the petition, given that the governing party would know exactly who wanted a recall election. The decision was not referred to the courts or to the province's privacy commissioner. *Vancouver Province* columnist Michael Smyth wrote that Robert Patterson came too close to the "partisan mud-slinging of the province's dirty political wars," and accused the Elections BC head of "spending more time rolling through the political slop than befits anyone holding such a lofty office as his." ("Into the mud pit," Michael Smyth, *Vancouver Province*, 3 February 1998.)

Garry Nixon purposely spent $1,330 more than the law allowed and was informed his fine was $13,300. And, instead of facing Nixon in front of a judge, the NDP government took a back-door approach; they obtained a certificate from the BC Supreme Court that ordered the accountant to pay the fine without his day in court.[26]

The Taxpayers Federation spent $47,000, was warned it was under investigation, but never heard back. Since the CTF never registered under the law and threatened to take Elections BC to court, that presumably explained the lack of action. Elections BC also never fined the National Citizens' Coalition, probably because prosecution of an American-based advertisement would be impossible.

In comparison, between taxpayer-financed ads that the government ran right before the election announcement, and the effect of NDP and labour ads during the election, one advertising executive figured that government, the New Democratic Party, and big labour spent $10 million.[27]

Barely a week after the provincial election ended, an Alberta court struck down another federal law that restricted citizen advertising during elections. It found the rule against third-party ads infringed the right to vote: "Insofar as these impugned restrictions severely limit the ability of third parties to participate in the very communicative process which allows [a] citizen's vote to be 'informed,' they undermine the rights of citizens to vote. Thus, this is the antithesis of an informed vote in a free and democratic country."[28] Undeterred, the BC government kept its own gag law on the books and used taxpayer money to fight for an obviously unconstitutional law.

Mr. Nixon goes to court

None of the Elections BC fines were ever paid. Garry Nixon and others challenged the government to prosecute them; it never happened. Instead, the law itself was soon under attack. Nixon, the National Citizens' Coalition, and Pacific Press went to court to have sections of the Election Act declared unconstitutional and inconsistent with the Charter of Rights and Freedoms.

On the issue of published polls, *Vancouver Sun* editor Patricia Graham testified the law compelled papers to print information they did not consider newsworthy (reams of statistical data), itself a case of interference with press freedom. That, she argued was forced expression.[29] In addition, there was a practical problem: Under the law, a paper could not print leaked opinion polls if it did not have the original statistical data, no matter how reputable the firm that commissioned the poll.[30]

And whether the government liked it or not, a poll *is* news because it offers a snapshot of what the public thinks at a given moment. Restricting that news was censorship. Critics argued the press has a duty to be responsible, but as the judge pointed out, "a responsible press is an undoubtedly desirable goal, but press responsibility is not mandated by the Constitution and like many other virtues, it cannot be legislated."[31]

In any case, the NDP's concern over false polls was entirely hypothetical. As pointed out in trial, and fully admitted to by government lawyers who defended the gag law, there was no evidence that a falsified election opinion poll had ever been published in British Columbia. Besides, the gag law would not prevent an intentionally false poll from being printed; not so long as faked statistical data went with it.

What was *not* hypothetical was an election-time poll that revealed Liberals and Reformers split the vote in sixteen key ridings across the province. That Liberal-commissioned poll was leaked to *Vancouver Sun* columnist Vaughn Palmer in mid-election. The *Sun* decided not to print it because background information was not given, a violation of the law if published. Voters who cared little for the NDP and wanted to vote strategically might have liked to see how others intended to cast their ballots. But, as the *Sun* editor argued in court, the publishing gag effectively prevented an informed electorate.[32]

The NDP vs. the constitution

The Attorney General claimed this was the only time the law prevented a newsworthy poll from being printed. The judge concluded that once was too often and for that and other reasons, struck down the law as unconstitutional. Editors, he wrote, should not have to think about criminal charges just for doing their jobs:[33]

> *The exercise of a fundamental freedom under the Charter ought not to hinge upon the ability of the press to successfully defend itself in the event of a criminal or quasi-criminal prosecution by hoping for a "favourable" interpretation of s.235 or that its "due diligence" will succeed. This type of risk should not have to be run in order to exercise fundamental Charter rights. This type of chill ought not to be cast over such a fundamental freedom.*[34]

In retrospect, the *Vancouver Sun* should have thumbed its nose at the law and published the poll. To obey the questionable law, even briefly, let the government succeed with its temporary and unconstitutional high-stakes gamble.

The judge also carved up the attempt to limit citizen group ads. He found that government lawyers relied, wrongly, on dubious 1990 Lortie Commission findings regarding third-party advertising in the 1988 federal election.

As it was, the author already disavowed the study on which the Lortie Commission based its report. Professor Richard Johnston from the University of British Columbia, argued that his original conclusions were wrong; thus by extension so was the Lortie Commission and so were government lawyers: his study could not be interpreted as arguing third party advertising had any effect. That conclusion was never challenged by other witnesses at the trial or by any other empirical study.[35] Regardless, what *did* have an effect on the public, as Richard Johnston argued, was political party advertising. The judge agreed:

> *I accept the evidence of Professor Johnston under cross-examination who testified that advertising by parties in election campaigns matter. I conclude that spending, particularly well crafted spending by candidates or political parties in election campaigns, likely can have an effect on voter intention. However, I also conclude that, unlike party and candidate advertising, there is no evidence that would allow me to conclude that third party advertising or spending has an impact on voter intentions.... I find that there is no empirical evidence that third party spending during election campaigns has in the past affected voter intentions in Canada.*[36]

Ironically, an unconstitutional gag law introduced to stop the presumed unfair influence of "third parties" during elections instead revealed again that *political parties* sway voter intentions. That might be because citizen groups never spend the vast amounts of money political parties do, or because their ads are not as slick. But whatever the reason, any law that bans citizens or groups from spending amounts equal to political parties – as if parties alone had some inherent right to debate issues – can be described with many adjectives, but "fair" is not one of them.

Postscript: the Canadian temptation to gag

In retrospect, the bill revealed (again) the hypersensitivity of some Canadian politicians about free-spirited debate. Those who vote for speech restrictions during elections reveal their assumption that voters are a nuisance. And one is left to wonder what kind of restraints on free speech might be drafted if politicians did not have to justify them to courts empowered to enforce constitutional guarantees.

The 1996 election gag law (and others) took away, temporarily, one of the few antidotes to the concentrated power that exists throughout Canada's political system. Majority governments are virtual monarchies for up to five years and leaders wield immense control of that power via extreme caucus discipline. And where independent and spirited public debate is seldom seen (along with independent politicians), free speech – the last refuge of opposition – is even more critical.

A successful bluff

In the 1996 election, the NDP won more seats than the opposition Liberals with *less* of the popular vote; 39 percent compared to almost 42 percent respectively; that meant seat by seat battles were key to an election victory. As the centre-right vote split between the Liberal and Reform parties, it is entirely possible that a published poll about vote splitting might have changed the 1996 election results. In retrospect, while New Democrats knew the gag law had no long-term shelf life once a court dissected it, the short-term calculation was a brilliant tactical gamble. The bluff paid off with five more years in office.

7

Gagging Mother Teresa

"I'm sure you can identify all the fascists who now work on your hospital administrations, but we can't simply fire them all. We'll have to change the way these people think."[1]

Glen Clark, speaking to a Health Employees Union seminar in 1993

It is difficult to imagine a more controversial topic in modern North American discourse than abortion. Forget the rule about not discussing religion and politics in polite company. Debates on those topics by the most spirited Oxford dons pale in comparison to the verbal flare-ups that result over whether abortion represents a denial of life, or freedom of choice.

Given its controversial nature then, it is precisely such a topic that should be used to measure a government's tolerance of ideas, especially when that government is wholly committed to one position without compromise. Free speech is the first test of a government's *actual* as opposed to professed tolerance. Anyone can favour free speech in the abstract but Voltaire's famous dictum – "I disapprove of what you say, but I will defend to the death your right to say it" – is forgotten most easily in the specific.

Hot enough for you? The debate in BC

When the NDP first came to power in 1991, there was no question where it stood on abortion. It was just over three years since the Supreme Court threw out Canada's abortion law. In response, Parliament passed what could fairly be called a pro-choice bill in pro-life language. Neither side was happy about the bill, but it mattered little since the Senate killed Parliament's replacement version by one vote. Abortion on demand was, *de facto*, the law of the land, and most politicians stayed as far away from the debate as possible. The exception was in British Columbia.

The Social Credit government in the 1980s, when led by Bill Vander Zalm, attempted to cut government funding for abortion. Supporters of the move argued that if abortion was just like any other medical procedure (as pro-choice advocates maintained), then, like any other procedure, abortion could be de-listed under the province's medical plan. Opponents of the move blasted the Premier for imposing his morality on other British Columbians.

That this was a stretch was not open for rational debate at the time. Fact was, services were added or de-listed as the priorities of the provincial Ministry of Health changed. But abortion funding was not about the expenditure of health care dollars. For both sides, it was about politics and appearances.

As for the NDP, their position on all of this was clear, as Point 11 of their 1991 election platform stated:

> *A New Democrat government will guarantee access to, and fund, reproductive counselling and abortion services in hospitals and community health centres in all parts of B.C. The power of hospital boards to deny such services will be ended.*[2]

As soon as the NDP entered office, little time was wasted on fulfilling their election pledge. A task force on abortion was set up, one million dollars was earmarked for Vancouver's two free-standing abortion clinics, and another $300,000 was allocated to abortion information.[3]

Well, there goes democracy...

In addition, 33 regional hospitals across the province were ordered to provide abortions, whether their boards authorized them or not. Unlike some provinces, British Columbia's hospital boards were a combination of appointed and elected directors. Anyone from the general public could vote for hospital board candidates providing she first joined the hospital society.

The result was that pro-lifers won control of some boards and cancelled abortions in hospitals under their jurisdiction. Pro-choicers won in others and made sure it was available. The debates were messy and divisive, but then that was local democracy. The stack-the-meeting approach employed by both sides could be improved upon; all the government need do was make hospital board elections part of the municipal or regional election process. But that would not have guaranteed the NDP's preferred policy outcome province-wide. It was easier to scrap elections, which they did shortly after the 1996 election.

That later move by the NDP to cut off pro-life groups at the hospital board level was preceded by an earlier manoeuvre – one to make sure they were never able to get near a hospital or abortion clinic entrance in the first place. All the NDP needed was an excuse and, as it turned out, a criminal nut with a gun provided one.

The November 1994 shooting attack on Vancouver doctor Garson Romalis (who was again attacked six years later) was a cowardly, immoral act by someone who, presuming he was motivated by a professed pro-life sentiment, did not understand or practise morality.

... and free speech

Nor did the attacker understand politics. The attack gave the government the excuse it needed to introduce a "bubble zone" around abortion clinics and ultimately hospitals. In an early 1995 news conference, then Premier Mike Harcourt claimed that "the level of organized violence and intimidation has increased, not just here in British Columbia, but in other areas of North America."[4] Later in the same news conference, the Attorney General downplayed the more conclusive tone of Harcourt's remarks. Colin Gablemann pointed out that the newly established Criminal Harassment Unit (CHU), set up specifically to deal with possible abortion clinic violence was just then "attempting to determine that very question."[5]

They did not have to wait long for the answer. Later the same day, CHU Sergeant Geramy Field noted that "there was no evidence of any increased harassment."[6] By the end of the press conference, the premier backtracked, and pointed out that "individual women who are using the clinic are at very little risk from the experience we've had to date." When pressed, Harcourt blamed the media for the proposed bubble zone bill. "It's because of the media interest in the story and because of apprehension by doctors and health care workers. The Attorney General and I are trying to be as honest as we can with you."[7]

Honesty aside, the NDP was selective in who would lose their right of protest and free speech. Harcourt's claims about the pro-life movement could also be applied to British Columbia's occasional violence-prone labour disputes at least as often as pro-lifers.

Bad violence and good violence

In a test of consistency that fate herself must have designed, three weeks *after* the attack on Romalis, labour protesters attacked construction workers (who belonged to a different union) in Port Alberni who attempted to get to their work site.

Union leader Len Werden helped set the incendiary torch by promising "there will be blood in the bloody street."[8] And the battle was on. One non-union employee of TNL construction went home with a broken cheekbone, a police officer was injured, and a BCTV camera operator was thrashed.

In contrast to the abortion-doctor attack, where the government set up a specific law-enforcement team, then Attorney General Colin Gablemann did not set up a "Criminal Harassment Unit" to monitor members of the IWA. And Werden's over-the-top rhetoric did not lessen his chance of marching in May Day parades with his labour friends in government. Quite the opposite, six years after his fiery words mingled with blood, Werden posed for the cameras as a candidate for the NDP leadership. It would be similar to pro-life activist Betty Green running for the leadership of the BC Liberals – except that Green never committed or condoned violence.

Similarly, the environmental movement never had the right to peaceful protest banned in specific locales via government legislation, with the cabinet deciding arbitrarily which locale would be off limits next. Despite the occasional episode of damaged forest machinery[9] or spiked trees, acts that were physically dangerous to loggers, there was never a bubble zone placed around forests preventing anyone with Birkenstocks and granola from loitering around old growth trees.

To deal with militant unions and over-the-top environmentalists, or Operation Rescue protests earlier in the decade, government and businesses used injunctions and anti-stalking and anti-harassment laws.

But then the government did not actually have evidence that abortion clinic demonstrators were a criminal threat, at least to any greater degree than your average environmentalist or union member.

On that point, probably the only media outlet in the province that took a pro-life editorial position was *BC Report*. That magazine asked for the report completed by the Criminal Harassment Unit (CHU) on the pro-life movement in BC. The government denied the request but the magazine obtained a copy anyway. The police report found no violations of the Criminal Code's anti-stalking and harassment sections, and no proof of any organized conspiracy against abortion clinics.[10]

While there were criminal, tragic, and isolated cases of violence surrounding the abortion debate – the Romalis attack the most obvious example – the bubble zone legislation was not about public safety. Loggers and construction workers could make a better case for bubble zones. It was about political allies: Union members and environmentalists were more likely to vote NDP than members of the pro-life movement. Friends who share the same vegetarian dip were one thing; opponents who dip communion wafers in wine and quote Mother Teresa were quite another.

We don't defend *that* free speech

The NDP's passage of a law that restricted certain words around clinics was probably helped by an Opposition that had not yet found its legs on economic issues, never mind the principle of free speech. One would think though, that the latter should have come automatically; free speech is about the only thing opposition parties have in the way of power to influence the public and the press.

But then the Liberal critic already flip-flopped once on this issue. When in 1991 the NDP steamed ahead on abortion access and started thumping on elected hospital boards, opposition health critic Linda Reid responded with an endorsement: "I commend you on this initiative."[11] Later the same day the position changed, and her press release lectured the NDP about the need to respect democracy.

The Liberals proved similarly clueless about why free speech and freedom of assembly in front of abortion clinics were worthy principles to defend even if one was pro-choice. Instead, all but one Liberal MLA and the provincial Reformers jumped on the anti-free speech bandwagon in the June 1995 bubble zone vote. The Access to Abortion Services Act banned any protest within 50 metres of an abortion clinic. A protest was defined as "any act of disapproval or attempted act of disapproval, with respect to issues related to abortion services, by any means, including without limitation, graphic, verbal, or written means."[12] Penalties for breaking the law were severe: up to $5,000 and six months in jail the first time, double the fine and jail-time for a second offence.

Given that Voltaire's love of free speech had so few friends in the Legislature, where MLAs could say absolutely anything without fear of being sued, one might hope that others outside the parliament buildings might be more protective of principles and constitutional rights. Such hopes were often misplaced.

Heads, we like free speech; tails, we don't

In late June 1995, one week before the bubble zone legislation was proclaimed into law, the BC Civil Liberties Association blasted the proposed restrictions. In a news release, the Association argued it was "not persuaded that peaceful protest, or the peaceful expression of views, so interfere with a woman's access to abortion that a constitutionally protected right to free speech must be overridden.[13] At the time, the group argued for injunctions when necessary and better enforcement of those injunctions.

But after the legislation came into effect, NDP MLAs lobbied the BCCLA board. After meeting with NDP MLAs and abortion clinic supporters but not pro-life groups, the board caved in to government pressure and voted to support the government's law after all.[14]

In a rambling press release worthier of a politician who discarded a former principled position in exchange for votes, BC's staunchest defender of free speech (until then) flip-flopped. Apparently, all that late June stuff about a "constitutionally protected right to free speech" was just a lapse. Governments *could* ban free speech about this issue in certain areas of the province. In the choice between Mother Teresa-types praying openly around an abortion clinic and a gag-happy government, the on-again off-again civil libertarians supported the latter.

The media, whose salaries hinged on the constitutional exercise of free speech, were more critical of the new law. Given that journalists dislike restrictions that damage that freedom, they are generally more sympathetic to the plight of protesters being carted away.

That understanding of the importance of free speech had its exceptions. *Vancouver Sun* columnist Stephen Hume argued that the Romalis attack meant "moderate [pro-life] supporters stand to forfeit their own right to expect tolerance from a free and democratic society governed by the rule of law."[15] Hume would likely never apply that broad brush to moderate natives if a hot-headed protestor acted criminally, but guilt by association was thought applicable here.

Two other *Sun* columnists saw the threat to free speech and association more clearly, and the selective nature of the government's attention span vis-à-vis violence, the union and environmental kind versus the pro-life variety.[16] But even the "you're-not-being-equally-repressive" line was a rather weak defence of the right to sell your ideas in the naked public square via your voice. The *Vancouver Province,* which took a pro-choice position, pointed out that "even a frown could be cause for arrest by the politeness police."[17] It also slammed the law as another example of the NDP's approach to free speech: "[It] ends where the NDP's intolerance level begins"[18] and sarcastically asked whether the next bubble zone "would be for those who advised people not to vote NDP?"[19]

In the end, a newspaper a couple thousand miles away dissected the entrails of the law and pointed out that the flaw in Bill 48 was that it was a *law*, not merely an injunction. Injunctions are temporary, legislation is not, and the provincial cabinet had the final say over what hypothetical protest might cause harm. No case ever need be made before a judge as is necessary for an injunction. Henceforth, pickets and prayers about abortion were banned whenever and wherever the NDP cabinet decided. As the *Globe and Mail* editorialists argued, the law banned harmless acts of protest.[20]

Speak up, I can't hear you pray

That it did. After the law was enacted, Vancouver police informed pro-life protesters near the clinic that while they could pray, they would be arrested if those prayers advocated a pro-life message. Constable Anne Drennan spelled it out quite clearly in case there was any confusion:

> *If someone is praying silently, or so quietly that no one can hear it, it's probably all right. If there's any indication in the prayer, or any suggestion that the prayer relates to the abortion issue in any way, it's a contravention of the terms of the act and we'd arrest them. If they read the Lord's Prayer or the 23rd Psalm, that's okay, but a reference in the Bible that's something to do with abortion, that's what we'd act on.*[21]

The *Globe and Mail*, like most newspaper editorial boards, was pro-choice. But unlike the provincial government, many opposition MLAs, and the BC Civil Liberties Association, its editorial board and most others understood that what was at stake had nothing to do with the immediate issue, i.e. abortion. What was under attack was the underlying principle that guarded the free exchange of ideas in the philosophical and political marketplace, even, perhaps especially, in front of an abortion clinic.

Dissidents and the state

Fair-minded supporters of the bubble zone legislation argued that the law prevented physical intimidation: Regardless of one's view, Canada allows abortion and thus abortion-seekers and providers deserve protection from physical intimidation. Yes, they do, as do politicians such as Jean Chretien, but the federal government never placed a permanent verbal bubble zone around the Prime Minister because of occasional clashes with protestors. In a free society, and on any issue including and especially that which is controversial, the right to protest is critical if society cares to ever reconsider any issue, no matter how controversial.

Privileges and rights of the present are the result of dissidents from the past. The future deserves the same opportunity to hear from present-day dissidents, including in an area where the debate is most keen and opinions most sure. As there is no ironclad guarantee of physical safety even in a police state, the right to assemble and to speak should not be constrained in such a general way as through bubble zone legislation. Besides the constitutional importance, such rights are proof of a society and government that, although sure of its own convictions, is modest enough to allow that it may be mistaken.

Four years later Vancouver's Crown Counsel would have a chance to prove their unbiased enforcement of the rule of law regarding violence in the abortion debate. In 1999, three University of British Columbia students attacked a pro-life display, overturned tables, tore down signs, and destroyed pamphlets. The incident was videotaped and the Crown agreed there was no lack of evidence for charges. But even though the same counsel threw the book at a 25-year-old pro-lifer who passed out roses within the abortion clinic bubble zone – and ended up in jail for 55 days as a result – no charges were pressed against the UBC vandals. "Not in the public interest" was the reason.[22]

Apparently free speech was not the only principle damaged by the NDP's bubble zone law. So too was the unbiased enforcement of the rule of law.

RAESIDE
Victoria Times Colonist - Dist. BY KOKO PRESS INC.
raesidecartoon.com
B.C.
NDP
POLICIES

8

Witch Hunt Anyone?

Folly at the Human Rights Bureaucracy

"Some stores even post signs in their entrance saying 'only four juveniles allowed at one time'. This is overt discrimination against young people yet there is little our Commission can do for them."[1]

- Mary-Woo Sims, Chairman of the BC Human Rights Commission

Theatre of the absurd

Does the hard-working, immigrant owner of the local 7-Eleven have the right to tell teenagers to buzz off if he thinks they are about to shoplift him blind? Or how about a quota on the number of teenagers allowed in the store at one time who can mess up the slush machine?

Well, *currently* that right exists. And for good reason: teenagers, especially males, are statistically more likely to commit a crime (including petty theft) than anyone else. And, lucky for the 7-Eleven owner, the BC Human Rights Code does not yet prevent "age discrimination" against those under nineteen. But as Mary-Woo Sims, chairman of the BC Human Rights Commission, (an NDP-created and appointed body) argued, such discrimination would be off limits in a world she ruled.

If youth under nineteen did not have access to the Human Rights Commission for complaints against convenience stores, they were about the only group that did *not* get a hearing in the 1990s. Over the course of the decade, New Democrats set in motion a human rights bureaucracy that combined woolly-headed academic views about rights with the NDP's own distinct political bias.

But the rights evolution that occurred in the 1990s was part of a larger debate, one not at all limited to British Columbia. Rights are rarely defined now how 19th-century classic liberals would have meant them, i.e. activities people do in the absence of state prohibition. Traditionally, if individuals secured the right to worship as they liked, could protect their family from a state's nanny-like tendencies, and were able to speak freely in the public square, such accomplishments were considered a pretty good start on a free and just society. Post-1968 in Canada, governments vacated the bedrooms of the nation and what happened there might interest clerics, philosophers and parents, but the state maintained a "don't ask, don't tell" policy. For some, those and other protections from the state were no longer enough, thus the crusade for new and improved rights.

Sims' concern for teenagers who could not go into the 7-Eleven whenever they chose was laughable, altogether too serious, and trivial all at the same time. Only a country that already provided a vast cornucopia of protected rights could afford to debate such silliness as that which Sims equated with tragedy. Yet, absurd as it might be, her view was consistent with the emerging rights philosophy that those who appointed her espoused; one's business is not primarily a private sphere where a voluntary exchange of goods and labour take place. Nor is a conscious collective (as in the case of a private university or a church) really private. Instead, they are generous exemptions of space from government until such a point at which the state wishes to have its say.

But as British Columbians discovered in the 1990s, the problem with the march of the new rights brigade was its overreach; the attempt to extend newly created rights into uncharted territory threatened to take away more classic liberal freedoms.

Rights a la carte

The first major NDP change to the human rights laws came in 1992. New categories for protection were added; a $2,000-limit on awards was lifted; and class action lawsuits were permitted for the first time. Post-1992, if a British Columbian felt wronged on the basis of any category in the Act, not only could the Council impose a cash penalty, the complainant could take the same party to court and penalize them with a second damage award. This threatened to turn all claims into big business, big-dollar, legal festivals. Even frivolous claims might attract legal attention given the example of similar U.S. legislation, where weak claims would be settled out of court because companies preferred to cut their losses rather than engage in a protracted legal fight that would be even more costly.

Can I see your tattoo?

The 1992 changes were a prelude to a much more expansive role for the province's human rights industry. In 1993, Bill 33, the Human Rights Amendment Act, banned any public expression that "indicates discrimination" or "exposes a person or group of persons to hatred or contempt."[2] If the definitions of discrimination, hatred and contempt were vague, the forms of communication to be scrutinized were not: they included any publication or statement; any public display; any notice or sign including posters, banners or pamphlets, and even tattoos, emblems and lapel pins.

Conversations and personal letters were exempted from the law, for the time being, though a later version of the Council would recommend putting computer disks and drives under the definition of a "public place."[3]

Not done yet

By 1995, the NDP expanded the law yet again. Bill 32 split the Council of Human Rights into three organisms, each with its own possibility for mischief: the Human Rights Commission, the Human Rights Tribunal, and the Human Rights Advisory Council.

Besides the expansion of a bureaucracy that had its own ideological axe to grind, the 1995 amendments opened the door to mandatory affirmative action akin to the American approach. For a government that rhetorically bashed the empire to the south when convenient, they had little compunction about stealing one of the worst U.S. ideas when it came to race relations. Attorney General Ujjal Dosanjh defended the possible imposition of quotas upon private business as hardly newsworthy, noting that the NDP promised just such changes in 1992.[4]

A defence of free speech

It would be difficult to find any British Columbian who would not endorse human rights laws, this author included. But not everyone defines those rights in the same way. Try and ban all hurtful speech and most Canadians, save a saint, would end up in jail on a bad day. The ability to criticize or compliment depends upon the availability of free speech; men and women are complex creatures whose beliefs, attitudes, and outlook are shaped by a thousand different forces, many of which are not recognized by individuals themselves.

Culture, religion (or the lack thereof), location, parents, life experience, literacy, an understanding of history and science, and innumerable other influences shape who people are and how they think. Those who find themselves on the receiving end of criticism may not care for it, but at points - especially in public debates about what kind of civilization we want, it is necessary all the same. A free and democratic society must not only allow but also encourage critiques of the status quo. And that applies as much to questions of morality as it does to economic policy, foreign affairs and the proper size of the state vis-à-vis Gross Domestic Product. To debate certain moral or economic questions is not to presume state involvement or abdication, promotion or discouragement; the point of free speech is to have the debate. Democracies do not survive in spite of disagreements among their citizens; they exist and thrive precisely *because* of clear, well-defined, and aired differences.[i]

Of course, there have always been limits on free speech; defamation laws exist as one example. The restriction on yelling fire in a crowded theatre is another. But defamation laws prevent actual, provable lies from being spread. And barring the village idiot from yelling fire prevents possible physical injury. In both cases, a penalty is possible because harm has been suffered in a way that causes obvious loss. Most laws punish people for their *acts*; hate crime laws target people for their opinions.

Laws to prevent speech, even that which most decent citizens agree is offensive, presume to reach into the past and "correct" someone's formative influences. But in reality, such a ban cannot do that; it simply restricts, in public, expressed thoughts. Such laws also reach into the future and attempt to declare what one generation sees as divisive or hurtful as the end of discussion on that subject. Spirited public discussions even and especially on controversial subjects, are best aired, not banished to fester in the dark.

"So-called freedom of speech"

But human rights laws, which once protected liberties of one variety or another, have lately been used to restrict those same freedoms. Predictably, those in favour of the new definitions endorsed the post-1992 changes. Moreover, those who clamped down on free expression argued the law would not imperil free speech but would merely determine whether someone had been discriminated against.

If only it were that easy. One woman's discrimination is another man's loss of a date. One problem with the law was in its *own* lack of discrimination, i.e., a clear definition of what hate and discrimination meant. The

---

i. Division, especially when referred to in the political sense, is often assumed to be harmful. That is a simplistic notion. Some who are divisive are merely ahead of their time; later, they're honoured with statues. Think of Winston Churchill's warnings on the danger of Germany's direction in the mid-1930s, and the original, elitist dismissal of his concerns. There are of course, divisive people who are merely cranks. But the harm is not in the divisions, which exist in any society. The harm comes when there is no way to resolve differences, and if there is no rule of law to enforce what, at least temporarily, has been decided.

Supreme Court of Canada contributed to the intellectual muddle when it allowed for such laws. By a slim 4-3 majority in 1990, the country's highest court allowed for narrowly defined hate legislation. Naturally, those interested in criminalizing attitudes wanted to stretch the court's allowable parameters. To no one's surprise, BC's NDP government was one of the first to try.

In defence of the intellectual rubbish behind their changes to the Human Rights Code, NDP MLA Jan Pullinger argued that hate speech was easy to identify: "We're not talking about an academic or intellectual debate, or about two people talking to each other. We're talking about hate literature, hate propaganda, and those kinds of activities that target a group because of race, religions, or other things that identify and single out a group… The so-called freedom of speech to distribute and promote hateful literature and ideas that target another group is an abuse."[5]

Pullinger's justification was intellectually weak; besides the practical problem of defining hate consistently and impartially, the more serious question was whether a government had any business attempting to prosecute people based on their words anyway. Laws that restrict even offensive talk, inevitably favour groups close to the politicians in power; had such a law existed in 18th-century England, slave owners could have sued newspapers for printing "hate literature" if those papers excoriated those that trafficked in human cargo.

When a government restricts speech on grounds that someone's feelings may be hurt, they also risk a ban on a new perspective that may contribute to a better society. If hate laws had existed in 1930s Britain, an English Nazi could, hypothetically, have sued Winston Churchill for unflattering remarks. The example is a stark one and on purpose; society needs cranks and nonconformists (and I put Churchill in the latter category) in the event that a commonly held view is wrong. And if nothing else, wrongheaded views, like balloons, are more easily shot down in full public view over an open field than hidden behind a mountain.

Social Credit MLA Harry DeJong pointed out that the early 1990s revisions could, technically, place the Talmud in the category of hate literature.[6] After all, the Old Testament contained prohibitions against letting witches live. For that matter, if the Human Rights Commission had its way and could end the religious exemption from the federal hate crimes legislation, Pope John Paul II could have been hauled in front of the Human Rights Commission. All he need do was reiterate on BC soil, church doctrine that gay behaviour was against Catholic teaching. And *BC Report* editor Terry O'Neill argued tongue-in-cheek that liberal commentators "might be prevented from conducting one of *their* favourite sports – bashing white European males. After all, mocking them could breach the new code in the areas of ancestry ("European"), race ("white"), and sex ("male").[7]

Of course, none of the above scenarios were likely to happen. The author of Deuteronomy is long dead and thus unavailable for prosecution, and, even if the federal government followed the Commission's recommendations, it would be difficult to serve a summons to the Pope. And O'Neill's cheeky hypothetical was impossible given that white males were already defined as part of the oppressing class *because* of their ancestry, race, and sex. As such, the law was not against all nasty speech; it all depended on whose favourite political ox was gored.

Kafka calling

On controversial and politically sensitive issues, one could hazard a guess as to what would elicit the attention of the human rights bureaucracy. Impolite public statements about gays or natives by white males would likely land one squarely in the Tribunal's sights; unpleasant public words about heterosexual white guys by native leaders or the Pope by gay activists would likely *not* lead to the star chamber. But even then, the precise line in the sand between acceptable speech and offensive words might shift, as the "context" and the skin colour, gender, minority or majority status played a large role in what constituted an offence and what did not.

So, in addition to the squishy definition of hate, another concern about BC's rewrite of the human rights law was its after-the-fact nature. One characteristic of the rule of law is that legal requirements must be clearly spelled out in advance. You cannot be convicted of breaking a law introduced after the act in question, nor convicted if the law is murky about what constitutes an offence. Following banana republic legal thinking: hate, and a multitude of other less-than-virtuous actions and thoughts (and whether they would be of concern to the human rights bureaucracies) was defined largely on context. It was akin to parking meters that required different amounts of money on alternate days and at various hours, with no sign that indicated what parking rates actually were.

Thus, in an ever-shifting weightless legal universe, principles of free speech were defined according to context, not as inviolate rights, clearly defined in law that individuals possessed apart from government.

White men can't speak

None of the concerns mentioned by critics caused government MLAs to rethink their approach; instead, they fervently defended their changes to the Human Rights Code. NDP MLA Graeme Bowbrick mocked the possibility of an unfettered marketplace of ideas. It was, he said, usually white men who argued for such things, and besides "...using prosecution, where appropriate, serves a very important symbolic purpose in combating hate in our country and in our province."[8]

Thus, Bowbrick broke the first rule of a fair intellectual fight: he argued someone's views are irrelevant because of who they are, as opposed to whether their argument makes sense or is (alternately) incorrect. It was also absurd: a white man used his free speech to argue in favour of a restriction on the speech of others, and then claimed the views of *other* white men should be ignored because, well, they were white men. Bowbrick, a lawyer with presumably some training in logic, should have known better.

Moreover, it was not just vanilla-skinned males who argued such laws injured the right to free expression. Dissenters from the original 1990 Supreme Court decision, which allowed for such laws, included Madame Justice Beverly McLaughlin (later the Chief Justice). The NDP might mock the marketplace of ideas, but McLaughlin did not. "The law-abiding citizen who does not wish to run afoul of the law will decide not to take the chance in a doubtful case. Creativity and the beneficial exchange of ideas will be adversely affected."[9]

And prosecuting someone for her language was hardly "symbolic." Tribunal prosecutions could inflict real penalties on violators. Graeme Bowbrick also overlooked the inconvenient fact that decisions from the Human Rights Tribunal were hardly similar to a court of law. In a real courtroom, higher thresholds existed for convictions, such as the rule against admitting hearsay evidence, and, just as important, proof of guilt beyond a reasonable doubt.

In the emerging clash between classic liberal rights and the new rights, the latter eroded such protection from the state. In the debate over the 1993 changes, Liberal MLA Wilf Hurd argued that Canadians did not create the Charter of Rights and Freedoms only "to then hand it to a quasi-judicial body to analyze. We didn't pass our fundamental rights and freedoms, and ask some appointed body that could potentially rule without the benefit of evidentiary introduction to somehow make a ruling."[10]

NDP MLA Jan Pullinger argued that every piece of legislation passed was subject to interpretation under the Charter of Rights and Freedoms.[11] Technically, yes. But in reality, a charter challenge might cost a million dollars or more against a phalanx of taxpayer-financed government lawyers. Anyone without that kind of money and subject to an unconstitutional ruling by the Human Rights Tribunal would just have to take his or her medicine.[ii]

Hurd's point was later borne out by at least two appointments to the Human Rights Commission. Neither Chief Commissioner, Mary-Woo Sims, nor Deputy Chief Commissioner, Harinder Mahil, listed any legal training in their public resumes. Instead, they both showed a history of activist leftist causes with obvious NDP links.

Sims worked under the Ontario NDP government of Bob Rae on various racism and gay rights projects, and the requisite union links were there as well. Mahil spent a lengthy amount of time in union activism with the IWA and anti-racist organizations. None of that is particularly good or bad in and of itself; less racism is a positive goal to work for and unions and gay activists have every right to promote their agendas. But it does suggest a penchant for activism, when what is needed in a quasi-legal institution is more nuanced and neutral legal judgment. Activists are rarely objective on matters closest to their heart.

Fishing anyone?

Another problem with BC's fresh approach to human rights was that the Human Rights Commission could act without a complaint ever being lodged. So, a private business could find itself investigated, judged, fined, and ordered to "shape up" in some way, on no other basis than someone on the Commission or in the bureaucracy thought it would be a nice day for an investigation. Put another way, the human rights bureaucracy was, post-1995, able to act as cop, prosecuting attorney, mediator, judge, jury, and executioner, all without so much as an initial complaint ever having been filed.

---

ii. Supporters of the Human Rights Commission et al. as currently structured might argue that just as a constitutional challenge is expensive, so too is court time for a person wrongly fired by their employer. Fair enough, but the necessity for some form of a human rights body to adjudicate disputes does not mean it must have the expansive reach that it now does. Nor does it justify appointments to such a body that lack legal training. (Tribunal judges usually possessed legal training; it appeared Commission directors did not.) The "wings" of such bodies can and should be clipped without hurting the proverbial bird.

Human rights = forced speech: a test case

"Did I not tell you just now that we are different from the persecutors of the past? We are not content with negative obedience, not even with the most abject submission. When finally you surrender to us, it must be of your own free will.... It is intolerable to us that an erroneous thought should exist anywhere in the world."
- O'Brien, from George Orwell's *1984*

The new approach to combating discrimination, in whatever form as defined by the Human Rights Commission/Tribunal/Council was pregnant with possibility. For example, given the new bureaucracy's sensitive approach to discrimination claims based on sexual orientation, combined with the traditional importance placed on free speech, a collision of the "new" and "old" rights was guaranteed. And it was not long before the new approach to human rights bagged a high-profile victim.

In 1997, Kelowna Mayor Walter Gray was asked by the Okanagan Rainbow Coalition to proclaim Gay Pride Day. The Coalition probably thought it was a slam-dunk, given that the mayor regularly issued proclamations on everything from the SPCA to Boys and Girls Clubs.

But, if gay advocacy groups wanted to test how far the new human rights apparatus would go, and if the Human Rights Tribunal cared to flex its muscles, Kelowna made a choice target. The city was long a bastion of conservatism, fiscal and otherwise. Politically, the city supported the Social Credit party since the 1950s when W.A.C. Bennett gave up his hardware business and began his 20-year rule of British Columbia. After his defeat, his son, Bill Bennett, took the reigns of the party and continued to represent Kelowna in the Legislature. In the 1990s, it placed Liberal MLAs in office only (apparently reluctantly) when it became clear the Socreds were dead and the provincial Reform party was a non-starter. Federally, it voted Conservative for decades until a more conservative entity, the federal Reform party, took its place and also its overwhelming election-time pluralities. As for NDP candidates, whether federal or provincial, they were always cannon fodder for the more conservative options available.

Given the nature of the city then, which was regularly refilled with more conservative retirees from Alberta, Kelowna would make an inviting target for an NDP government wishing to make a political point through a bureaucracy: They got their wish. Gray signed the Gay Pride Day proclamation but not before crossing out "Pride." The Mayor, not one given to overt displays of religious belief, was, by his own account, an infrequent Anglican. He was also a former broadcaster who built up two Kelowna radio stations later sold when he became more involved in local politics, first as an alderman, then as a popular mayor.

Gray's objection was simple: he was not going to endorse that which he did not take pride in: "If I have difficulty saying I'm proud of the gay and lesbian lifestyle and I sign a proclamation, I'm being hypocritical."[12] Some did not like Gray's position, but that was never the point: the question was whether the mayor's signature should be forced.

The group that demanded the proclamation wanted recognition so that gays were "encouraged to take pride in themselves," as their letter to the Mayor stated.[13] If Gray was a vegetarian who believed eating meat was wrong, and refused to proclaim a "Support Beef Producers" week, or a deep green environmentalist who refused to sign a "Tribute to Foresters" proclamation, it is unlikely the Tribunal or anyone else would have cared. Similarly, an atheist mayor who refused to proclaim a "Christian Pride" week would also not have been hassled by the Human Rights Tribunal. And in any of those cases most Canadians – gay, straight, or otherwise – would likely have rushed to defend the right of a politician to not sign a document that crossed their own beliefs.

But then most people might presume that a forced signature, any more than forced speech, would never be ordered by any government or public body under the guise of, of all things, human rights. Like so much else in British Columbia in the 1990s, the right *not* to speak, write, or sign could not be taken for granted.

Turning free speech on its head

The Rainbow Coalition, which apparently had little room in its spectrum of colour for those who cared about more traditional freedoms, launched a complaint with the Human Rights Commission. The case was a clear example of the conflict in modern political thought about human rights. Which is more important? The right to as little interference from the state as possible, or to have one's preference/lifestyle/orientation/religion approved, endorsed and highlighted by a representative of the state, even if that overrides the first, more basic and long-held right?

As it was, under the federal law dealing with hate crimes, no one ever came across a passage that made it clear that *not* signing a document, or *not* speaking or writing certain words, would lead directly to the star chamber of a human rights tribunal. Predictably, that is not how the lobby saw it. One Rainbow spokesman argued that it was not a free speech issue since Gray was a publicly elected official,[14] as if that made any difference when a bureaucracy attempted to force his hand into signing something he did not care to initial.

The hearing took place in Kelowna in the autumn of 1999 and included all the absurd trappings of a kangaroo court. There were the usual clichés that emanate from the modern victimhood culture. First up was the original complainant, Quentin Hughson. He claimed Walter Gray's refusal to sign the proclamation was a "a slap in the face."[15] Up next were anonymous complaints. This was unlike even banana republic show-trials or normal Canadian courtrooms where accusers must confront the accused. Thus, a faceless Ms. "T" testified she felt insulted by Gray's change of wording on the proclamation. Another anonymous complainant, Ms. "B," like Hughson, also felt the mayor's decision was "a slap in the face."[16]

And then the experts came out for the affair. Professor Becki Ross, a professor of Women's Studies at the University of British Columbia, testified Gray's action communicated a "message of intolerance because he eliminated the one word that has been so central to the queer struggle for liberation."[17] Not to be stopped there, Ross described Gray's decision as "tantamount to a public insult, which is mean-spirited, short-sighted, and damaging to positive, respectful relations between people of all sexualities in and outside of Kelowna." Ross testified that the mayor was in effect saying, "I will not say there is anything to be proud of."[18]

Well, yes, he was. But whether Ross approved or disapproved was irrelevant. Walter Gray had a constitutional freedom to sign, or not, just as a vegetarian mayor had the right to not be proud of carnivores. Well-intentioned people might and do disagree on what is right, wrong and to be held in high esteem. At stake in the Gray trial was something quite basic: the right to dissent from someone else's moral view and actions - even as a public representative – and not be forced to endorse it upon threat of legal punishment.

Re-education and 1984

If victimhood is endemic in today's culture, so too is the belief that money makes up for it all: the Tribunal ruled against Walter Gray and the Rainbow Coalition wanted him fined $10,000 and the money turned over to them. They also demanded that Gray and other members of Council undergo a three-hour "unlearning homophobia" session to be organized by the complainant himself. For dessert, they demanded a Gay Pride proclamation, preferably with Walter Gray's signature on it. It echoed of O'Brien's lecture to Winston in George Orwell's *1984*: "Shall I tell you why we have brought you here? To cure you! To make you sane! Will you understand, Winston, that no one whom we bring to this place ever leaves our hands uncured?"[19]

Tribunal officer Carol Roberts declined to fine the mayor, though in another adopted banana republic custom, she did warm to the idea of the re-education session. However, since Gray informed her he learned a great deal from the testimony of Professor Ross, Roberts felt "the involvement of the Mayor in this case goes some way to achieving the educational objective sought by the Complainant."[20] Thus, given that Gray jumped through some re-education hoops already, no session was ordered. *1984*'s minister of re-education, O'Brien, would have been more persistent, but proud of Carol Roberts and the tribunal nonetheless.

The presiding officer had slightly more trouble with the prospect of ordering a gay pride proclamation. Roberts was, she said, "not unmindful of the coercive nature of such an order."[21] Mindful or not, she promptly swallowed any misgivings and ordered the coercive proclamation anyway. Thus, the BC Human Rights-As-We-Define-Them-Tribunal took away Walter Gray's right to sign whatever he deemed appropriate as a representative of his citizens and his own conscience. The right to classic liberties – not to be coerced by the state to write, say, or endorse that which one does not care to do, for whatever reason – was overruled and the new "right" (for someone not to have their feelings hurt) won.

In response, Gray refused to sign any further proclamations, period. Some councillors offered to sign the proclamation in his place. That showed a remarkable thickness as to what was at stake; the right to not have words inserted into one's mouth via the threat of state-imposed fines and re-education sessions from a kangaroo court, less interested in traditional human rights than in obvious political agendas. Council never attempted to limit the free expression of the Rainbow Coalition, which regularly received permits for gay pride parades in Kelowna. Pity that the coalition and the NDP-appointed human rights bureaucracy could not extend the same courtesy to Walter Gray.

The attack on the mayor was also offensive from another angle. Gray was a former Social Credit heavyweight and a skilful politician, well liked both in Kelowna and among his colleagues in the Union of BC Municipalities. He could have easily rallied the conservative city and his fellow municipal colleagues against the NDP on a number of occasions. Despite that influence, he chose to cooperate and work with an NDP government; he preferred consultation and cooperation to confrontation. In return, Gray was subjected to a political attack by the NDP-appointed activists. Occasionally, he was sent notes from cabinet ministers on government stationery that chided him for his position.

In an ironic twist several years after the complaint was first lodged against the mayor, gay pride parades began to drop "gay" from the parade titles and instead stuck with only "pride." It appears Gray's persecution by the Human Rights Tribunal probably could have been avoided if only he crossed out the *other* word.

Visions of the anointed: the Commission's blueprint for the future

The NDP changes to the Human Rights law eroded traditional human rights, at least as understood by the average citizen and accepted *de facto* as a decent balance by classic liberals, now often called conservatives. As to why the government and their appointees thought such changes were necessary, one need only examine Commission documents to understand how its staff viewed other British Columbians. It is useful reading as their influence and this debate will be with us all for some time.

In their blueprint for the future, "A Call for Action - Combating Hate in British Columbia," the Commission examines Canada's past and present and finds a hate-filled country that must be cleansed, preferably with a little help from the Commission itself:

> *Hatred against First Nations' people, Blacks, Jews, Chinese, other visible minority immigrants, gays and lesbians, religious minorities and women, has unfortunately been an enduring legacy of the Canadian experience.*[22]

A rather curious view of history, that. Many Canadians who fought Nazis in the Second World War might object to such a blanket condemnation of Canada's past. Immigrants of every colour and creed who fled to Canada over the past two centuries, in part to escape lunatic governments and the uneven application of the law, might also take issue with the report's assumptions. Such immigrants might resent the implication by the NDP-appointed commission, that their neighbours are closet racists in their hearts: 'systemic,' to use a favourite term of the new rights czars.

But as Thomas Sowell has argued elsewhere, those who consider themselves the most forward-looking are in fact "most likely to look backward at a history that is beyond anyone's power to change."[23] In a desire to reach back and correct historical wrongs, impossible as it is, such utopians "create new injustices among our flesh-and-blood contemporaries for the sake of symbolic expiation… but only believers in the vision of cosmic justice are likely to take moral solace in that."[24]

In the same blueprint for the future, the Commission argues that the hate crimes law was built on the foundation of the *Criminal Code* section that requires a high threshold of proof before a conviction is obtained. "Then," the Commission states, "it is only reasonable that provincial hate-crime laws "build on such a foundation."[25]

That sounds reasonable, but "building on such a foundation" actually means skirting the Criminal Code's purposefully onerous requirements and its necessary exemptions. The BC Human Rights Commission does not care to build, but to erode that foundation. Those federal requirements and exemptions are meant to preserve viewpoints and moralities apart from those officially held by the state. After all, if the state restricts some views from being expressed, what if commonly accepted thinking on a subject is incorrect?

The same position paper wants religious freedom provisions stripped from the *Criminal Code* "to ensure that hatred is not being perpetrated under the guise of religion."[26] Apparently, convicting priests of hate crimes is not yet easy enough.

All of this begs the question of whether hate crimes, if Canada must have them over free speech, should be left to the courts with higher thresholds for proof. That is preferable to an appointed, activist bureaucracy with little regard for classic liberal freedoms and a desire to escape the few restraints on its power as now exist. While some of what that human rights bureaucracy promotes and guards is well meaning, necessary, and reasonable, the zealousness to invent new rights trampled on cornerstone freedoms. Most basic, gone was the right to affix one's John Henry to a document without coercion. At the very least, the wings of the human rights bureaucracy should be clipped.

By overthrowing classical definitions of freedom in exchange for coercive speech codes, the NDP's law and their appointees traded pillars of concrete for flimsy sticks of wood. Justice requires a firmer foundation.

At the end of it all, changing the law one more time to accommodate Mary-Woo Sims' desire to hassle 7-Eleven owners looks entirely moderate in comparison to what else is planned.

The NDP *v.* Property Rights

NDP cabinet minister Andrew Petter, a law professor at the University of Victoria before entering provincial politics in 1991, once argued that the Charter of Rights was an enemy of the welfare state. This was in contrast to conservative critics of the Charter that argued it allowed for judicial activism of a more liberal nature. Petter's views, especially on private property, reveal much about the one-time BC Attorney General.

> *The first thing that must be recognized about the Charter is that it is, at root, a 19th century liberal document set loose on a 20th century welfare state. The rights in the Charter are founded upon the belief that the main enemies of freedom are not disparities in wealth or concentrations of private power, but the state. Thus one finds in the Charter little reference to positive economic and social entitlements, such as rights to employment, shelter or social services. Charter rights are predominantly negative in nature, aimed at protecting individuals from state interference or control with respect to this matter or that.*
>
> *Consider the right to equality in section 15. That right does not impose upon the state any positive obligation to undertake measures aimed at eliminating societal disparities in wealth and power.*
>
> *The negative nature of Charter rights combined with this selective view of state action remove from Charter scrutiny the major source of inequality in our society – the unequal distribution of property entitlements among private parties. At the same time, they direct the restraining force of the Charter against the arm of the state best equipped to redress fundamental economic inequalities – the democratic arm, consisting of the Legislature and the Executive.*
>
> *The inclusion of property rights, in particular, would act as an additional spur to judicial protection of established interests against the redistributive and regulatory policies of the welfare state.*[27]

FINALLY, GLEN CLARK COMES UP WITH A JOB CREATION PROGRAM THAT WORKS:
BARRISTERS & SOLIC
IN
HELP WANTED
RAESIDE
www.raesidecartoon.com
VICTORIA TIMES COLONIST - DIST. BY KOKO PRESS INC.

9

The NDP *v.* the Law

"I prefer the evidence of Mr. Sheehan to that of Mr. Clark..."[1]
- Mr. Justice Brenner in Sheehan v. Clark

Legal eagles

Throughout their time in office, BC New Democrats provided perhaps the greatest single career and earnings boost to the province's lawyers. Barristers and solicitors who never dared hope for a Whistler condo, a summer getaway in the Okanagan, or that third BMW, found that dreams *do* come true, if only they could find work defending the provincial government.

To wit, given that lawyers were kept busy by the NDP, so too were judges. The public may not know it, but the severest critiques of BC's New Democrats came not from the opposition Liberals, BCTV, nor the Fraser Institute. Despite the verbal acid poured on government MLAs by talk-radio hosts and political columnists, none were as critical as BC judges, who had regular encounters with the abuse of power honed to a fine art by some of the province's elected officials.

An entire legal course could be taught on the court cases lost by the NDP or by individual New Democrats. Here is a partial list:

1995-1997

In 1995, Frank Dixon won a case against his former employer, the Crown corporation, BC Transit. Glen Clark, the minister then responsible, appointed Dixon as president two years earlier and ordered him to get tough with the absentee-prone union. After the new appointee followed Clark's directive, BC Federation of Labour boss Ken Georgetti was unhappy and Clark flip-flopped. Dixon attempted to reform the company anyway and was fired. The government first denied Dixon's statement of claims, then tried to arrange an out of court settlement,[2] and later lost the case outright.[3]

In 1996, the government went to court to gain an injunction against a federal government plan to buy back fishery licences.[4] The attempt failed.

In 1997, in another fishery-related action, BC launched a lawsuit in American courts that aimed to force American states to abide by a Canada-U.S. salmon sharing agreement: U.S. courts dismissed the $325-million lawsuit.[5] Also in 1997, Surrey and Vancouver blocked the NDP government in court after it tried to force slot machines into those cities.[6]

1998-2000

In 1998, the government's attempt to siphon additional gaming proceeds from charities was ruled invalid by the BC Supreme Court. The judge ruled that the action breached the Criminal Code in its attempt to massively increase gambling.[7] Mr. Justice Owen-Flood:

> *The real ambit of the new Regulation becomes apparent: it encourages and facilitates a massive and unparalleled expansion of charitable gambling in British Columbia and then enables the Government to take the largest piece of the greatly enlarged pie. The regulation is something of a two-faced Janus, as it expands the breadth of charitable gaming in the Province, but then appropriates the bulk of the proceeds for the Government.*[8]

After that case, the government passed "neutron bomb" legislation to prevent charities from claiming damages: Attorney General Ujjal Dosanjh's Bill 50 retroactively shielded government from any claim connected with its failed attempt to siphon off charitable money. That legislation was introduced on a Friday afternoon, hidden in a miscellaneous statutes bill in mid-July. The courts have not yet struck down Bill 50, but it deserves a dishonourable mention for its brazen nature.

Another loss included the BC Hydro case where Glen Clark wrongly fired Hydro president John Sheehan. On Clark's first day as Premier in 1996, he fired Sheehan after it was publicly revealed that top Hydro executives (with NDP connections) stood to profit from the corporation's investment decisions. In the end, the judge ruled that the executives did nothing amiss. He *did* find that Clark knew of that possibility (for executives to invest), in direct contradiction to both his public claim at the time of the 1996 firings, and his later testimony in court.[9]

In another high-profile case in 1999,[i] former MLA, BC Finance minister, MP and NDP heavyweight Dave Stupich plea-bargained away 64 counts

---

i. See Appendix A: Turning Tommy Douglas in his Grave – The Nanaimo bingo scandal.

The home that charity built? In the Nanaimo Commonwealth Holding Society scandal that involved former NDP MLA, MP, and BC Finance Minister Dave Stupich, the judge wrote that by 1989, at least $1 million in charity money had been dealt with in a fraudulent manner. As a condition of sentencing, Stupich was not allowed to visit his $800,000 home on Gabriola Island. On prime real estate with a view of passing ferries and Vancouver Island, the 3,440 square feet house contained six bedrooms, three bathrooms, manicured gardens, a swimming pool, and a hot tub. *Vancouver Province* photo, used by permission.

and pleaded guilty to one charge of fraud involving more than $5,000 and one count of running an illegal lottery. Democratic Publications, the newspaper arm of the New Democratic Party also pleaded guilty to two charges of operating an illegal lottery scheme in connection with the scandal.[10]

In 2000, the NDP government's attempt to sue tobacco companies for health costs was declared invalid;[11] their election gag law against citizen groups and the media was found unconstitutional;[12] and Bob Ward's defamation case against Glen Clark over fast ferries (Clark called him a crank) proved successful.[13]

But as the NDP's second term drew to a close, the most dramatic legal and media circus was yet to come: on October 20th of that year, former Premier Glen Clark was charged with two criminal counts – defrauding the government and breach of trust. The charges stemmed from his alleged role in the granting of a casino licence to his neighbour, Dimitrios Pilarinos.[14]

Will that be a personal cheque or the taxpayer VISA?

Under the Socreds, if the duties of a civil servant landed them in court, the public paid the bills; politicians were on their own. Legal battles could be costly for a politician, but until the NDP, lawyer fees were billed to the MLA, unless their party paid for it or unless money was raised through sympathetic donors. Bill Vander Zalm's defence in allegations of criminal misdeeds (charges he was later acquitted on) cost him half a million dollars. In the late 1980s, then Attorney General Bud Smith hired his own lawyer in a controversial case where a contract awarded to Smith's Socred friends was not prosecuted, a decision made in his ministry.

After the NDP came to power, the policy was changed and politicians could be funded by taxpayers on a case by case basis. A short time later, after the Nanaimo bingo scandal broke, the policy was made more generous yet again: legal costs would henceforth be covered whenever a politician needed a lawyer.[15] For crack legal minds with NDP connections, it was open season on taxpayers.

In an increasingly litigious society, it was reasonable that a politician's legal bill be covered when lawsuits arose because of their official duties and on matters under their authority. But some New Democrats abused the privilege as legal help was also used for matters related to personal conduct.

Glen Clark illustrated this divide perfectly: in the case of the Bob Ward defamation suit, it was reasonable that a politician publicly defending a government project (the fast ferries) might be given government-paid legal help. But Clark's alleged personal actions led to criminal charges over the granting of a casino licence, and such matters were not his bailiwick but those of the cabinet minister responsible for gaming. There, the government took care of Clark's legal bills but promised that Clark would have to repay them if found guilty. Besides the possible difficulty of collecting, it was an odd precedent. If a bank manager was subject to criminal charges over a hit-and-run, it was unlikely his employer would foot the legal bill for off-work actions. Clark's casino charges were not much different.

Beside the tax-funded legal pot available for MLAs, money was also made available for political appointments to launch legal missives against opponents, usually the media. In early 1999, Glen Clark aide Tom Gunton went after journalists critical of his murky role in the 1996 fudge-it budget affair, including Mike Smyth of the *Vancouver Province*. The Premier's communications director Geoff Meggs warned other media they might be next.[16]

In Pursuit of Carrier Lumber

"These notes trace in reasonably direct and cynical terms the very pattern of decisions I have found to emerge from the documents of events themselves. There was in fact a high level decision to kill Carrier..."[17]

- Honourable Mr. Justice W.G. Parrett

Despite the multitude of choices, one case best demonstrated the lengths to which the NDP went to steamroll businesses and individuals in pursuit of a political agenda. Largely unreported until judgment day, Carrier Lumber *v.* the Crown revealed in damning completeness, a government's willingness to bulldoze the rule of law and cynical provincial bureaucrats more than willing to carry out political directives no matter how ethically and legally flawed. Worse, the government, in cynical fashion, appealed the case, ostensibly to save taxpayers a damage award; in reality to avoid having to cut that cheque before an election.

In September of 1997, Prince George-based Carrier Lumber filed a statement of claim against the government of BC for breach of contract, deceit, and the wrongful suspension of the forest licence it had been issued fourteen years earlier. Halfway through the trial, Carrier stumbled upon crucial government documents that were deliberately hid from both Carrier and the court.

In his judgment two years later, the presiding judge expressed surprise that the facts of the case were not already widely broadcast across the country. He thought it extraordinary, both for what it exposed about the government of the day and for what it revealed about the press. His best explanation for the lack of media interest was that the remoteness of the events and the trial, far from the urban areas of the lower mainland, caused the case to be overlooked.

Justice Parrett's observations were insightful. Had the case been heard in downtown Vancouver instead of Prince George, national reporters would have filed daily dispatches about allegations of corruption, contract breaking and cover-up. Had that happened, it is likely that NDP cabinet minister Dan Miller, at the centre of the judicial censure, would never have become interim premier in August 1999, one month after the judgment was handed down. The case against the government, the ministry of Forests, and Miller, was the most damning legal indictment the NDP regime had yet received. The defendants in the case were revealed as cynical, deceitful, and contemptuous, both of the court's authority and the rule of law.

The background

In May 1992, in an attempt to placate several north-central British Columbian native bands who were increasingly forceful in asserting their land claims in the area, then Premier Mike Harcourt, Economic Development Minister David Zirnhelt, and Forests Minister Dan Miller met with Chilcotin chiefs at the 108 Mile airport. The Premier and ministers promised that there would be no timber harvesting in the band's traditional territory without their consent.

But the promise was not the government's to make: Carrier Lumber, a Prince George-based firm with an acknowledged reputation for innovation, good corporate citizenship, and superior relations with natives, possessed Forest Licence A20022 since 1983. As part of a salvage operation to combat the Mountain Pine Beetle, the licence gave Carrier the right to harvest five million cubic metres of forest, a substantial amount of it in the Beef Trail Creek area, the land at the centre of the dispute.

The Chilcotin fire-trap

Ironically, in light of the government's later actions, it was Carrier that was pursued by the provincial government to log the area, not vice-versa. In the late 1970s, the Crown desperately wanted the area cut because of the pine beetle infestation that threatened to ravage the region's forests and heighten the risk for out of control forest fires.

That there was any logging wealth to fight over would have been a surprise to anyone just a decade earlier. The Chilcotin plateau had never before been harvested and for good reason: The area was remote, and expensive to log in comparison to preferred lower-level regions where trees grew quickly and more densely. In comparison, the Chilcotin plateau was semi-arid, had sparse timber stands and access was difficult. Thus, it was hardly the preferred choice of any logging company interested in a profit.

Once the beetle infestation hit the region though, substantial amounts of timber were infected and dying; the result was a looming catastrophe both environmentally – there was a growing risk of wild fire – as well as financially. As the beetle spread, large stands of timber were killed off and by 1984 the infestation was described as the largest insect disaster known to mankind.[18] To grasp how much money was at stake, given that the area would one day have to be cleared and replanted at a substantial cost, the government only had to examine a much smaller area that it earlier sought to have harvested.

In 1981, a 550,000-cubic-meter parcel was auctioned off but no one cared to bid: the tenure offered was not long enough to justify the investment, the timber quality was poor, and the area too remote. After a similar auction one year later also failed to attract much interest, the ministry of Forests estimated the cost of clearing, seedlings, and replanting at $430 million, not including what the province would lose from the value of the existing crop. That was for an area 1/360th of what the ministry thought might be lost if the pine beetle continued to spread.

It is in this context the provincial government looked for a forestry company to control the growing infestation. And in a last-ditch effort, the Crown offered up an unprecedented five-million cubic meters of timber for harvest over ten years: only a timber licence of that size might attract a company given the enormous capital investment required

Despite the offer, the Ministry of Forests had few takers; all wanted money up front for hauling off the dead timber. Only Carrier Lumber's proposal assumed all the cost and risk. As a plus, when the logging was complete, the government would be $19 million richer in taxes and stumpage fees.

Socred harassment

In 1987, the provincial government added tough new silviculture requirements for forestry companies, and by 1989, it was only then becoming clear that the beetle infestation had tapered off due to severe winter cold in the middle of the decade. The combination of new silviculture requirements and a changed forest would later make Carrier unnecessary to the ministry of Forests. At the time though, Carrier was under the impression that the original deal was still a deal. After all - they had a contract.

Instead, in what became known as the "bombshell" letter, the ministry of Forests wrote Carrier in May 1991 and demanded that Carrier put up a security deposit for replanting costs; the new silviculture costs were estimated at between $15 million and $30 million. As Justice Parrett wrote, given that it was the government that was legally bound to provide almost a million dollars to Carrier for regeneration, not vice versa, the ministry's later demand amounted to an arbitrary $16-million to $31-million change in the original forest licence:[19]

> *I have not the faintest hesitation in finding that an imposition of costs of this magnitude seriously jeopardized Carrier's whole operation in the Chilcotin and that if known at the outset would have precluded the project from ever beginning.*[20]

The new silviculture obligations, never part of the original forest licence, later became the stated reason for junking Carrier's contract. The real reason had to do with native land claims, claims which were increasingly frequent and noted by governments. In Carrier's case in particular, blockades slowed Carrier's progress in harvesting the full five million cubic meters. In addition, the machinations against Carrier within the ministry of Forests continued to grow. The company, Justice Parrett later wrote, was being set up as "part of a carefully calculated scheme to divert attention and lay the blame for the failure of this licence on Carrier."[21]

Plagues, pestilence, blockades and the NDP in power

As rotten as Carrier was treated after 1989, things became much worse after the NDP came to power two years later. By then, Carrier had established five mills in the Chilcotin region; an industrial presence in one of North America's more remote areas that had been created from scratch. But that investment was soon undercut.

It was no secret that the new government in Victoria was quite sympathetic to native land claims. But Carrier always maintained a good working relationship with native communities, and thus was the last company that a government, Socred or NDP, should have sacrificed in the chess game over native land claims.

But by 1992, Carrier had not yet cut half the trees it was promised in 1983. That was due in large measure to native and government bickering over chunks of land the company was supposed to harvest. In addition, the pine beetle plague had subsided, and as more native blockades took place, internal ministry memorandums warned that if Carrier simply turned in its licence and walked away - a distinct possibility at that point, that action would "result in a major economic blow to the Chilcotin region."[22]

At this point, Premier Mike Harcourt was briefed of the dispute and his staff laid out two options: Option One was that the Province repeat in writing the offer by the Forest Service, that no road building or harvesting could take place until resolution of a joint venture proposal. Option Two was that the Province give in to native demands for control of the area.

Both scenarios were rotten for Carrier. The second option was a death sentence for the company's mill in the area, and it would have set a terrible precedent for future land claim negotiations. "Name it and it's yours" would have been the message.

The first option (and the one the bureaucracy recommended) was not much better. As the writer of the memorandum to Harcourt recognized, the implication of Option One – no permits issued until resolution of the dispute – was that it required agreement by Carrier. Even if Carrier accepted, and there was no legal reason why they should, such a stall may not have satisfied native grievances anyway.

Mike Harcourt, David Zirnhelt, and Dan Miller at 108 Mile

> *The events of this meeting would have enormous repercussions to Carrier and potentially to the whole Province of British Columbia.*[23] *- Justice W.G. Parrett*

On May 13, 1992, Mike Harcourt, Forestry Minister Dan Miller, and Economic Development Minister David Zirnhelt, flew to 108 Mile, and met with Chilcotin chiefs at the town's airstrip. This time, unlike previous meetings between the former Socred ministers and some native leaders, the new premier made a promise that led directly to the lawsuit, one that may yet cost taxpayers hundreds of millions in damages.[24]

Did the premier and his ministers give away Carrier's legal rights to harvest timber? Justice Parrett:

> *It is clear that during the course of this meeting Premier Harcourt promised the Nemiah people that there would be no harvesting in their traditional territory without their consent. The fact that this commitment was given is not even disputed, indeed, in a case marred at every turn by issues of document disclosure the documents on this point clearly and unequivocally demonstrate that this commitment was made.*[25]

One day later, the scope of the premier's promise was set out in a memorandum from David Zirnhelt to Forestry Minister Dan Miller and also to Aboriginal Affairs Minister Andrew Petter. There were five points, but the first one set off a chain reaction of bureaucratic cover-up, duplicity, the withholding of documents from the judge during trial, and a stinger of an accusation from the judge that zeroed in on the premier and ministers themselves.

The memorandum stated that "the result of the meeting of the Premier, myself, and the Tsilhqot'in Chiefs is as follows: The Premier agreed that ...

the Minister of Forests will send a letter to the Nemiah Valley Indian Band stating that no cutting permits or road building permits will be issued unless agreed to by the Nemiah Valley Indian Band."[26] Justice Parrett:

> *In a single statement, any remaining hopes of Carrier harvesting their full volume in the time remaining on their licence were dashed, but the significance of that event pales in comparison to the other implications.*[27]

What happened next is worth reprinting from the court transcript verbatim. Phillip Halkett, a career civil servant who was deputy minister of Forests in 1992, was called to testify in the trial launched by Carrier:[28]

Q: *And here in Mr. Zirnhelt's letter, this memo, you see the following, paragraph 1 of his May 14th memo: "The Minister of Forests will send a letter to the Nemiah Valley Indian Band stating that no cutting will be issued unless agreed to by the Nemiah Valley Indian Band." I would suggest to you, Mr. Halkett, that that is a very significant departure from the law as it is spelled out in the Forest Act?*
A: *Correct.*

Q: *That being a very experienced civil servant you would have, I'm sure, seen that immediately upon reading it, you would have appreciated the effect of that?*
A: *Correct.*

Q: *And you are now presented with a situation where the Premier and a Minister of the Crown have made such – apparently made such a statement to five Tsilhqot' in Chiefs?*
A: *Correct.*

Q: *What was your reaction when you saw that?*
A: *In polite society?*

Q: *Yes, yes.*
A: *The Premier had no authority to make that promise.... You cannot by verbal statement transfer lawful authority to any Indian Band, you cannot – another way of putting the same thought is you cannot by ministerial statement by any Minister transfer jurisdiction from the Provincial Crown.... And you cannot do that on the authority of any person, even if that person is the Premier.*[29]

After Harcourt's promise to the Nemiah band, senior civil servants recognized the mistake and his own ministers tried to minimize the commitment.[30] That failed, as the Nemiah had a full understanding of what the premier committed to and were not likely to forget it.

Sacrificing Carrier Lumber

After early 1992 and Mike Harcourt's promise, Carrier's demise was assured. After nine years, only half the promised timber, and tens of millions invested because of the 1983 government pleadings, Carrier's financial interests and legal rights were treated as dead. The only question was how the government would justify the action. Justice Parnett:

> *It was time for damage control and a plan to divert attention. In my respectful view these briefing notes demonstrate nothing less than the evolution of that strategy in a Ministry that was cynically prepared to use Carrier when it suited them and to sacrifice them when it was in the Ministry's interest.*
>
> *This is nothing more and nothing less than another part of the Ministry's attempt to alter reality and protect their own positions. It is part of an overall scheme which included the writing of self serving and demonstrably untrue memos and correspondence, the holding of "secret" meetings without the knowledge of key and materially interested parties, and the suppression and withholding of key documents which would fully reveal their conduct.*[31]

Welcome to the jungle

The bureaucracy recognized that Premier Mike Harcourt had no authority to ignore a legal contract, but for whatever reason – a lack of backbone, bureaucratic laziness or arrogance – civil servants within the ministry opted to obey their political masters rather than the rule of law. In the chess game between disgruntled civil servants and politicians, the quickest way to derail a political gambit is to leak a memorandum. Right or wrong, many an ambitious cabinet minister has had their plans derailed by a lowly bureaucrat and a strategically placed brown envelope. In this case, no one bothered, despite having all the right moral and legal reasons.

But there was another reason for Carrier's demise: forestry bureaucrats despised Carrier owner Bill Kordyban. As Ken Drushka, the *Vancouver Sun* forestry columnist noted, "Officials in the forestry ministry had long considered Kordyban to be a pain in the ass."[32] Kordyban built a business on unorthodox methods of forestry where others would have gone broke, he held strong views about forest policy, and he hated the NDP.

The feeling was mutual: "The NDP government of Mike Harcourt saw him as the devil incarnate, a right-wing lunatic easily disposed of," wrote Drushka. And civil servants within the ministry of Forests did not live up to the first part of their title: evidence in court produced a bureaucrat's cartoon with Bill Kordyban slumped dead across a stockade wall with an arrow in his back.[33] Given the animosity of the bureaucracy and the government, it was easy for them to conspire against Kordyban, "first to kick him out of the Chilcotin, and then to defeat his legal challenge," as Drushka later wrote.[34]

So in the summer of 1992, a draft briefing note was circulated with three options on how to cancel Carrier's licence. The draft version included Option Three, the one recommended by the bureaucracy: to describe Carrier as "acting contrary to law" because of "their failure to accept silviculture obligations."[35] As the judge wrote, it was a "strategy designed to obscure the real events, and try to minimize the fact that they were prepared to sacrifice Carrier to leave themselves and the government an open field to deal with the aboriginal issue."[36]

The Ministry recognized that there were risks to this blunt instrument of Carrier's demise. It would send a signal that forestry companies could be sacrificed in conflict areas (i.e., where a native claim existed), and 400 jobs would be lost. More disturbing was the possibility that Carrier might *accept* the new silviculture obligations.[37] Should that happen, the Ministry would be back to square one with natives.

Did then Forestry Minister Dan Miller suspend Carrier Lumber's licence and effectively kill the contract? Or, as claimed in court by the Crown, did Regional Manager Mike Carlson do it alone? In court testimony, Carlson claimed that he alone made the final decision,[38] an assertion the judge refused to believe.

The missing briefing note

Mike Carlson apparently had an advanced case of amnesia. All the pages in the draft briefing notes were prepared for the minister. Carlson's handwriting all over the margins and the note itself recommended Option Three, with its stress on the silviculture "problem" and not the blockade, as the option the minister should choose.[39] Justice Parrett questioned Carlson repeatedly as to why, if he was so focused on this being his decision and no one else's, was there no comment in the margins that this briefing note was not to go to the minister. Carlson said he had no recollection. The judge was not satisfied:

The Court: *Then why did you participate in the process of preparing a briefing note that's going to the Minister for him to apparently consider that recommendation? I'm sorry, Mr. Carlson, I just don't understand why you would do that? Can you help me with that?*

Carlson: *Not having any recollection of any discussion I can't offer any help, I'm sorry....*[40]

The final version of the briefing note was never produced at trial. Did Dan Miller see a final briefing note, and sign off on Option Three that killed, illegally, a binding contract Carrier had with the Crown? Justice Parrett did not buy Carlson's assertion that he alone gave the order to kill Carrier:

> *Putting it as simply as I can, I simply don't accept his evidence on these two points. Indeed, his evidence on these two aspects of this action is so distinctly out of harmony with the preponderance or probabilities as to stretch credulity beyond the breaking point. Mr. Carlson would have me believe and accept that having been concerned enough in the fall of 1991 to request and obtain a legal opinion, that the decision to suspend Carrier's licence fell within his sole discretion and that he would never permit anyone to interfere with it, he then participated in the drafting of briefing notes which he read over, added comments on, and then, in Reeves' words, approved in principle....*
>
> *The difficulty with that evidence is that even in the first draft that he admits to reviewing, the issue of suspending Carrier's licence, is, by that briefing note, referred to the Minister, for decision....*
>
> *The existence of these briefing notes, the fact they are designed to elicit a ministerial decision, the express wording of this recommendation, Carlson's review of this briefing note, and his approval of it in principle, are all utterly inconsistent with his own sworn testimony that no one was going to be allowed to interfere with his statutory decision making power.* [41]

Missing documents and the suppression of evidence

For the judge to piece back together the events within the ministry of Forests back in 1992 was due to either plain luck or divine intervention: take your pick.

The trial was already underway in 1997 when a chance meeting between a Carrier manager and members of the Ulkatcho Indian Band led to the discovery of massive amounts of Crown documents, one of which bore the signature of the minister of Forests.[42] Carrier, which had a good relationship with native bands, was given the documents. In another stroke of divine intervention for Carrier Lumber, the trial was temporarily suspended at the time due to the illness of a major witness. Had it not been for that sickness and the Ulkatcho Band, the facts of the case might never have come to light.

With the discovery of new items materially relevant to the case, the court compared the list of documents that the government submitted versus the documents turned over by the Ulkatcho. (The original copies were in the ministry's own files.)

The two lists were starkly different, and the judge blasted the ministry for withholding materially relevant documents from the court and called their disclosures "selective."[43] He noted that even after this event, the government still refused to fully comply with his order to produce any and all documents relevant to the case:

> *The rules which apply to these types of proceedings must apply equally to all and are not to be avoided or ignored by the petulant arrogance of senior bureaucrats....*
>
> *The explanations offered to attempt to explain the defendant's massive failure are completely inadequate to offer any reasonable overall explanation. While some aspects of the defendant's failure to disclose may be attributable to simple arrogance and a refusal to accept the proposition that they are subject to direction from the court or accountable for their actions, the disclosure in a number of key areas is indicative of active and careful suppression of evidence....*
>
> *I am equally satisfied that there are still documents which have not been disclosed which bear directly on the way in which key decisions were made.*[44]

The high level decision to kill Carrier

Justice Parrett traced the various briefing notes, the letters to Carrier, and the conflicting testimony given by ministry officials, and then shredded the credibility of key Crown witnesses, including Mike Carlson:

> *I conclude that a meeting took place with the Minister late on the afternoon of June 10, 1992, and that at that meeting a decision was made to announce the three month moratorium and to instruct*

> *Carlson to suspend Carrier's licence. It is improbable that a decision of such magnitude would be taken without a briefing note setting out the options for the Minister. This was in fact the very system designed and implemented by Deputy Minister Halkett and to which he demanded rigid adherence....*
>
> ***I conclude on the whole of the evidence that a final form of the briefing note was placed before the Minister and was the basis of the decisions taken that afternoon.*** *Those decisions found expression in the Minister's letter eventually finalized on June 15,1992, and in Carlson's letter the next day.*[45] (Emphasis added.)

In case anyone thought the judge was finished with the bureaucrats and the minister in question, he then delivered the final judicial cut. Not only was Dan Miller at the centre of the decision to pull Carrier's licence, in contradiction of Mike Carlson's discredited court testimony, but someone or some group of individuals deliberately withheld key documents from the trial:

> *The absence of the final briefing note put before the Minister, any records related to the meeting, which in my view clearly must have taken place, and any documents other than the one draft communicating directions arising from the meeting must be considered an attempt to conceal the events and to "set up" the evidence advanced at trial that Carlson, as the statutory decision maker, was the only person involved in the decision to suspend....*
>
> *I conclude that such documents clearly existed and that they have been deliberately withheld.*[46]
>
> *These notes trace in reasonably direct and cynical terms the very pattern of decisions I have found to emerge from the documents and events themselves.* ***There was in fact a high level decision to kill Carrier****.... It is difficult to conceive of a more compelling and cynical example of duplicity and bad faith. The words "managing perception" may have a gloss which seems to carry with it some high purpose. The reality is, at least in this case, little more than a process of altering reality by concealing the truth and presenting a fabricated cover story.*[47]
>
> *As the Plaintiff's counsel said at the opening of this trial, "This case is about the primacy of the rule of law, and the subjugation of the sovereign to it."*[48]
>
> *The conduct of the defendant traced through these reasons is, in*

my view, conduct unacceptable under our common law or to the Canadian public generally. When the power of the legislator or the bureaucrat is abused it is in this country subject to the review of an independent judiciary. The power of review must be carefully exercised and jealously guarded for it is the foundation of the protection of the citizen from the power of the state. Where, as in the present case, the impugned conduct is unconscionable... the court is compelled to intervene.[49] (Emphasis added.)

Still in denial

Less than one month after the judgment, and the day after he was sworn in as interim Premier, Dan Miller still claimed the case was all about 1987 changes to silviculture requirements.

I do recall when I was the minister...from my recollection it was a very straightforward issue. The law had been changed in 1987 by the Social Credit administration, conferring on licence holders an obligation to do the silviculture. In that particular instance there was a great deal of difficulty that, in fact, started in the Social Credit administration in having that company accept their silviculture obligation. I became the minister and I made efforts to resolve the issue and at the end of the day the decision was made, I think by the ministry, to pull the licence on that basis.[50]

One month after a judge put Dan Miller at the centre of the decision to illegally revoke Carrier's licence, the new premier still blamed the Socreds, argued $16-million to $31-million in new silviculture obligations could be retroactive, and blamed the ministry for the decision to pull Carrier's licence.

It was his story and he was sticking to it. The next day, Attorney General Ujjal Dosanjh appealed the case.[51] That put off the inevitable damage award, estimated by some at $150 million,[52] until after the next election.

NDP
HEADQUARTERS

RCMP INVESTIGATION INTO NANAIMO BINGO SCANDAL CONTINUES.

UJJAL... ANY CHANCE OF CLOSING THE NANAIMO COURTHOUSE?

RAESIDE

Victoria Times Colonist.

HEY FIRST NATIONS PEOPLE! GOT A HANKERIN' FOR A CHUNK OF B.C.?
WELL C'MON DOWN TO CRAZY GLENS!... WE GOT DEALS FOR YOU!
WE'RE BLOWING THE ENTIRE PROVINCE OUT THE DOOR! NO MONEY DOWN AND NO PAYMENTS, ...EVER!
YOU WANT THE CARIBOO? PEACE RIVER? VANCOUVER? WE GOT ALL THE BIG NAMES HERE AT CRAZY GLENS!
NO CREDIT? NO PROBLEM! NO LEGITIMATE CLAIMS? HERE AT CRAZY GLENS... WE DON'T CARE!
...AND AS OUR DOORCRASHER SPECIAL, WE'RE THROWING IN VANCOUVER ISLAND.
RAESIDE
Victoria Times Colonist. Dist. by Koko Press Inc. www.raesidecartoon.com

10

Congratulations, You're Fired

"Get with it; get into the modern age. Stop fighting the old racist battles of the past."[1]
- NDP Cabinet Minister Ian Waddell, on opposition to the Nisga'a Treaty

In real life, people pay exorbitant fees to lawyers to win a case in court. If successful, and should those who lose the original case appeal, chances are the plaintiff will continue the costly legal battle to protect the original judgment. And usually it pays to keep the same attorneys. In BC politics in the 1990s, the normal rules rarely applied.

On the radar screen: this land is whose land?

On October 23, 1984, a pivotal statement of claim was filed with the Supreme Court of British Columbia. The case, later known as Delgamuukw, concerned an area in northwest BC (equal to the size of Nova Scotia) and whether it was owned by the Crown, i.e., the Province of British Columbia, or the Gitksan and Wet'suwet'en Indian bands. The latter argued that aboriginal title had never been extinguished because British Columbia formalized few treaties in the colonial period.

Later court battles and decisions would alter the province's political, jurisdictional, and economic landscape; in the meantime, the main battles were still fought in the political realm. By the late 1980s, native bands in BC grew increasingly bold about asserting that no treaty meant no formalized deal, which in turn meant title was still theirs in some sense yet to be determined.

The definition of ownership meant vastly different things depending on the native leader in question, and the final Supreme Court of Canada decision on Delgamuukw was still more than half a decade away when the NDP took power in 1991. But there was little doubt about the early 1990s message from natives to politicians: the provincial and federal governments should make up for lost time.

The traditional BC position

When British Columbia entered confederation in 1871, jurisdiction over native inhabitants and the land was transferred to Ottawa under the terms of the *British North America Act, 1867*. As was clear from the Terms of Union, Ottawa assumed certain obligations:

> *The charge of the Indians and the trusteeship and management of the lands reserved for their use and benefit shall be assumed by the Dominion Government, and a policy as liberal as that hitherto pursued by the British Columbia Government, shall be continued by the Dominion Government after the Union.*[2]

As the late Mel Smith pointed out elsewhere, treaties were, after that point in time, unquestionably a federal responsibility, assuming they should be negotiated at all.[3] New treaties or not, natives in British Columbia were treated similar to natives elsewhere in Canada. Sometimes quite badly, sometimes more fair than elsewhere in Canada, and never as well as Canadians in the 1990s would rightly think of as just.

Over the next several decades, a reserve system was set up in BC similar to what occurred in the rest of Canada, and natives were eligible for the full range of programs, subsidies, and tax exclusions regardless of the existence of BC-specific treaties or not. They were also denied the right to vote, among other racist acts, and locked out of economic participation by virtue of their placement on reserves that were communally, not individually, owned.

By 1924 the federal government, via an Order-in-Council, formally acknowledged that BC satisfied the 1871 Terms of Union. The process, now complete, met the "full and final settlement of all differences between the governments of the Dominion and the Province."[4] As Smith puts it, "Such an acknowledgment by the federal government is support for the long-held provincial position that BC had fully discharged its obligations to its Indians *though it had done so differently from the rest of Canada*."[5] (Emphasis added.)

The end result was that by the late 20th century, British Columbia possessed 1,634 of Canada's total reserves of out of a total 2,323.[6] Out of 2.68 million hectares in Canada, 344,000 hectares were in British Columbia, or 12.8 percent of the total, while BC had seventeen percent of Canada's status Indians.[7]

Natural sympathy

Canada in 1991 was not Canada in 1871. Discriminatory laws on voting and other acts of citizenship ended 30 years before and the department of Indian Affairs spent billions of dollars every year in an effort to ameliorate the admittedly awful condition of many Canadian natives.

Modern-day Canada was also different from 1871 in other significant ways. Tens of millions of additional people lived here and were either immigrants themselves or the result of parents and grandparents who migrated. Many of those – kulaks from the Soviet Union, Jews from just about anywhere, or other refugees from lunatic dictators that blemished the 20th century – also had their own tragic story to tell that could equal the tragedy of what many natives endured at various points in Canada's history. Tragedy produces sympathy, and Canadians, at least those who knew enough of their own family history and that of their mother countries, were sympathetic to fair claims for settlement from any quarter. In fact it was *that* sympathy and sense of fairness from the 97 percent of the population who were not native that enabled native claims to reach a higher profile than ever before.

That said, as understandable as the native position was on that level, it was also reasonable to expect politicians to negotiate fairly but keep in mind that the original British settlers of the province were long dead. And no matter how fashionable it was (and is) to create government policy based on skin colour and ethnic heritage, it was a leap of logic to make a 20th-century immigrant from Italy, South Korea, Nigeria or China responsible – in any sense – for policies enacted by 19th-century immigrants from England.

It also stretched reason to assume that every late 19th-century action could or should be compensated for in the 1990s, or even to argue that every decision taken by early colonial rulers was always intentionally harmful and culpable in the modern legal and moral sense.

Such assumptions would doom any country on the planet to endless debates of the sort British Columbia endured in the 1990s. Present-day citizens of every jurisdiction in the world would, under such a premise, pay for a very long time for actions committed by historical figures long dead. And such a standard would also catch native North Americans in the compensation trap as much as anyone else. No one's ethnic history is blood-free.

Land values and immigration

The land claim debates of the 1990s also had another faulty assumption: that the present-day value of land should be the reference point in treaty negotiations. Settlers, pre- and post-1867, made Canadian land more valuable through agricultural use and its development. That land value was the result of decades, if not hundreds of years' worth of improvements made on it. It required duplicity to argue that such territory was stolen, and then demand compensation *for* that land based on worth given to it by immigrants, whose existence and efforts increased its value. It was a contradictory claim but one often advanced in the 1990s.

In 1991 for example, the 200-strong Fort George band near Prince George filed a claim with the federal government that sought more than $500 million in compensation for its claim to most of downtown Prince George.[8] For anyone to think that such land was worth that amount of money and not consider the effect of tens of millions of immigrants who moved into Canada (and what that meant for land values in the country) was fanciful. And the improvements made to such land occurred in part because of the concept of property rights and wealth creation that English immigrants and others brought to North America.

One supposes that the claims of the 1990s were fine as a starting point for negotiations, but there were inherent contradictions in the assumptions. That should have been pointed out on occasion.

The missing demand

Because of natural and understandable sympathy for natives and some agreement with the idea of compensation – even if agreement on the specifics was elusive – there was widespread support in the late 1980s and early 1990s for some form of compensation. As it was, the Canadian public long funded a federal department of Indian Affairs with the understanding that such funding *was* the way past wrongs could hopefully be ameliorated. However mistaken that notion was, and how incomplete and unaccountable some funding models were, Canadians did not, contrary to popular and more elitist political mythology, ignore the native question; had they in fact done so, the department of Indian Affairs and its multi-billion dollar budget would never have existed.

A better explanation was that most Canadians simply did not know what more could be done. Another was that many endorsed well intentioned but fatally flawed approaches to native policy. Few argued against the status quo. Former Alberta Social Services Minister Mike Cardinal (and a native himself) once argued government welfare destroyed the initiative and independence of a generation of natives. He was right about the dependency trap, but only a native Canadian could point to the destructive effect of the dependency culture without the risk of being labelled a racist. Problem was, few Canadians had any ideas on how to improve on what existed.

Any alternative such as individual ownership of land was seen as a threat to the communal nature of some reserves.[i] The idea was not welcomed by native leaders, either because they did not understand the spur to wealth

---

i. The lack of understanding of the importance of property rights is hardly limited to some native leaders. Few government MLAs in BC understood why the concept was crucial to wealth creation and improved living standards.

creation that property ownership would create, or because they *did* understand it and feared it as a threat to their power, which it was (and is).

Individual property rights combined with a local taxation base spurs accountability and would put native leaders in the service of native property-holders, the exact reverse of the current system. And every society on the planet that advances economically does so on the basis of such a model. When native leaders continually rejected such ideas, other Canadians simply gave up or already bought the status quo arguments and thought little else could be accomplished. Both segments continued, through their taxes, to write cheques from Indian Affairs in ever-increasing amounts. Canadians have not been as uncaring or uninterested as some would suggest; they have been paralysed by either fear of being labelled racist or by a belief that the Indian Act was as much as could be done, tragic and as harmful as the Act was.

Native leaders asked for everything but what was most likely to ameliorate the rotten environment in the long term. Few thought to remove the worst roadblock to native prosperity and improved living standards: the lack of full individual property rights and all the protections and incentives that such rights might have provided.[ii]

Reserves were still owned communally and thus could never be used for individual collateral. Without that, there was little incentive for individual improvement to the land since there was no long-term benefit to such actions. As a consequence, there was no significant local tax base from which to promote responsible taxation and expenditure decisions by the band. Instead, money was transferred from a distant colonial capital to be dispersed as leaders saw fit. The incentives were and still are structured in the wrong direction.[iii]

But if that right of individual property with all its benefits and risks was not yet realized, it was due to many native leaders themselves and to non-native politicians who could not consider natives as anything but dependent on government – an assumption which was neither historical, fair, nor necessary.

---

ii. There was some progress on this question in the Nisga'a treaty, though it remains to be seen if the way the treaty structured property rights will actually lead to the kind of property rights ultimately necessary for wealth creation. More on this in the next chapter.

iii. For more on why individual property rights matter in terms of wealth creation, see Hernando de Soto's *The Mystery of Capital* (Basic Books, New York, 2000). The Peruvian author makes a convincing case that free markets and the wealth they create are possible only when individuals can leverage privately owned property to obtain capital.

Slip-sliding away: the shift in the provincial position

By 1987, with the creation of a Native Affairs Secretariat and then a full-fledged Native Affairs ministry one-year later, British Columbia's position as regards native land claims shifted. Not long after, the formal demands for compensation became more explicit and expensive.

In one sense, there was nothing wrong or excessive with the demands of native Canadians; it never hurts to ask (or *demand,* for those who didn't care to recognize Canadian sovereignty). All negotiations, including court battles, have a starting point and the list, expanded as time went on, just happened to be the shopping expedition for many of BC's native bands.

But in real life in the 1990s, treaties meant not a whit insofar as the federal department of Indian Affairs, and funding, was concerned. The push for treaties was a reach for more money, control, land, and in some cases, sovereignty association of the kind that would make a sovereignty-seeking Quebec government deliriously giddy.

That was all part of bargaining, but just as native Canadians could, as a tactic, demand a fairly long list of items in exchange for an end to official grievances, it made parallel perfect sense for the Province to have the strongest possible hand of its own to play. After all, the provincial government was still responsible to ensure stability and continuity with regards to natural resource use (forest licences and mining permits to name a few), never mind property rights in general. Mess with that – the backbone of the BC economy – and everyone would lose.

Thus, land-use stability and provincial sovereignty of the land were not unreasonable barriers to honourable settlements, unless of course, sovereignty itself was disputed. As it turned out, that was precisely what was at issue.

When the Delgamuukw case arrived in court in 1991, the Province (under the Social Credit party at that point) argued that right or wrong, and whether everything British settlers did was completely awful or fully virtuous (the truth likely somewhere in between) the Crown had full ownership of British Columbia's land base, without exception and without compromise or infringement.

The 1991 Delgamuukw trial

Lawyers from the Vancouver firm of Russell & DuMoulin argued the case on behalf of the Crown. The firm's lawyers attended to microscopic detail during the 347 days of trial over a three-year period. Thirty thousand pages of transcript were produced and 50,000 pages of written evidence were submitted. The law firm knew the case and the province's history better than any university professor, premier, or cabinet minister.

When, on March 8, 1991, Chief Justice Allan McEachern handed down his verdict after one year of deliberation, the 394-page judgment was clear: title had been extinguished, completely, during the colonial period.

> *Aboriginal persons and commentators often mention the fact that the Indians of this province were never conquered by force of arms, nor have they entered into treaties with the Crown. Unfair as it may seem to Indians or others on philosophical grounds, these are not relevant considerations. The events of the last 200 years are far more significant than any military conquest or treaties would have been. The reality of Crown ownership of the soil of all the lands of the province is not open to question...*[9]

First, we fire all the lawyers

But that was March of 1991. By October, the 16-year reign of the Social Credit government was over and the New Democratic Party was in charge. Five months later, in a Kafkaesque manoeuvre, the government sacked the winning legal team in Delgamuukw and brought in Swinton & Company. Their lead lawyer on the case, Bryan Williams, spearheaded a campaign of equal justice for native people in the late 1980s. Like any claim to justice, the fine print definition is what counted, as well as whether or not the proposed remedies could in actual fact rectify the original injustice.

As it concerned the original and successful Delgamuukw case, and despite his obvious sympathies with the plaintiffs' view of what was just as it concerned land claims, Williams argued his bias would not hurt BC's defence in the next court of appeal trial.[10] He was, he said, "retained to argue the government's position. And I will."[11]

Problem was, the government position had changed. Attorney General Andrew Petter reminded critics of the firing that there were new rules on the legal playing field: "People forget there was an election last fall. The McEachern decision on Delgamuukw was argued for by the former client. There's now a new client."[12] Social Credit House Leader and former native affairs minister Jack Weisgerber was blunt: "The decision [by the NDP government] to replace Russell & DuMoulin is a deliberate attempt to sabotage its own case."[13]

Bull's eye. As it happened, the British Columbia Court of Appeal, which heard the case barely one month after the original legal team was fired, watered down the next Delgamuukw verdict, though not quite as much as claimed by aboriginal apologists. That happened later when the 1997 Supreme Court of Canada verdict cut the legs off the McEachern judgment to such an extent that some aboriginals claimed the Court endorsed everything up to and including nationhood. That was an exaggeration, given that the Supreme Court did not specify what aboriginal title meant, only that it existed in some form. But try telling that to a native blockade on a major BC highway on a holiday weekend.

Delgamuukw goes to Ottawa

The Supreme Court, in a bizarre ruling that only further confused government, business, and natives, left the meaning of aboriginal title largely undefined, and let it be known that negotiation was preferable to litigation. This was convenient, since it allowed the Supreme Court to accede to the popular academic notion of aboriginal title without having to get specific.

Thus, in the space of six years after the New Democrats took power, the entire land base, fisheries, mineral rights, property rights, and the future direction of development in the province of British Columbia was thrown into a weightless universe where ground zero was impossible to determine. Ideas matter. And the NDP's decision to fold the strong (and winning) provincial hand in the legal realm mattered more than most.

Any aboriginal attempt to take actual physical possession of the Hotel Vancouver was unlikely to come to a successful conclusion. But in rural areas of the province – in the forests, fisheries, and mines, where much of the province's wealth was created – the Supreme Court of Canada verdict was a "do not disturb" sign.

Many of the NDP's economic policies during the 1990s were destructive enough on their own. Added to such disasters was the 1991 decision to fire the successful legal team in the original Delgamuukw case. That led directly to conflicting property claims, less investment, and higher unemployment both for natives and other British Columbians.

Of course, the Supreme Court could have written the same 1997 judgment even if the Russell & DuMoulin team had been kept as the Province's counsel. But the fact that the new provincial government ran away from the original McEachern decision and pursued an opposite political strategy makes that scenario highly implausible. Fact is, no one argued for the original winning 1991 BC Supreme Court decision. New Democrats and their legal counsel believed strongly in pushing for a type of native self-rule that had more to do with affirmative apartheid than with classic liberal freedoms based on the supremacy of individual rights. Their policy on native issues led directly to politics of exclusion based on race. To them, the imperfect-in-practice but worthy goal of colour-blind rights and responsibilities was old-fashioned.

Eventually, one treaty would come to symbolize all that was wrong and muddle-headed with the NDP's approach to land claims issues.

THE NISGA'A TREATY WILL PAVE THE WAY TO GUARANTEE THE SECURITY AND TRADITIONAL WAY OF LIFE FOR THE NEXT GENERATION
LAND CLAIMS NEGOTI
...OF LAWYERS.
RAESIDE
VICTORIA TIMES COLONIST–DIST. BY KOKO PRESS INC.
www.raesidecartoon.com

11

Provincial, Discriminatory & Illiberal

A Brief Guide to the Nisga'a Treaty

"The provincial and federal negotiators had to agree to a racially based government to give aboriginals control of their lands.... If a racially based government isn't offered to aboriginals, they will not sign treaties."[1]

- Premier Glen Clark in 1998, on the Nisga'a treaty

Insofar as government giveaways are concerned, the betrayal of core political and civil principles – equality and voting rights without regard to race – was always the more critical reason the Nisga'a treaty should have been rejected.

The treaty was a case study in just how far modern governments strayed from the protection of individual rights and how willing they were to sacrifice the same on the altar of collective entitlements. Despite the fine rhetoric that came from supporters, the Nisga'a treaty was as far from Martin Luther King's vision of a colour-blind society as one could possibly travel. Many who negotiated, voted for it, and supported the treaty were well intentioned, but good intentions are not enough in the realm of rights. The treaty was a perfectly modern example of noble hopes, legitimate desires for reconciliation between natives and non-natives, but also overwrought guilt, mushy philosophical thinking on rights, combined with the 20th century's full-time grievance industry. It is almost superfluous to mention that lawyers were in the thick of it all.

Given the treaty area – a pocket of land in northwest British Columbia (as remote from most of BC as it was to the rest of the country) – it should never have been much of an issue. But the core dispute – whether individual or group rights would prevail in a modern country – thrust it into the spotlight. While those British Columbians uncomfortable with the treaty might not be able to articulate why, even a vague familiarity with it prompted gut-level questions.

BC's own Charlottetown Accord

In that sense, the treaty became British Columbia's very own Charlottetown Accord. Like the Accord, defeated by Canadians in a 1992 referendum, the treaty possessed constitutional implications with serious repercussions for land use, taxation and expenditure decisions by senior levels of government. It was also a template for other treaties despite the many denials of backers on that point. (No other band with negotiating skills would settle for less than the equivalent of what the Nisga'a won. Other bands might take cash instead of land, but all had their calculators out after the Nisga'a deal.) And similar to some proposals in the Charlottetown Accord, the Nisga'a treaty divided Canadians based on skin colour.

The Accord's proposal to entrench native self-government was one reason that proposal failed in 1992. But BC's new government MLAs skipped over that important point and decided to recognize native self-government without ever defining what it meant. One important difference between the Charlottetown Accord and the Nisga'a treaty was the existence of a referendum; no province-wide vote ever took place on the Nisga'a deal or even on treaty negotiating principles in general.

The NDP knew of the philosophical similarity between the Charlottetown proposal and the Nisga'a treaty and thus never took the risk. Contrary to the assertions of its proponents, the Nisga'a treaty was about rights defined by race but that is not how the government sold it. Premier Glen Clark cast the issue as one of minority rights: "I find it repugnant to ask the majority to vote on the codification of minority rights."[2]

Clark and his MLAs knew that any attempt to put the treaty before the public was likely to meet with failure. Daniel Savas, vice-president of the polling firm Angus Reid, said the treaty would lose "big time" in a referendum.[3] In 1998, Premier Glen Clark even expressed doubt that the treaty could pass a free vote in the Legislature.[4] Given those doubts, the provincial government spent $7.5 million in taxpayer money in a vain attempt to convince the public it was worthy of their support.[5] It even produced a one-sided video of the treaty for schools.[6]

The land mass

The treaty settlement land included 62 square kilometres of existing Nisga'a reserves and was supplemented with 1,930 square kilometres, an area equivalent to seventeen times the size of the City of Vancouver.[i] One positive was that the treaty appeared to give property rights to the Nisga'a in fee simple, similar to how most other Canadians held their land. There were some exceptions however, including limits on expropriation by other governments and private interests.[7] And in a major departure from other fee simple practices, the Nisga'a government possessed the sub-surface mineral rights,[8] and that put the new Nisga'a rulers on par with federal and provincial governments. In addition, the Nisga'a gained a major say in wildlife resource management in a much larger area, the Nass Wildlife Area comprising 14,217 sq. km.,[9] an area seven times larger than the settlement land itself. The land portion of the treaty was mostly uncontroversial. What attracted more notice was the action on the political landscape.

A guide to the NDP spin – the dollar questions

The provincial government made much of the fact that the Nisga'a treaty would end tax exemptions for Nisga'a natives, a step forward in treating all Canadians as equal. While it was true Nisga'a natives were on a timetable to pay provincial (but not federal) sales tax after eight years and income tax after twelve, that one-step-forward in ending race-based tax exemptions was undone by multiple steps backward as other exemptions took their place.

The treaty ensured that the Nisga'a community was exempt from provincial stumpage tax.[10] Provincial acts that legislated mining, petroleum, natural gas, and property transfer taxes also did not apply. Provincial resource royalties were ended on Nisga'a land,[11] as were licensing fees, and royalties on fish and wildlife entitlements.[12] Normally, eliminating a multitude of taxes would be positive, but the Nisga'a treaty made such exemptions conditional on skin colour.

Moreover, unlike similar privileges under the Indian Act that could be removed with the stroke of a legislative pen, race-based tax exemptions in the Nisga'a treaty were effectively set in concrete as the Nisga'a had to agree to eliminate such exemptions in future. And, unlike the municipal model the new Nisga'a government was purported to be, the Nisga'a gained the power to impose income, sales, and stumpage taxes should they so desire, though such taxing powers were never available to mere municipalities.

Ironically, while certain tax exemptions and privileges were cast in stone, the Nisga'a claim upon the greater Canadian public purse was yet open-ended. In addition to the almost half-billion dollars worth of land, cash and resources transferred to the Nisga'a, the existing annual $29 million Nisga'a

---

i. Vancouver's population was half a million. An estimated 2,000 to 2,200 Nisga'a resided in the treaty territory.

subsidy was to rise to $32.1 million.[13] Thus, Canada's taxpayers were scheduled to pay $160.5 million over the first five years in *addition* to settlement costs, with only an obligation from the Nisga'a government to try and reduce such fiscal transfers thereafter. The NDP government sold the treaty as a path to Nisga'a self-reliance, but the subsidies were scheduled to continue *ad infinitum*.[ii]

But despite the quasi-federal/provincial taxing potential given to the Nisga'a, self-sufficiency was unlikely. There was little incentive, since Nisga'a individuals were still eligible for every federal and provincial program, service, benefit and subsidy available to native and non-native alike. Treaty recipients received all the benefits of being full participants in the Canadian mosaic, without the parallel responsibility of paying for much of it. Moreover, under the terms of the treaty, tax revenues created in the Nisga'a territory could be diverted under the justification of long-term investments for the band, while other taxpayers were still obligated to support the Nisga'a government.[14]

Also of note was that because the Nisga'a administration was the creation of two other governments, it was inevitable that it would be more costly than a normal town council for a community of two thousand people. Most towns and cities fall or thrive largely on their local tax base. They cannot expand local government much beyond what property owners are willing to endure; too much taxpayer feather plucking can cause a hiss. But government-created creatures suffer no such reactions. Instead, the Nisga'a government wanted semi-nationhood status along with the bells and whistles; they mostly received it but at everyone else's continual expense.

For those who thought no price was too high as long as it settled BC's land claim fights, the Nisga'a treaty was sure to disappoint. It was not quite as final as its backers claimed: the treaty was open-ended and contained at least 50 areas yet to be negotiated or where "ongoing" consultation was required.[15] Moreover, if more generous terms were given in the up to 60 other treaties to follow Nisga'a, the Nisga'a treaty could be ratcheted up to meet such settlements.[16] The end result was that the provincial government might spend buckets of money to ratchet up treaties they falsely advertised as "final" or end up in legal battles over such provisions. Given the attrac-

---

ii. The chief federal negotiator, Tom Molloy, told the *Globe and Mail* in 1998 that he expected that fifteen years after the agreement was signed, the Nisga'a would provide, at most, 25 percent of the initial taxpayer transfers to the Nisga'a government. Under that scenario, taxpayers in the rest of Canada would have to fund at least $400 million in transfers over the first fifteen years of the treaty in addition to the settlement cost. The treaty was sold to the public as final, when in reality it was open-ended on a number of issues, this one included.

tive legal fees at taxpayer expense for all concerned, it was possible both scenarios could occur, as judges ordered generous interpretations of such porous agreements.

Debunking the municipal myth

In the debate over the treaty, New Democrats often claimed the new Nisga'a government would be similar to municipal governments. The official government pamphlet on the treaty informed the reader that "the Treaty allows the Nisga'a people to govern themselves in a way comparable to a municipal government."[17]

One had to wonder what municipalities the NDP referred to: Surrey and Nelson never possessed power over citizenship,[18] culture,[19] health services,[20] children and family services,[21] adoption,[22] elementary, secondary, and post-secondary education,[23] cultural property,[24] management of fishing resources, and ownership of mineral and timber resources.[25] The Nisga'a government gained jurisdiction in all those areas as a result of the treaty.

In the attempt to portray the Nisga'a government as just another municipality, a supplementary claim was that federal and provincial laws would be paramount over Nisga'a legislation. In November 1999, Aboriginal Affairs minister Dale Lovick stated that "this treaty gives the Nisga'a people the opportunity to manage resources on their own lands – *subject to BC and Canadian laws*."[26]

Wrong again. In seventeen sections, the treaty stated that in the event of an inconsistency between a particular Nisga'a law and federal or provincial law, the Nisga'a law or settlement legislation (the treaty) prevailed to the extent of the conflict.[27] But then Dale Lovick knew that; he said as much earlier that year in the Legislature. In January 1999, the same Aboriginal Affairs minister stated that "the paramountcy of Nisga'a laws is intended to ensure that the Nisga'a will, first, have primary authority over matters that are internal and integral to their own culture."[28] Lovick did not dispute that select Nisga'a laws would trump some provincial and federal ones; he defended it as absolutely necessary. His later comment was political spin, and untrue.

The Nisga'a Nation,[iii] as the new government was labelled on the treaty

---

iii. Curiously, while the official version of the treaty made reference to the Nisga'a government as the "Nisga'a Nation," pamphlets sent to British Columbians used no such language that might hint at such sovereignty. In the brochures, the reference was made only to the "Nisga'a Tribal Council." The references to the provincial and federal governments though were consistent in both documents.

cover, resembled a nation-state, not a municipality.

Self-sufficient?

Given the vast areas yet to be negotiated, along with the possibility for multiple Crown corporations and Nisga'a public agencies, and the large swaths of jurisdiction the new government was responsible for, self-sufficiency was and is highly unlikely. Many Nisga'a will likely be employed by some level of Nisga'a government, or as one of the many negotiators who will iron out the 50 or so areas yet to be straightened out. One hopes to be wrong on this point, but it appears few will be in the private sector where the wealth created would help the Nisga'a band become independent of greater Canadian subsidies. Thus, the treaty did not, as claimed by the NDP and others, act as a final relinquishment of other Canadians' debt to the Nisga'a, nor did the treaty do much to promote private sector wealth creation.

Orwellian democracy, equality, and race

No example better illustrated all the long-held liberal democratic principles which the BC NDP put on the table and bargained away as if it were a poker chip, than the issue of equal voting rights on Nisga'a land. Compromise is always a part of politics, but some things were once thought beyond political horse-trading: equality under the law and the ability to vote for those who would govern you. After the treaty, citizenship in Canada might as well have come with two passports.

Defenders of the treaty said they could not understand critics who claimed it would create a province divided by race and laws. Some argued it was not about race but property rights.[29] This argument might have been more credible if Nisga'a property rights were defined consistent with how such rights applied to other Canadian governments and individuals. Instead, federal and provincial governments were restricted in their expropriation rights, as were private commercial interests. The final decision on such matters would be up to the Nisga'a government, a body that would be selected, as it happened, on race.

In defence of the treaty, NDP MLAs argued that the Nisga'a would establish a democratic government. This was similar to the comment by the chief federal negotiator Tom Molloy that the Nisga'a territory would be democratic because "every adult Nisga'a has a vote." Dale Lovick went even further and stated that "the treaty does provide for the representation of Nisga'a and non-Nisga'a, including the election of non-Nisga'a."[30]

Lovick's comment was a half-truth. The relevant sections of the treaty provided that the Nisga'a government would consult with non-Nisga'a about issues that "directly and significantly affected them."[31] The definition of "directly" and "significantly" could be subject to interpretation, and a subclause allowed for "other comparable measures" in place of voting rights.[32] So, while the treaty mentioned that a future Nisga'a government could provide for the possibility for non-Nisga'a to vote on occasion, it was not guaranteed.

Moreover, while non-Nisga'a citizens were not directly taxed at the beginning of self-government, there was no barrier to federal and provincial governments allowing the Nisga'a government that authority in the future. (After all, these same governments negotiated the treaty that cemented the racial exclusion.) In the meantime, non-Nisga'a living on Nisga'a land had their right to vote for a government that might affect their life negotiated away.

Glen Clark vs. Dale Lovick

In public, government MLAs themselves differed as to whether the treaty was about racial privileges. In 1999, Dale Lovick claimed "treaties such as Nisga'a do not create 'race-based' enclaves."[33] This was the exact opposite of what Premier Glen Clark, who claimed the treaty as his own, stated the year before:

> *The provincial and federal negotiators had to agree to a racially based government to give aboriginals control of their lands.... If a racially based government isn't offered to aboriginals, they will not sign treaties because the status quo – where non-aboriginals already do not vote – is better.*[34]

Clark had a valid political point. In a negotiation, it was difficult to convince one side to risk giving up control of their government one day when the existing arrangement would never compel such. (Leaders with almost unlimited power in their jurisdiction, native or otherwise, are always reluctant to surrender it.)

But then it was a bit much for proponents of such treaties to argue they had created a democratic government on Nisga'a land. And it begged the larger question: should any government anywhere in Canada exclude potential voters based on race? Defenders of the treaty, and even those not particularly enthralled with it, regularly endorsed the concept of native self-government without defining what they meant. But in most cases, such self-government implicitly included the idea of voting rights based on race. There

---

iv. This assumption also begged the question of whether governments should promote or protect one culture, especially in immigrant cultures such as Canada.

were many arguments in favour of such an exclusion, but usually they could be boiled down to the defence of native culture and tradition.[iv] But such a defence would be anathema if applied anywhere else in Canada or the world. Immigrants to Quebec (assuming they were citizens) could vote in referendums even though they were more likely to favour Canada over separation.[v] Israel allowed non-Jews to vote despite tremendous ethnic and religious tensions in that area of the world. The governments that negotiated the Nisga'a treaty said, in effect, that Canadians could be institutionally separated based on their race.

The decline of progressive thought

The NDP's definition of democracy twisted the word beyond recognition. After all, it used to be thought that democratic governments were ones that every adult could vote for *regardless of race*. Exclude some adults in an area where a government has influence over their lives, and it was no longer a democratic government, unless defined in some Orwellian manner. What was created – or cemented given the existence of such already on native reserves – was precisely what treaty critic Mel Smith claimed, what Glen Clark admitted, and what Dale Lovick denied: race-based enclaves.

Granted that voting rights irrespective of race would have meant that some native reserves could have been swamped by non-native voters: the Westbank Indian reserve near Kelowna has 500 natives and 7,000 non-native inhabitants.[35] But then, Canadians of Asian descent are a growing percentage of the population in greater Vancouver, perhaps already a majority in suburbs such as Richmond. Would any 20th-century politician who considered himself a political sophisticate ever endorse withholding the vote from non-whites in that city? Would they ever write up a provincial Election Act to turn the right of voting into a privilege?

The Nisga'a treaty was written to ensure that voting was a privilege, to be defined, determined and decided by a particular government at its leisure, and not a core political right to be exercised regardless of race. British Columbians might have been curious to know what gave any politician or

---

v. Given the existence of race-based voting rights already on reserve land, there is an obvious political difficulty, and in some cases a treaty-based difficulty, with a move to universal voting. It is further granted that most native leadership would strenuously oppose it along with individual property rights. But that reality hardly justifies the philosophical defense of such anomalies. Those who argue for voting restrictions on such a basis are in the uncomfortable position of defending ethnicity as a basis for government. Such a position is anything but liberal.

negotiator the belief that they could turn a long-fought-for political and civil right into a mere privilege. The existence of the 1997 Delgamuukw decision - while it recognized aboriginal title and presumed treaty negotiations, certainly did not mandate voting rights based on race.

Still, the NDP believed itself to be on the side of progressive thought. Glen Clark said Opposition critics of the treaty "appealed to the worst in human nature."[36] MLA Harry Lali portrayed critics of the treaty as racist hicks who missed out on his own virtuous upbringing:

> *I'm proud to say that growing up, my parents were very open-minded and tolerant of people of different colours and taught us children – I'm the youngest of six children – to be that way throughout our lives, to respect differing views and at the time to be respectful and mindful of people of different ethnic groups and colours. Unfortunately, there are too many British Columbians who are not as tolerant in their viewpoints, especially when it relates to aboriginal people.*[37]

The last sentence was rich in self-absorbed arrogance. But besides the assumption about other British Columbians, Lali might have noticed that his own party reversed the definition of what was once considered progressive: urban liberal thought used to believe that sectarian division based on race, religion, or ethnicity was an embarrassment, a holdover from the nineteenth century. As British Columbians closed in on the 21st century, they woke up to find a government that argued for a return to 1849.

PRE-EVICTION PARTY:

NDP

B.C.

DEPUTY MINISTERS

RAESIDE

Victoria Times Colonist- Dist. by Koko Press Inc. www.raesidecartoon.com

12

Sweden or Switzerland?

"Clearly, the previous administration, combined with the Mulroney administration, has done more to discredit politicians, political life, and those who serve in this very difficult environment than anybody else that's gone before."[1]

- Glen Clark in 1992

Final exit

The NDP is not the problem. Oh sure, New Democrats in power have been *a* problem, even to their own interests, whether or not they yet realize it.

But the 1990s were the last gasp for New Democrats in their present form. They came into office on a promised wave of raging moderation but succumbed to pride, believed overmuch in their own prejudices, abused their power and learned too little too late.

By the end of their second mandate, there were signals the NDP altered course, albeit slightly. Taxes were lowered marginally, the worst anti-business rhetoric was (mostly) dropped, and the party legislatively acknowledged the importance of balanced budgets, though not without a fight from the unreformed core, including many MLAs. Insofar as economic debates were concerned, the war of ideas was fought in the 1990s and the NDP lost. Tax relief, deficit and debt reduction, balanced budgets, cautious government spending (at least in theory), and other prudent fiscal policies – ideas rarely talked about ten years ago – are now mainstream in Canada.

But because those policies are widely assumed as sensible, it is difficult to discern how genuine New Democrats are in such matters, especially close to an election. Four years elapsed between the infamous 1996 budget and the "honest books" legislation finally passed by the NDP. And it took much media exposure, several auditor's reports, and just a little embarrassment to prod the government to do the right, obvious, and thoroughly ordinary action: lay out real numbers and assumptions in budgets.

Similarly on balanced budgets. It took nearly a decade for the NDP to return to a position they once championed in opposition: deficits are impractical and impossible to justify on a medium to long-term basis because they redirect dollars away from programs and tax relief to bondholders. The party's sudden return to common sense hints at political desperation.

On other matters, it is worth noting that, unlike the 1970s, the NDP did not openly nationalize more industries in the past decade. That was partly due to a changed public attitude; in the light of day, the government could not pursue blatant economic interventionism post-Bill Bennett (who began privatization before almost anyone) and Ronald Reagan and Margaret Thatcher who franchised the concept. But the NDP did create more Crown corporations, which in some cases amounted to a milder version of the same philosophy. And it was within the relative darkness of new and old Crowns that much bungling and the waste of tax dollars took place; Forest Renewal British Columbia and BC Ferries were prime examples.

At least on tax relief, the NDP did begin (under Joy MacPhail's term in Finance) to cut the top marginal rate, and in that, showed some recognition of reality. But the cuts were minor and grudging, and one suspects the NDP has yet to understand why such relief is crucial for BC's future prosperity. MacPhail claimed to be a fiscal conservative though that was difficult to discern from her record in Finance; she did reform welfare somewhat in her role as Social Services minister.

Besides MacPhail, there was at least one other MLA with clout that argued against the government's high income-tax policies and also their love of government ownership. For all his political faults, Dan Miller, while interim premier, called into question the desirability of high marginal tax rates[2] and even the government's ownership of forests: he once mused about junking the "Soviet-style system."[3]

Miller's candour while temporary premier was refreshing, and had it not been for his involvement in the Carrier Lumber case and his irresponsible tenure as minister accountable for BC Ferries, he would have been a smart choice for a permanent NDP leader. He was less ideological than most, and understood that the party's flirtation with green purists will one day drive a wedge between private and public labour and split the party.

It is speculative, but if Joy MacPhail or Dan Miller really were "new labour" politicians a la Tony Blair, there was no way to demonstrate it given their surroundings. Blair followed the reforms of Margaret Thatcher and John Major which made Blair's moderation politically possible, both in his own party and in public. Of course, MacPhail never won the leadership of her party and Miller never wanted the crown. But even if either one had captured the leadership post-Glen Clark, it is difficult to conceive of a radically different NDP from what British Columbians were served up in the 1990s.

After all, a supposed moderate, Mike Harcourt, did follow a right-leaning government in 1991 and tilted hard left in a hurry. And Harcourt's caucus and cabinet included Miller and MacPhail. Besides economic issues, the NDP busily interfered in people's lives to the detriment of free speech and free association. Whatever claims individual MLAs might make to occasional temperance on economic issues, there were no moderate New Democrats when it came to gag laws, appointments to an overzealous human rights bureaucracy, and pushing their luck in court on a number of fronts.

One small step for the NDP

One enduring achievement, for which any honest critic should credit BC's New Democrats, is a freedom of information law that is among the best in the country – a law passed despite the objections of Glen Clark.[4] Unfortunately for the party in power, the legislation helped to damage their reputation as it proved to be the source of much embarrassment for the government; it helped reveal their glaring incompetence, political interference, and shoddy budget practices.

There were other accomplishments. New parks and an emphasis on women's issues were laudable, even though the party could and should be criticized for doctrinaire approaches that offended as many people as they pleased. On women's issues, equality of opportunity was one thing and wholly desirable. Affirmative action was quite another and anything but fair. On the environment, most people liked the idea of new parks. But a complete ban on mines in the Tatshenshini – potentially worth $40 billion – was a costly sacrifice to purists. Every time British Columbians hear NDP MLAs complain that Alberta is resource-rich and thus has choices BC does not, they should recall how, in general, New Democrats tied up resource development in knots and in specific cases banned it completely. Alberta's Conservatives might be quite cozy with the oil industry but it beat the NDP approach of thumping a major industry.

Pride, prejudice and power revisited

If a few individual New Democrats made steps towards moderation in their rhetoric in the late 1990s, "moderate" is not yet a label that can be applied to the NDP as a whole. A moderate government would return to the private sector what is properly their business, i.e., business itself. There is no economic or moral justification for a government to run retail stores, even if they happen to sell alcohol. In the 21st century, there is no reason why British Columbians should not be free to choose which company will insure their car from the risk of an accident. (They already insure their homes and their own lives from among a competitive selection of would-be insurance suitors.)

The only reason British Columbians cannot do so now, in those and other areas, is that the government has the power to deny them that choice. And the reason the NDP denies citizens competitive choices is because that party is intimately tied to the money and volunteers that organized labour, especially public sector unions, provide. It is a convenient closed circle for those involved but not for those outside the well-worn ring. The circle needs to be cracked open, permanently.

Put another way, after the NDP's pride (in their moral superiority) weakened and prejudice (in their economic ideas) ebbed away, there was little left but undivided and undiluted power. And they used it, sometimes ruthlessly, almost always to favour allies at the expense of the greater public good. By the end, governing was about power politics and not much else. And that trumped sensible decisions about spending, taxes, and competition in the provision of services.

Cynics may argue that favouring allies at the expense of one's political foes is a pretty apt definition of politics under *any* government. But the difference this past decade was a regime whose friends consumed an ever-greater share of the available capital without creating new wealth. In that game, most British Columbians ended up on the losing side. And it created a society bogged down by special interest group politics under loftier justifications.

The curse of concentrated power

Thus, the NDP played out a valuable object lesson for British Columbians in the 1990s: the abuse of concentrated power.

Mike Harcourt thwarted a regulatory review and killed proposed multi-billion dollar mines because there were few legislative barriers that could slow him down. A gag law was introduced that muzzled debate during an election, (despite the fact that similar laws were struck down by courts elsewhere) because New Democrats despised free speech and could, for a time, prevent it.

Fast ferry costs skyrocketed, as they were destined to from the start, because no one could call the minister responsible to account, publicly, in front of a bi-partisan committee with cameras rolling. The government-controlled committee that did exist could be shut down at any time, and it was, because ruling MLAs had the power to do so. On Forest Renewal British Columbia, where $2 billion was at stake, the story was repeated yet again.

Similarly, an environmental review process and budget controls could be skirted on SkyTrain because a premier wanted a visible pork project ready in time for the next election.

In short, a government elected in 1991 with less than 41 percent of the vote, and in 1996 with 39 percent of the vote, obtained 100 percent of the power. The NDP, elected by a minority of popular votes, ruled to please that minority.

The object lesson

Given the cost of the object lesson of the Nineties, not only financially but to damaged institutions, core freedoms, and public trust in politicians – already low in the early 1990s when the NDP took office – British Columbians must ensure that such lessons are never repeated.

As it is in Canada, premiers and prime ministers can rule as four- or five-year monarchs with little challenge to their authority. This is unlike Great Britain, from which Canada's institutions of power are derived, where MPs are far more independent. In the United States, there is the added safeguard of an institutional separation of power between the president and two branches of Congress, a separation that prevents any one individual from exercising complete power for a four-year stretch. There, even a president with a majority in the Senate and the House of Representatives usually negotiates with Congress to see his budget passed. A president facing the opposite party in both houses of Congress must always cut a deal.

Contrast that situation with Canada. In provincial legislatures as in Parliament, politicians often act as rubber stamps, in a process that pleases neither them nor their constituents. Independence is shown behind a closed door if ever, and a politician's ability to argue publicly for a position opposite that of their party and leader is non-existent.

Dispersing power

If British Columbians do not want another run of Mad King Clark one day, they must ensure any new government relinquishes *some* political power for the sake of a more sane political future. If sole control of the levers of political decision-making is not separated quickly, the new politicians in Victoria will become intoxicated with the deceitful allure of the belief that "if only *I* am in charge, all will be well." Once that is swallowed, diluting power to prevent future egregious abuses will be next to impossible.

And such changes are as necessary for the politicians as they are for citizens. As much as MLAs must properly represent the concerns of their constituents to government, not vice-versa, they also need room to represent their own views and conscience to the public and to the government. It is not healthy for representatives to be either a mere lightning rod for inflamed public opinion, as often happens on immigration debates, or on jingoistic and backwards nationalistic appeals (anti-free trade rhetoric comes to mind). Neither should a brilliant and thoughtful politician have her real views neutered by a leader and party; uninformed debates and a bored, jaded public are the inevitable result of such smothering.

Politicians must be able to engage the public with a novel idea without the danger of their own party ousting them from caucus. Similarly, representatives must be able to buck the party establishment on occasion with the knowledge that their home base, i.e., local voters, will likely come to their defence. That means that power must not reside wholly in the premier's office, nor completely in the notion that a politician must always do "what the voters want," as if every voter had an idea of what that is on every issue. (In Canada though, it is the former scenario that has long been problematic, not the latter.)

Canada needs the equivalent of the recently retired American senator, Democrat Daniel Patrick Moynihan. Thoughtful and independent politicians are rare in Canadian politics – not because they do not exist, but because they are severely constrained from frank public speech and positions.

So, broadly, what change is necessary and how can it be attained? Here, in general terms, is what must occur. All would work to disperse power more widely and make government more effective in both the financing and provision of public goods. Just as critical, the following would let political ideas bloom.

Change # 1: parliamentary and legislative reform

Concentrated power must be diluted and separated. No single politician should be allowed almost all the cards of power, as is now the case. Without institutional divisions, power will remain with the premier's office as naturally as gravity pulls mountain water toward the ocean.

Thus, bi-partisan legislative committees *with teeth* must be the rule, not the exception, and they must be given legal protection to function continually, in public, without being shut down prematurely as happened over the fast ferry investigation.

In that case, the NDP majority on the public accounts committee gagged the committee from exposing wrongdoing. That could never happen in the state of Washington because there are at least three bi-partisan committees that oversee the public ferry system. Their existence prevents any one side of the state legislature from covering up the incompetence and misdeeds of politicians and partisan appointments. Such committees exist in theory in

British Columbia but rarely in practice and never with the freedom they ought to possess.

Other legislative reforms should include a scheduled debt repayment plan. Interest on the total provincial debt is now more than $2.5 billion a year or almost half of all the personal income tax collected. Put another way, every British Columbian could see a personal income tax reduction of half what they now pay (without touching a penny in program spending) if the provincial debt did not exist. Of course, $35 billion in debt does exist and must be repaid. But if provincial tax relief is to be permanent, the debt must be chopped away at in every single year. British Columbia is far behind our main Canadian competitor, Alberta, on both taxes and debt. Relief of both must be an urgent priority.

Tougher balanced budget legislation (so it includes capital expenditures) should be passed into law. Taxpayer protection legislation is also needed – that protects taxpayers from arbitrary increases to their cost of living, courtesy of the political class. Money is power and if politicians want more of it, citizens should first have a vote on such plans.

Money belongs first to those who earn it and create it – not to governments. Those who think taxpayers must justify their pleas for tax relief have it backwards; governments are the creation *of* and in service *to* citizens. Governments and those that lead them must be made to justify their takings from citizens, not vice-versa. Those who argue the reverse are always on the road to serfdom.

Change # 2: electoral reform

The disaster that was the Nineties in British Columbia should never be allowed to repeat itself, whether the party in power is left or right. The electoral system must change to more properly represent more British Columbians.

A number of options are available to change the electoral system. For example, run-off ballots, where, if no candidate receives 50 percent of the votes cast plus one, the top two candidates square off in a second election. (Preferential balloting may also accomplish this task.) Critics argue that this would still allow a government to be elected by a minority of voters,[i] though it would be an improvement on the existing system.

There is also the single transferable vote (STV), as advocated most re-

---

i. If a government is elected with only 51 percent of the seats, and each of winning MLAs also received only 51 percent of the vote (while losing candidates for the winning party received no votes), it is in theory possible for 26 percent of voters to elect a majority government.

cently by Nick Loenen, a former Social Credit MLA. It is worth serious consideration. Loenen's proposal – a form of proportional representation – has merit and should be examined closely. (His ideas were borne out of his own frustrations as an MLA in the last Socred government.) In effect, BC's 75 ridings would be collapsed into 15 and each would have from three to seven MLAs. Voters would rank individual candidates from one party, or more than one party as they so choose. Loenen has argued that this change would more closely link the MLA to her constituents and weaken the concentration of political party power.[ii]

Loenen's proposal has tremendous merit, though I would argue that any change to the way British Columbians elect their MLAs must be accompanied by other reforms that allow for citizens themselves to directly affect legislation. Electoral reform is important but just as crucial, and perhaps more so, is the transfer of some political power back to citizens themselves. In 1991, 80 percent of British Columbians voted for citizen initiative legislation and recall laws. While the NDP reluctantly passed enabling legislation in the mid-1990s, the laws were designed with so many tripwires as to make them virtually unusable by voters, which was precisely the aim of Ujjal Dosanjh (who wrote the law) and his colleagues.

Change # 3: effective recall

The threat of recall proved enough to unseat Vancouver Island Liberal MLA Paul Reitsma in 1998 (he resigned rather than face a recall petition that was about to succeed). But the law has thresholds that are absurdly high in comparison to other jurisdictions, and they must be lowered. Citizens need and deserve levers they can pull vis-à-vis a government they believe is on the wrong course.

Granted that recall is primarily reactive – but it allows citizens to fire an MLA for reasons *they* choose – not ones pre-approved by politicians or opinion-makers. The arguments against recall are almost always based on elitist arguments about when its use would be "proper." Reactive campaigns are necessarily rare, but occasions arise when it is necessary. As such, the ultimate decision as to the "proper" use of recall should be up to citizens themselves.

Recall, even as a threat, is a useful tool to remind MLAs about who sent them to Victoria. Odd as it may seem, it also benefits the MLA vis-à-vis their leader; it allows them to buck their own party and leader with the

---

ii. For a thorough and thoughtful analysis of electoral reform, and why BC in particular needs it, see Citizenship and Democracy, by Nick Loenen, Dundurn Press, 1997.

reminder that citizens could take back the mandate of an MLA, and, depending on the government's majority, the mandate of a government itself. In that sense, while recall can threaten a political career, it can also strengthen the ties between an MLA and voters. It forces MLAs to engage in the debate of ideas with their constituents on a regular basis – not a bad thing for either politicians or citizens.

Change # 4: effective citizen initiated referenda

More proactive than recall is citizen-initiated referenda. Because the 1995 law was designed not to work, not a single referendum has taken place in British Columbia. Beyond making the law workable, it can and should, as noted by the late Mel Smith, be made binding on governments.[5] As long as the law requires Legislature involvement and provides for the role of the Lieutenant Governor to sign it into law, binding referendums are wholly constitutional.

Such referendums are desirable in that they will institutionally separate power from the Legislature. Currently, politicians and *only* politicians can initiate and pass laws. Moreover, in British Columbia, power is in one legislative body, and in practical political terms, in the premier's office.

Referendums serve as a check on concentrated power and this dilutes, reasonably, the power of the Legislature and thus the premier's office. Designed with appropriate petition thresholds (so as to put a referendum question on the ballot) and then a simple majority of voters for ratification, such a law would preserve most of the power of MLAs, but not all of it in its current unassailable state.[iii] In comparison, MLAs would still be more powerful than most of their counterparts in the U.S. House of Representatives and state legislatures, but there would at long last be an effective check on elected representatives, should British Columbians choose to exercise such power.

---

iii. Some who favour citizen initiated referendums argue that super-majorities should be used, i.e., a successful initiative should require 50 percent plus one overall, and approval in two thirds of the province's ridings. This would be a gross double standard. Currently, MLAs can obtain their seat with far less than even 50 percent of the vote, never mind some additional requirement. Even under some electoral reform proposals, prospective MLAs would not require more than half the votes cast plus one. The hurdle for a successful initiative should hardly be higher than that required for election to the Legislature. A simple majority (50 percent plus one) for an initiative would already be a higher percentage than that obtained by 45 MLAs when elected to the provincial legislature in 1996.

Objections to referendums

The objections to citizen-initiated referendums are many, most of them weak and all answerable. Here is a summary:

Citizenship is undermined, complicated issues are reduced to simplistic yes-no alternatives, special interests will "buy" referendums, MLAs will lose their representative role, and – to choose an extreme argument – referendums will poison our water because voters will choose a 90-percent cut in tax over clean water.

Such objections are spurious. Far from weakening citizenship, referendums prompt public interest in serious affairs of state and promote healthy debate. Citizen-initiated referendums were held in many Alberta communities in 1998 on the issue of video lottery terminals after the machines were forced into municipalities by the provincial government. For good or ill, most communities kept VLTs but at least a controversial issue was fully debated, thought through, fought, and settled by citizens themselves.

Similarly, the 1992 Charlottetown Accord referendum prompted many to ponder and debate Canada's constitution. Canadians would never have bothered to seriously read up on constitutional matters without a direct say in the final decision. It should also be noted that "yes" forces in that referendum outspent "no" forces by thirteen-to-one, had most elite opinion on their side including the cheerleading CBC, and still lost. So much for bought referendums.

Along the same line of argument, some that oppose citizen referendums argue that special interest groups might influence the process, a laughable objection: they *already* influence the political process. Those who want to "buy" a referendum will have to splurge for much more than they now spend on wine and cheese for government MLAs. 1,582,701 British Columbians cast votes in the 1996 election. In a referendum where a simple majority was required, a successful ballot measure would require 791,351 votes for a win. That is much more difficult than convincing half of the MLAs in the Legislature, or even just a few key cabinet ministers.

Idea contests

In addition to the reasonable dilution of political power, referendums are contests of ideas. They force backroom interests and arguments out into the town square, where the merits of specific proposals can be considered and debated by all, not just a few. Referendums encourage civic participation and require that proponents and opponents of an initiative defend their arguments in public. Such idea contests engage and focus the minds of citizens, and force us all to ponder an issue more deeply.

Contrast that with elections, more often the equivalent of beauty pageants. Individual candidates are excruciatingly careful to avoid controversial or specific ideas. Candidates and parties produce bland brochures, meaningless television commercials, and platforms often designed with as little substance as possible, so as to offend few voters.

And far from endorsing simple solutions, referendums would force politicians to face tough issues early and to make choices. If in 1980, Pierre Trudeau was forced (via a referendum measure) to confront chronic deficits and to balance budgets over the course of his mandate, Canada's debt and accompanying interest payments would now be substantially smaller.

Opponents of referendums often point to a particular law passed by a referendum in the United States that they dislike, as justification for their opposition. In other words, they dislike the particular result of a democratic vote; their favoured political cause lost and thus they dismiss referendums because there is no guarantee of the results they want. This is telling in that it reveals just how convenient the current arrangement of power is for established interests. Too bad. Politics and the public square are not the private property of MLAs, backroom staff, political parties, or those that finance them.

Voters: smart about MLAs but not referendums?

A frequent argument against referenda is that it undermines the public good. Citizens will think "only" as taxpayers (not a frequent occurrence over the past four decades in Canada though) and poison their children's water in exchange for a tax cut, assuming the scenario is ever that stark. That's a rather churlish view of oneself or one's neighbours, but it is similar to the assumption some politicians have of their constituents: that voters are not smart enough to choose "properly" in a referendum. That's a curious view, since such politicians must believe their constituents made an eminently wise choice when they picked their MLA.

Those crazy Swiss

Responsible government and referendums can and do exist side by side. Citizens in Switzerland – one of the most stable of all countries – have possessed robust referendum rights for 150 years. Citizens there initiate referendums on taxes, the army, the European Union, immigration and constitutional change.

Such debates have hardly made Switzerland unstable. In fact, countries with international disputes come to Geneva to iron out their differences. Apparently no one thinks the Swiss are irresponsible for having thought through and voted on such issues.[iv]

Diluting power with the package

A strong and identifiable link must be created between politicians and voters, in addition to a real check on political power (including that of political parties). Electoral reform, along with workable recall and referenda, are critical reforms as a whole package. Electoral reform alone will not accomplish the task; that merely re-scrambles the omelette of power. Where in that reform (by itself) is there an actual institutional separation of power, especially of the sort that would give *citizens* more direct input and control?

This point is crucial in any reform of BC's political balance of power. Our parliamentary system has few checks and balances on virtually unlimited power, save the courts. And recourse to the courts is expensive, time-consuming, and thus out of reach for most. In addition, judicial checks on power, while they prevent unconstitutional and illegal actions by governments, do not prevent mere stupidity from being foisted on citizens. Nor do the courts, as is proper, challenge what some would argue are undesirable but wholly constitutional laws.

Switzerland or Sweden: time for the choice

British Columbia has the opportunity to become the Switzerland of North America in economic, environmental, and political terms. Set in a spectacular natural setting with reasonable environmental safeguards, prosperous, and with robust participatory democracy, Switzerland is a fine jurisdiction to emulate; British Columbia could one day be envied throughout the world as Switzerland is now.

But that will require a choice by British Columbians, and it is a decision that goes beyond the simple (and as I write, expected) change of political rulers inside the corridors of power.

The decision is also about what kind of province British Columbia will become in the next ten years and beyond. Even Sweden – the model of a redistributionist state for those who admire envy as economic policy – has not made a mess of things quite the way New Democrats did in the 1990s in BC. But neither is Sweden a wealth creator of the type that a modern immi-

---

iv. During the recent Canadian federal election, much uninformed criticism was stirred up over the fact that one federal party (the Alliance) considered an initiative law with "only" a three- percent sign-up of citizens necessary to force a federal referendum. In Switzerland, if 3.4 percent of the population (about 50,000 people) signs an initiative petition, a referendum is automatic.

grant economy such as British Columbia requires.

The choice then, is between two distinct models. Will we as British Columbians, and regardless of the government in power, continue to drink from the chalice of envy, a philosophical and economic poison concocted in nineteenth-century England, a model that wreaked so much destruction in British Columbia over the past decade?

Or will we finally live up to our potential and work, live, and debate, as educated men and women, more than capable of creating prosperity, splendour, and good but limited government; and engaging in robust but civil political dialogues with each other as we chart our course in the new century?

Sweden or Switzerland; the choice is ours.

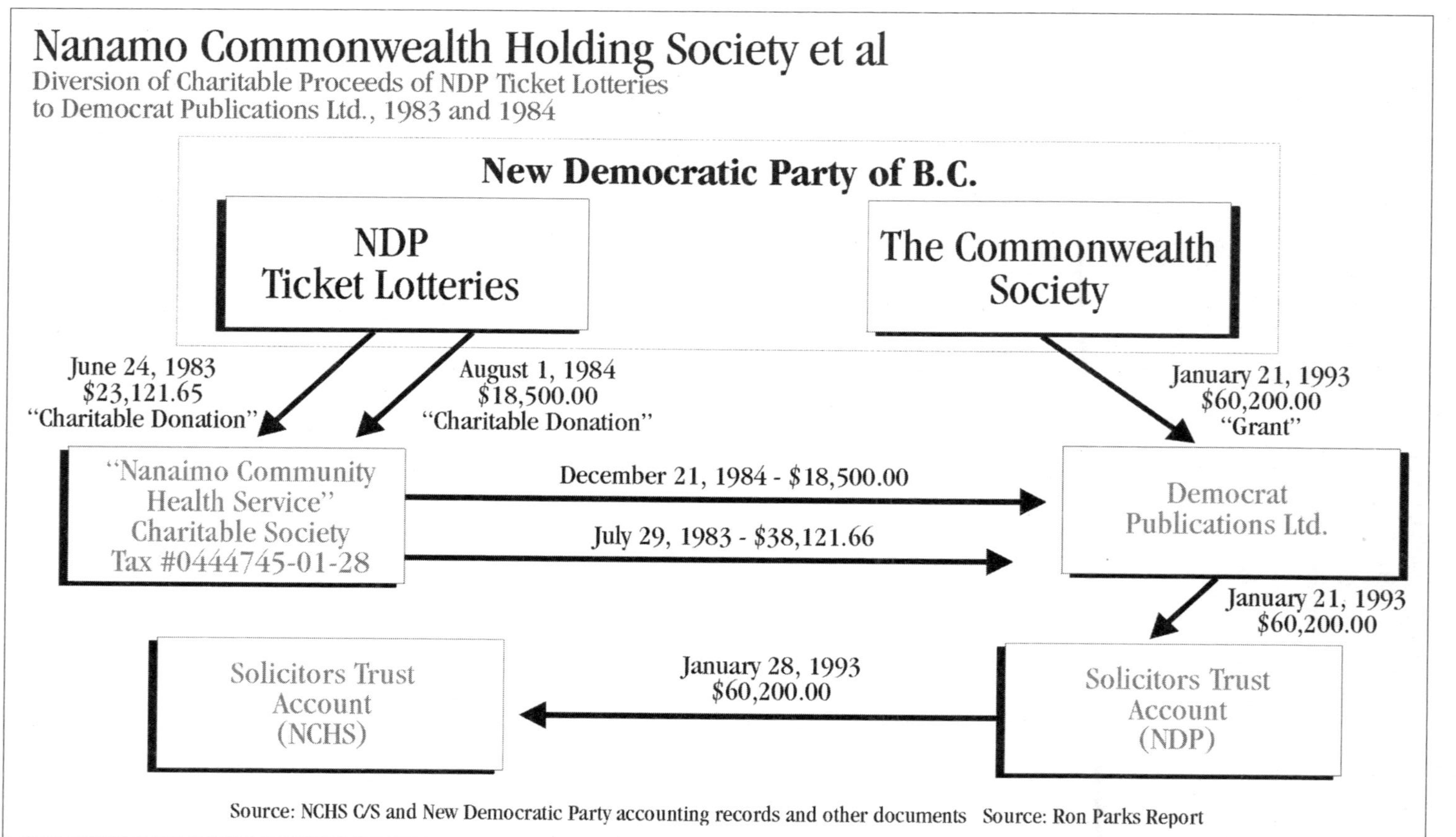
Nanamo Commonwealth Holding Society et al
Diversion of Charitable Proceeds of NDP Ticket Lotteries
to Democrat Publications Ltd., 1983 and 1984
New Democratic Party of B.C.
NDP
Ticket Lotteries
The Commonwealth
Society
June 24, 1983
$23,121.65
"Charitable Donation"
August 1, 1984
$18,500.00
"Charitable Donation"
January 21, 1993
$60,200.00
"Grant"
"Nanaimo Community
Health Service"
Charitable Society
Tax #0444745-01-28
December 21, 1984 - $18,500.00
July 29, 1983 - $38,121.66
Democrat
Publications Ltd.
January 21, 1993
$60,200.00
Solicitors Trust
Account
(NCHS)
January 28, 1993
$60,200.00
Solicitors Trust
Account
(NDP)
Source: NCHS C/S and New Democratic Party accounting records and other documents
Source: Ron Parks Report

Appendix A

Turning Tommy Douglas in his Grave

The Nanaimo Bingo Scandal

"Even now the extent of the fraud is not known with precision. It can be said however, that by 1989 nearly $1 million of society funds had been dealt with in a fraudulent manner by Mr. Stupich. What was returned, what was lost, and what remains to the benefit of Mr. Stupich in the final result remains unclear."[1]

- Mr. Justice Josephson, in sentencing Dave Stupich in 1999

No event broke the image of BC's New Democrats as honest brokers more than the revelation that its elder statesman, Dave Stupich, siphoned off charity money for personal and political ends. The public expected the NDP to spend more money than other parties; some voted for them for that very reason. Most people, including honest partisans, also knew NDP fiscal management was a tad less prudent than that of a British banker.

But the Nanaimo Commonwealth Holding Society scandal forever punctured the party's claim to moral superiority. Post-Nanaimo, the party no longer had an easy pass on the compassion card – the ace it often pulled out to justify its more loopy ideas. In addition to recklessness with the public purse, it turned out New Democrats had as many skeletons as any other party, perhaps more. Because New Democrats ripped apart the Socreds for dirty tricks in the 1979 election, the hypocrisy over the bingo scandal only added to the stench. After all, no one ever accused the party of the Bennetts and Grace McCarthy of charity rip-offs.

In the beginning

The Nanaimo Commonwealth Holding Society (NCHS) was a non-profit association set up in 1954 by the Co-operative Commonwealth Federation (the precursor to the NDP) to purchase meeting hall facilities in the Vancouver Island city, and by its own words, "to assist in the pursuit of socialist education."[2] In the early days of the party, local businesses were reluctant to rent space to the CCF and that hampered its effectiveness and growth.

In 1959, the Society bought its first bingo machine and eleven years later the NCHS was one of the larger bingo operators in the province. From its creation, Dave Stupich was involved as treasurer for the NCHS and the local NDP constituency association. Whether as an MLA, provincial Finance minister, a member of parliament, or through local involvement in the provincial and federal wings of the party, Dave Stupich *was* the NDP in Nanaimo. In him and through him, the local party had its being.

Behind the red door

NDP politics in Nanaimo had long been of the red-meat variety – an outgrowth of the hard-knock industrial relations that set the tone for class conflict at the turn of the century in the coal mining industry. The Nanaimo Commonwealth Holding Society was a key piece of the NDP's growth in the area. Dave Stupich, the NCHS, and the NDP built the most powerful political riding association in Canada. As one NCHS director and MLA Dale Lovick later bragged, they were "the biggest game in town, so powerful it could intimidate other parties into not even running candidates. It was our town."[3]

In the early 1970s, NCHS bylaw changes (approved by its directors) allowed it to hold real estate investments and also to lend money or provide loan guarantees "to any person or company having dealings with the society…."[4] That change included the possibility of lending to the Society's own directors. In effect, the NCHS could act as a *de facto* bank. In time, the Society did just that and later lent (and gave) money to an NDP newspaper, to New Democrat election causes, to a Dave Stupich friend in financial straits, and to Stupich himself.

As fun as it was to excoriate WAC Bennett and the Socreds in NCHS-owned meeting halls pre-1972, those right-wingers yet denied to BC the new socialist Jerusalem the NDP so desperately wanted to build. And then the son of WAC cut short the NDP's three-year experiment in 1975. Instead of some grand utopia built across the province by an omniscient NDP government, the party would have to settle for a smaller, more concrete version of paradise in Nanaimo.

By 1980, the Commonwealth Society was in possession of two meeting halls (which doubled as bingo parlours) and eight parcels of land across the city; they were to be developed as cash flow permitted. That year, one property was donated to an NCHS-related society for a 70-unit senior citizen's complex; another (the Commonwealth Centre) was to be the headquarters for all Nanaimo area bingos and for the NDP. Yet another project included plans for a twelve-storey hotel.

The NCHS funded its ambitious real estate ventures through bank loans and $2 million worth of debentures and co-ownership units, but the timing was awful. North America's worst economic downturn since the Depression was about to hit, and by 1981 the overheated North American real estate market was the first casualty.

The NCHS hotel project went under first but only after it swallowed up $1 million in Society money; a union pension fund bought it in 1983. The Commonwealth Centre (the ideological nerve centre of the NDP in Nanaimo) was second on the block and the Royal Bank took that over in 1985.

The real estate collapse left the Society broke. Ron Parks, the forensic auditor who late scoured their books pointed out if NCHS were a corporation, "it would have undoubtedly been put into receivership."[5]

Bingo money to the rescue

The socialist-turned-capitalist-developer project failed; it took trailer-park moms and grandmothers (and their bingo money) to pay off some Society debentures, but by 1984, the NCHS still owed $2.8 million including principal and interest. Most of the money was owed to loyal NDP supporters; thus, folding up the Society was not an option.

Debentures were one thing, co-ownership quite another. When the banks called the loans, co-owners lost their $1 million in investments, though as the Parks Report noted, they probably recovered some, if not all of their money back by utilizing the resulting losses for tax purposes.[6] The big bad investment-loss tax write-off for capitalists turned out to be of some use to financially incompetent socialists. Still, the loss stung, and it is a measure of the local NDP's strength that, despite the calamity, the city continued to elect NDP MLAs.

The charity kickbacks

Long before the NCHS found itself in financial hot water over the 1980s real estate bust, Nanaimo charities were required to kick back a portion of their bingo profits if they wanted any money from the Commonwealth Society. In the early 1970s and under provincial regulations, 25 percent of bingo

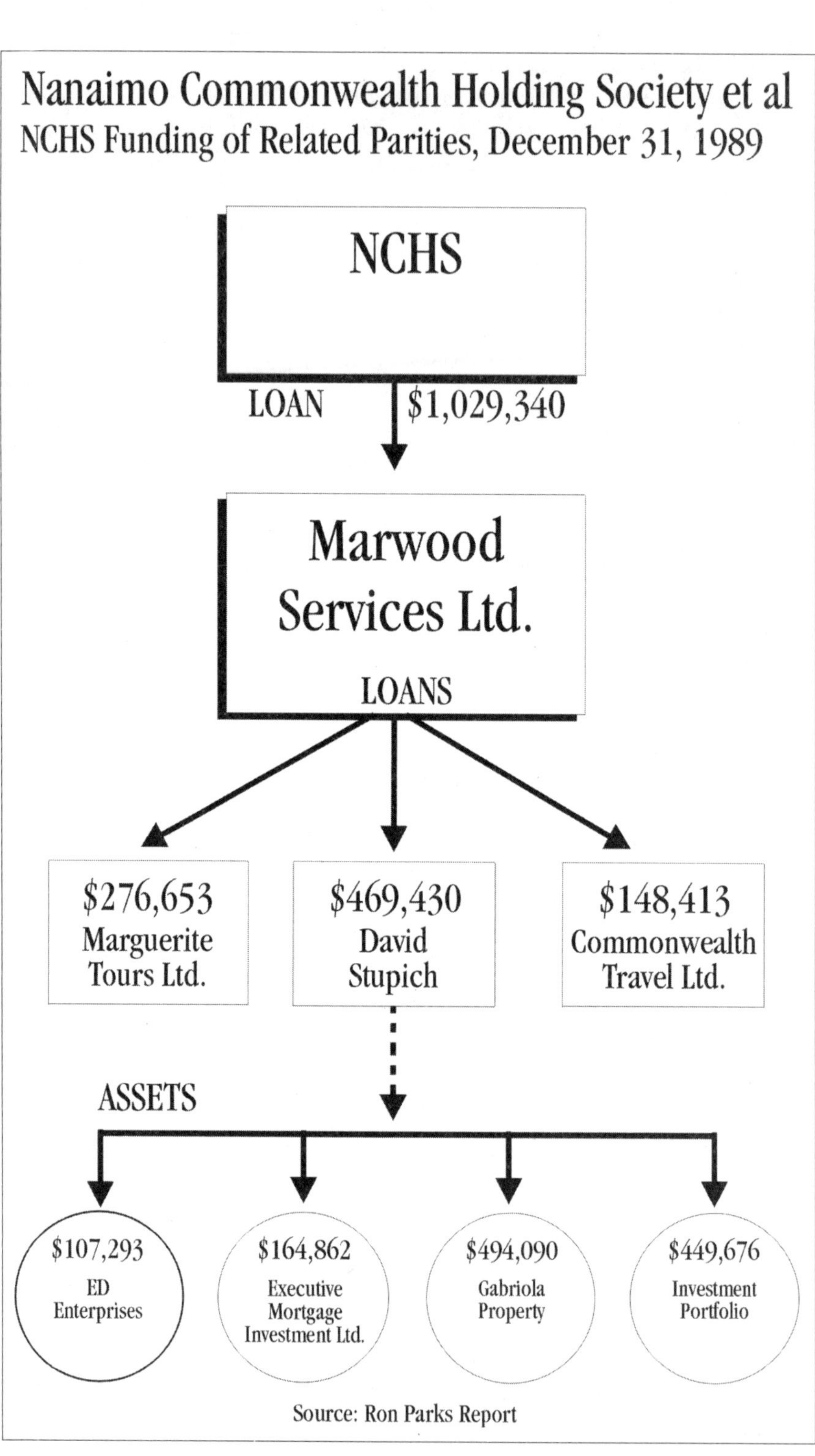
Nanaimo Commonwealth Holding Society et al
NCHS Funding of Related Parities, December 31, 1989
NCHS
LOAN
$1,029,340
Marwood Services Ltd.
LOANS
$276,653
Marguerite Tours Ltd.
$469,430
David Stupich
$148,413
Commonwealth Travel Ltd.
ASSETS
$107,293
ED Enterprises
$164,862
Executive Mortgage Investment Ltd.
$494,090
Gabriola Property
$449,676
Investment Portfolio
Source: Ron Parks Report

revenues were to be donated to charity, 59 percent to winners and at most, sixteen percent for operating costs. Some charities in the province, including the NCHS, skirted the regulations and kept the full sixteen-percent, needed or not. "Clarifications" from the province later reminded operators that 25 percent was a *minimum*, not a maximum contribution to charity. If the full sixteen-percent was unneeded for operational expenses, the surplus portion was to go to charity.

Pre-1974, to skim extra revenues from charities, the NCHS also charged "rent" to any charity that did business with the Society. In one rather stark admission, Dave Stupich wrote board member Frank Murphy in 1973 and explained how the Society circumvented government bingo regulations in order to keep more money:

> *From time to time, a cheque is turned over to me for donation to the Handicapped Workshop Society. I collect "rent" back from that society, on delivering this cheque, record as hall rent an agreed portion of it, and show any surplus between rent paid and reasonable hall rent as a loan from the B.C. Tomorrow Committee.*[7]

One police investigation affidavit revealed the kickback scam in all its infamy. In the early 1970s, the Nanaimo Vocational Workshop for the Handicapped received a $1,000 cheque from the Commonwealth Holding Society and it sent back a receipt made out in the same amount. It also sent back $900 as "rent." In other words, the charity received only ten percent of the donation that the Commonwealth Society reported to government. Sister Margaret Rowe, who directed the workshop, decided the workshop would no longer provide cover for the phony donations. After she informed the Society that future receipts would be made out for the actual amount – $100 – the bingo society cut off the charity completely.[8]

At the time, Dave Stupich justified the rip-off because the pilfered money helped further socialist education, a term that he defined quite broadly: "this socialist education has always been interpreted as meaning that the society will help the political activities of the NDP in whatever way is desired."[9]

The money laundering was ripe with scandal-potential. One day, a charity might not play ball as Sister Rowe decided, or after having submitted to Stupich's demands for a time, might blow the whistle on the scheme. Given that the above letter was written in 1973, it is remarkable that it took another two decades for the scandal to come to light.

All in the family: the NCHS Charitable Society

By 1974, Stupich found an easier, safer, and more profitable way to launder money: he created a new, parallel society with its very own charitable number. The scam was simple. The NCHS Charitable Society (*NCHS-CS*) was incorporated in 1974, granted federal charitable status, and henceforth could issue tax-deductible receipts. Besides Stupich himself, the board members included Harry Hackwood and Elizabeth Marlow, Stupich's common-law wife. Hackwood and Marlow later formed MarWood Services Ltd., an accounting firm that later filtered much of the bingo money loaned/given to other companies, the NDP, and to Stupich himself.

NCHS-CS (as opposed to the original and non tax-deductible society, NCHS) was useful in a number of ways: the *NCHS-CS* could more easily raise money as it had a charitable number. Moreover, the original society, which, as a condition of its bingo licence was required to donate money to charity, could now donate to its very *own* "charity," i.e. *NCHS-CS*.

To complete the circle, the parent society would charge the fake charity "rent." While other charities still received some bingo money, most cash stayed with the Society and its fake charity – not with, for example, the Boys and Girls Clubs. As reported later, 54 percent of the charitable donations made between 1970 and 1993 went to the NCHS's *own* "charity," *NCHS-CS*.

Questions begin to surface

Concerns about Society practices surfaced as early as 1978. The province's Gaming Branch inspector, Dan Currie, suspected bingo funds were misused, but his report gathered dust. He repeated the allegations two years later and questioned whether the NCHS charitable wing was an appropriate recipient for bingo funds. No detailed audit ever answered Currie's allegations.[10]

In 1982, the chief inspections officer of the Gaming Branch ordered Dave Stupich to stop accepting "donations" instead of rent from community groups. One year later, a detailed Branch report concluded that the NCHS Charitable Society received almost $700,000 in donations from the five bingo licences operated under the parent NCHS umbrella between 1979 and 1983.[11]

From there, directors within the Gaming Branch ran straight over a dead man's curve. Further investigations were stopped, and Carl Bolton (the inspector who prepared the 1983 report) was told by his director that NCHS was "a dead issue."[12] Society licences were routinely renewed without question for the next four years.

Given that the Social Credit government was in power in the 1980s, it is curious that an NDP-linked bingo society, already the subject of several critical Gaming Branch reports, was never properly investigated. As early as the 1970s, gaming officials suspected something was wrong. In 1978, one B.C. Lotteries official wrote "it appears to me that the Nanaimo N.D.P.

Association may well be one and the same [as Nanaimo Commonwealth]."[13]

Carl Bolton later told auditors that inspectors within the Gaming Branch "felt there was some sort of political or bureaucratic power that was sort of preventing us from doing that." He added, "whether that was real or not, is another question."[14]

There was at least one other reason why the scandal took so long to be revealed: Dave Stupich was one of the best-liked politicians in the province, even by opponents. His personal popularity explains in part why it took so long for the scandal to unfold. No one wanted to believe that such an avuncular and friendly fellow was a crook. As the judge who later sentenced Stupich put it "...it was this trust and reputation for integrity which enabled him to carry out the fraud for so many years without deception."[15]

The empire begins to crumble

By the spring of 1992, allegations made by Nanaimo resident Jacques Carpentier were beginning to crack open the Society. Past tips to RCMP were investigated but resulted in no charges; by 1993 though, the RCMP hauled off 75 boxes of NCHS banking, accounting and computer records from Marwood Services (Stupich's accounting practice). After the government stalled for another year, it finally ordered an independent investigation (though no public inquiry) and, with no co-operation from Stupich himself, Ron Parks scoured the accountant's books via a court order. Initially, the government attempted to restrict the audit to just 1988 and 1991. The auditor ignored the directive and sniffed beyond the boundaries anyway.[16]

Tell it to the judge

In 1994, four Dave Stupich-related societies – NCHS, *NCHS-CS,* Harewood Community Hall Association, and Harewood Social Centre – were charged with violating Section 207(3) of the Criminal Code of Canada that related to operating a bingo without making the minimum required donations under gaming regulations. The four societies pleaded guilty and were fined $55,000. NCHS was ordered to repay $100,000 in restitution.

Still, the NDP government refused to order a wider public inquiry into the sordid mess. In April 1995, the premier told the Legislature that the NDP was cleared by an internal report on the matter. The report, argued the premier, included a "review of 130,000 financial transactions that showed there is no evidence of any of those funds going to the BC New Democratic Party."[17] It was later revealed that the audit was shallow. Bank deposit slips that identified party donors had long been destroyed; the result was a superficial review and nothing close to an actual audit.[18]

Collateral damage: the Parks Report

When the long-awaited Parks Report was released in October 1995, autumn election talk was quickly replaced by the bombshells the audit contained not only about Dave Stupich, but the New Democratic Party: The report revealed that the Nanaimo Commonwealth Holding Society made two payments in 1983 and 1984 (worth $56,621.65) to Democrat Publications, the NDP's official newspaper. In 1993, after the scandal broke into the open, the NDP quietly repaid the money, $60,000 including interest, to NCHS. The payment was listed as a repaid "loan", which was false. It was a grant in the first instance, not a loan. But some of Mike Harcourt's own aides, who knew about the payment, never told the premier in 1993.

However, the premier was briefed in April 1995 by auditor Ron Parks about the early 1980s payment from NCHS to the NDP newspaper.[19] Also in June 1995, Finance Minister Elizabeth Cull briefed the premier on the contents of the Parks Report.[20] Mike Harcourt knew in June that, "there was one transaction involving the NDP"[21] according to his own words. Still, the Premier claimed all the way up to October that there was no evidence of questionable transactions between the NDP and charity money.

Immediately after the Parks Report was made public, Harcourt explained his actions this way:

> *The question arises why did I not inform British Columbians when I learned of that repayment. Well, let me be clear on what I knew in April.*
>
> *I knew of the repayment of the loan from my interview with Mr. Parks and from discussions I had after that with the president of the party. I had no way of knowing, as Mr. Parks makes clear in his report, that those monies were diverted from charities. I had been saying that I knew of no connection of the NDP and diverted charity funds and it is only with the Parks Report that I became aware that there was that connection.*[22]

Yet NCHS was all about bingos, about *charitable* bingos. And it was just convicted of stealing charity money the year before. What more did Harcourt need before he concluded that tainted money might have flowed between the NDP and NCHS sixteen years earlier? At the very least, why did Harcourt not at least dig a little deeper to find out what those around him knew? Instead, until October, Harcourt and Cull continued to state publicly that there were no questionable links between the party and NCHS. As *Vancouver Sun* columnist Vaughn Palmer (who did not question Harcourt's veracity, just his judgment) put it: "Welcome to the premier's world, prepare to suspend disbelief."[23]

Cull's credibility canyon

Meanwhile, the Finance minister demonstrated a canyon-like credibility gap on the issue: hours before the report's release in mid-October, Cull again referred to the party's review of its own books as an "audit"[24] and claimed it proved "there was no evidence that the party received tainted funds from the NCHS."[25] Three hours later, the Parks Report (which Cull read, shared with NDP political operatives, and briefed the Premier about in June) was publicly released. The numerous NDP-NCHS connections were revealed.[i]

Cull later claimed she struggled with "having knowledge of the Parks Report ever since I received it and not being able to discuss it."[26] Of course, she *had* discussed it, as far back as June with John Walsh and John Heaney, two of the government's top political guns.[27] Another New Democrat, Gerry Scott, was also at the June 1995 meeting. Scott, coincidentally, was at the NDP newspaper *The Democrat* when the party received one of the payments from the lottery scheme back in 1983.[28]

Given that the media went to court to obtain what Elizabeth Cull and other NDP staff read in June, the struggle had everything to do with keeping the report from the public in what everyone assumed was to be an election year.

All aboard the NDP caucus special

Besides the NCHS grant to the NDP newspaper, the 1995 audit by Ron Parks found other evidence of NDP-NCHS transactions. As Ron Parks wrote:

> *NCHS's financial statements for the years 1979 to 1982 disclosed amounts payable by NCHS to the NDP. Our investigation into these amounts revealed the following NDP-related accounts at NCHS[29]:*

Account Name	Period
NDP Caucus Special	1975 to 1985
NDP Headquarters	1979 to 1985
D. Stupich Campaign Fund	1979
DDS Campaign Fund	1982 to 1985

Besides the Dave Stupich connection and the four NDP-related accounts, the NDP profited in other ways from the Society. It turned out that NCHS

i. The Parks Report was released at 7:30 on a Friday evening. Viewers of the popular television series *West Wing* will understand the reason: governments often dump unpopular news late on Fridays in an effort to avoid much (or any) coverage of their action.

laundered corporate donations to the NDP (which were at the time publicly declined by the party). On the "in" side of NCHS ledgers, over $475,000 exchanged hands between the party and the society, almost half of it from secret corporate donations.[30] Also revealed in 1995 was that $12,500 was deposited into the account by someone with the initials "D.B."[ii]

On the cheque-writing side of the ledger, NCHS also helped out NDP MLA Bob Williams with $80,000 when he gave up his seat so Dave Barrett could regain a seat in the Legislature (after he was bounced by voters in the 1975 election). Stupich's own election campaigns were financed through the Society ($15,196) and NDP-related travel costs financed by the Society amounted to over $235,000 over the ten-year period.

In 1979, an NCHS-related charity gave money to the Vancouver East NDP in 1979 while yet another Society charity gave cash to Vancouver's civic New Democrats in 1990. NDP delegates to a 1989 convention had party-related costs covered by NCHS. All the while, many NDP MLAs used NCHS and later Marwood Services (a Stupich-related firm) to handle the constituency books.[31]

Ron Parks had this to say about the NDP-NCHS connection:

> *The campaign accounts held funds used to finance Mr. Stupich's election campaigns. This information, together with the findings from our examination of these accounts leads us to the conclusion that these accounts were in effect, a convenient source of funds for the NDP which was not recorded in the party's financial records.*[32]

Back to you Mr. Harcourt

When confronted by reporters about the revelations, Premier Mike Harcourt refused to fire the political staff who neglected to tell him about the 1993 reimbursement to Democrat Publications. He also refused to criticize then party president Patrice Pratt for what the media called an NDP cover-up. Instead, Harcourt blamed lawyers for advice they gave to the party to keep the $60,000 repayment a secret, this despite an ongoing RCMP investigation at the time. There was no cover-up by senior party officials Harcourt in-

---

ii. Speculation in 1995 centered quite logically on former Premier Dave Barrett. In public hearings five years later, Barrett confirmed the whispers; in 1983, he deposited $12,500 of a $20,000 donation into NCHS accounts shortly after that the election. The other $7,500 was given to his office manager for expenses. Barrett never revealed who gave him the money. The former premier also borrowed money from NCHS for his campaigns, money later paid back. ("Dave dealt in cash," *Vancouver Province,* 4 May 2000.)

sisted, and the only finger of blame was pointed to Dave Stupich. When asked whether NDP party executives were in the wrong, Harcourt's response was "no."[33]

Harcourt was not exactly a fountain of information. Two weeks after the damning report was released, *Vancouver Sun* reporter Justine Hunter was on the same return flight from the Western Premiers Conference in Regina along with the premier. She confronted Harcourt with information that one of his aides, Sharon Prescott, knew something of the $60,000 payback at the time it was made (in 1993). Since Harcourt vowed in 1992 to get to the bottom of the scandal, Prescott had deceived Harcourt, perhaps to ensure that Harcourt could truthfully state that he knew of no link between the NDP and NCHS. If that was the motive, it also had the potential to make Harcourt look less persistent than he should have been with aides and party officials.

Which is exactly what happened. Once the Parks Report was released, Prescott quickly told Harcourt of her 1993 knowledge – two weeks before the reporter asked about Prescott. But no heads rolled and nor did Mike Harcourt make public the fact that a senior aide withheld this information from him for two years.[34]

Hunter then asked whether anyone else, say top aide John Heaney, knew about the $60,000 repayment. The premier mused that Heaney might have known. After all, a year earlier, John Heaney researched the possibility of a lawsuit against the *Sun* for its suggestion that the charity money and the NDP were connected. Since the lawsuit was never pursued (given that there were NDP-NCHS connections), it now all made sense, sort of.[35]

So, two weeks after the scandal first hit the front page, Harcourt had not yet directly asked a top staffer, John Heaney, if he knew for sure about the 1993 payback. "I only talked to him briefly," replied Harcourt to the reporter's queries.[36]

By late November, Mike Harcourt resigned as Premier, not because he was personally implicated in the scandal, but due to his own sluggish response when the political fallout hit ground zero.

Dale Lovick and the lost memory syndrome

As for sitting MLAs closest to the affair, Nanaimo MLA and cabinet minister Dale Lovick suffered from memory loss. Lovick, who most days thought of himself as a bright and competent fellow, could not remember any helpful details at the 1999 hearings into the scandal. The MLA was an NCHS director during the period when the Society cut cheques to Democrat Publications but he did not recall such approvals. Nor could he remember payments to political accounts.[37] Lovick did remember that he received a monthly stipend from NCHS funds but apparently never thought there was anything untoward about such payments.

Lovick's memory lapses stretched credulity; Lovick told the RCMP two years earlier that he knew the NCHS paid NDP office rent and much more.

> *The office was staffed, pretty much full-time, by people whose salaries, I think, were paid by, okay, NCHS. If they went to a [political] convention, NCHS would frequently pick up the tab for a hospitality suite.*[38]

National Post columnist Mark Hume (who helped break the scandal in the early 1990s as a reporter with the *Vancouver Sun*) wrote that "now it's clear that of all the sitting politicians, he [Lovick] knew the most, the soonest – and he did the least about it."[39]

In the dock

By 1998, the RCMP concluded their investigation and recommended charges against Dave Stupich, his wife, daughter, former NDP party secretary Joe Denofreo, and former Premier Dave Barrett. Prosecutors soon laid 64 criminal charges against Stupich and the other alleged co-conspirators; Democrat Publications was also charged. Dave Barrett escaped charges after prosecutors concluded there was not enough evidence.[40]

How much money was diverted?

Between 1970 and 1993, over $18 million was raised by NCHS through its various bingo licences. $4.7 million was to go to charity.[41] In practice, large amounts were diverted to NCHS and then on to Stupich, his wife's company (Marwood Services), the NDP, and to an assortment of other recipients.

Of the $4.7 million, between 1974 and 1988 alone, almost $2.4 million flowed into NCHS-CS accounts, amounts that were then supposed to be redistributed to charities. Here is what Ron Parks found:[42]

So where did NCHS money go? For the period of 1984 to 1988, almost $1.3 million was loaned to Marwood Services from Dave Stupich's fake charities. Interest was not charged on the loans but Marwood, once in possession of the money, charged interest and earned a tidy return. During the 1987-1990 period, Marwood's total interest income was $173,000. None of that interest found its way back to NCHS, even though Marwood owed between $667,000 and $1,029,340 to NCHS at various periods during that time. As for how much "loaned" money ever found its way back to the original society, that was undetermined.

1974-1988		
	$	%
Donated by licencees to THE NCHS C/S	2,375,106	100
Less: Donated to charity by THE NCHS C/S	451,462	19
Shortfall	**1,923,644**	**81**

Dave Stupich: the champagne socialist

What did Dave Stupich gain at the expense of NCHS? For just the years between 1988 and 1991, $374,000 was the direct amount according to the best guess of auditors in their 1995 report.[43] But that figure doesn't capture the amount loaned/given to Stupich before 1988 by NCHS directly or via Marwood.

In court, one estimate pegged the amount Stupich used interest-free from NCHS (via Marwood) at $955,000.[44] It was never determined how much of the "borrowed" money, if any, ever made its way back to the Society. In sentencing Stupich, Justice Bruce Josephson noted that "even now, the extent of the fraud is not known."[45]

Dave Stupich maintained his innocence to the end. In 1999 testimony before the official inquiry into the scandal, Stupich denied that any Nanaimo charity was ever ripped off:

> *We met every one of our promises to give money for charities in Nanaimo. Have you heard from a single charity in Nanaimo that has complained we gave them less than promised? Not a one of them was given less money than promised.*[46]

That is not how the RCMP, Crown prosecutors, or Auditor Ron Parks saw it:

> *There were significant unauthorized and inappropriate uses of funds for loans to related parties and individuals, some of which remain unpaid; for diversions from charitable groups to NCHS to repay debenture holders and other debts arising out of commercial real estate ventures; for excessive administration fees; and for political purposes.*[47]

In 1999, Democratic Publications pleaded guilty to two charges of operating an illegal lottery scheme in connection with the scandal. Dave Stupich plea-bargained and pleaded guilty to one charge of fraud involving more than $5,000 and one count of running an illegal lottery. He was sentenced to two years less a day, to be served with an electronic monitoring bracelet from his daughter's Nanaimo home. The judge went easy due to a claimed case of advanced dementia. Charges against his common-law wife, daughter, and former NDP provincial secretary Joe Denofreo were stayed in return for Stupich's guilty plea and for 200 hours of community service by his relatives.

As part of the sentence, Dave Stupich was forbidden to visit his Gabriola Island home during his period of confinement. The 3,440 square foot home, built in 1984, had six bedrooms, three bathrooms, vaulted ceilings, a cedar shake roof, a wood fireplace, manicured gardens, a swimming pool and hot tub. Worth $800,000, the home sat on prime waterfront real estate with a view of Vancouver Island and the passing ferries.[48]

Shortly after the trial, Stupich drove his own car and made bank deposits in downtown Nanaimo without assistance. He even penned a well-researched letter to a Nanaimo newspaper defending the latest minimum wage hike.[49] The dementia was apparently not as critical as first claimed in court.

Appendix B

The Fudge-It Budget Chronology[i]

October 1994[ii]

Treasury Board staff make a presentation to Finance Minister Elizabeth Cull; they forecast revenues of $19.567 billion for Budget 1996.

January 1995

Chris Trumpy, then assistant Deputy Minister of Finance and head of Treasury Board staff, writes a memo to Cull to explore the possibility of using proceeds from Columbia Downstream Benefits. $135 million annually would be available and Trumpy urges Cull to apply it towards the growing provincial debt. He warns that debt-servicing costs are beginning to mount and BC risks a credit downgrade. Though the government has reduced the deficit and plans to balance the budget, the Achilles heel is rapid and unsustainable growth in non-operating tax-supported debt resulting from capital spending.

February 1995

In a briefing note to Finance Minister Cull, Treasury Board staff warn that Budget 1996 is headed for a "fairly large deficit." "$600 million to $800 million is likely."[1] The memo cautions the New Democrats against following the Socred lead down the road to "deception and dishonesty."[2]

Treasury Board staff forecast a Budget 1996 with revenues of $19.851 billion. ($20.126 billion with revenue "optimism.")

---

i. Dates compiled from *A Tale of two Budget Lies*, Canadian Taxpayers Federation, July 1997 and various newspaper accounts; original source documents from the British Columbia Ministry of Finance.

ii. Government budget years end on March 31. For simplification, the 1995-96 budget year is referred to as Budget 1995, and the 1996-97 budget year is Budget 1996.

March 1995

Budget 1995 is tabled in the Legislature. Cull announces a Debt Management Plan. The government proceeds to aggressively promote the Plan despite the fact that the government has already received warnings from its own staff that the targets set out in the plan were unreachable unless it took significant corrective action.

The Debt Management Plan forecasts revenues for Budget 1996 at $20.235 billion and a surplus of $25 million.

September 1995

Treasury Board stands by its pessimistic forecast. In background documents prepared for an NDP caucus briefing, it is made clear to the government that they "need to find $1.15 billion" if they are to balance the budget in 1996. Revenues are forecast at $19.905 billion with optimistic targets of $20.235 billion.

November 1995

A Forest Ministry revenue branch memo states that revenue is not coming in as expected for the 1995 budget year. They forecast $70 million to $120 million less than expected.

December 1995

Forests Minister Andrew Petter writes a letter to Cull warning her about a "significant drop" in revenue from Forestry, and in particular, the Small Business Forest Enterprise Program.

In presentation materials, Treasury Board staff forecast revenues of $19.977 million for Budget 1996, a quarter of a billion dollars below the official $20.235 billion figure in the Debt Management Plan.

January 1996

Treasury Board continues to forecast a deficit. Even using the optimistic figure - $20.235 billion – the shortfall is predicted to be as high as $725 million, according to a document entitled "1996-97 Budget - How's It Shaping Up," prepared for the transition team of Glen Clark.

February 1996

In February, an informal working group was formed that included Brenda Eaton, civil service head of the Treasury Board and Tom Gunton, an aide to Premier Glen Clark.[3] No notes were kept, but the Auditor General was later told that it was Gunton's "informal" job to scrutinize the assumptions used by the Treasury Board staff, of which Ms. Eaton was the representative.

On February 23, the Clark government is one day old and suddenly Treasury now has two sets of revenue forecasts. The longstanding estimate, which appeared in documents as far back as a year before, is still $19.948 billion. There is also now an alternative forecast of $20.785 billion - $800 million higher than Treasury Board estimates.

On February 26, in a line-by-line analysis of the alternative forecast, Treasury Board points out that *none* of it is supportable given existing forecasts by the provincial or federal governments. In spite of this, the alternative forecast becomes the Clark government's official forecast.

March 1996

March 8: Treasury board staff issue another warning against revenue optimism advising that "it is evident that the provincial economy has suffered a sharp decline." The province will start the 1996 budget year "in a hole."

March 12: Brenda Eaton, head of Treasury Board staff, responds in writing to the staff who submitted the March 8 memo. Ms Eaton makes no attempt to dispute the projections. "We've repeatedly made that point…, cautions I believe are well understood and documented."

Later that day, Premier Glen Clark tells reporters "We're on track for a balanced budget for the 1995-96 fiscal year and a second balanced budget next year."

April 1996

On April 30 in the Legislature, the NDP claims the budget year just ended (1995) is balanced, and that Budget 1996 will be also balanced, largely on the strength of a revenue forecast of $20.659 billion. Budget revenues are *$424 million higher than that forecast four months earlier* in the Debt Management Plan. Cull is asked where the extra money comes from. "Improved forecasting,"[4] is her response even though there are no internal documents to support this claim. Election 1996 is called that afternoon.

May 22, 1996

Treasury Board staff revisit the three-week old Budget 1996. "Revenue is expected to be $769 million below forecast," they write, citing optimistic budget forecasts. Revenues are now forecast at $19.890 billion compared to $20.659 billion in the "official" budget projections. The forecast deficit is now one billion dollars. Six days later, Treasury staff revise the forecast yet again with the deficit estimated at between $533 million and $1.038 billion.[5]

Election Day 1996 - May 28

The NDP win 39 seats with 39 percent of the vote. The Liberals win 33 seats with 42 percent of the vote, while two Reformers and one independent are elected. The NDP form their second majority government.

June 1996

June 21: Acting Deputy Minister of Finance Brenda Eaton provides new Finance Minister Andrew Petter with statements showing that the 1995 budget year will likely end up with a $235 million deficit.

June 26: The Throne speech includes a reference to a *second* balanced budget, i.e., the budget year that ended on March 31 and the current year.

June 28: Petter reveals to Victoria Times Colonist reporter Les Leyne that Budget 1995 will in fact have a deficit.

July 1996

Finance Minister Petter blames poor weather for delaying logging, and claims he did not know about the drop in revenues while he was Forestry Minister. This appears to be a contradiction of his 1995 letter sent to Elizabeth Cull while he was Forests Minister.

September 1996

After a copy of Treasury Board's grim analysis of Budget 1996 is leaked to the *Vancouver Sun*, Petter admits the 1996 budget surplus is also in doubt.

October 1996

Premier Glen Clark appears on to television to explain why the budget is out of line with what the NDP said during the election. "It's pretty obvious that everybody's forecasts were wrong. The largest most profitable institutions in the country rely on these forecasts to guide their decisions. And so do we." [6] This ignores the fact that Treasury Board's, professional, non-partisan forecasts were right all along.

January 1997

On CBC Radio's *Early Edition*, Finance Minister Petter admits the NDP went too far in claiming a balanced budget. "I think we did overstate the case during the election campaign."

Endnotes

Chapter 1: Pride & Prejudice, *and* Power

1. *Vancouver Sun*, 13 September 1996.
2. "Alberta Government Boondoggles Since 1980," Canadian Taxpayers Federation – Alberta Division, 1996.
3. "Unrestrained double-talk," *BC Report*, 27 January 1992.
4. Author interview with Mike Geoghegan, 3 October 2000.
5. Ibid.
6. "A flip-flop, a new leak: a typical 24 hours for the NDP," Vaughn Palmer, *Vancouver Sun*, 23 March 1995.
7. "The NDP is far from being a friend of whistleblowers," Vaughn Palmer, *Vancouver Sun*, 17 May 2000.
8. "The high cost of severance," *BC Report,* 10 February 1992.
9. "When Harcourt ministers and aides talk too much," Vaughn Palmer, *Vancouver Sun*, 12 April 1995.
10. "Sihota tuition fees spark conflict claim," *Vancouver Sun,* 23 November 1996.
11. "Socreds were saints compared to NDP," *Vancouver Sun*, 28 April 1994.
12. "Woman who lost money calls ex-minister's plight 'unfair and unjust'," *Vancouver Sun*, 6 May 1995.
13. "A flair that makes him a legend at the public trough," Vaughn Palmer, *Vancouver Sun,* 9 April 1999.
14. Ibid.
15. "Alberta's economy surges ahead to third-largest, ahead of BC," *Vancouver Sun*, 3 October 2000.
16. *Hansard,* 7 April 1993.
17. *Hansard,* 24 March 1992.
18. Speech to Simon Fraser University conference "Abusing Power: The Canadian Experience." 7-9 May 1998.
19. Ibid.

Chapter 2: Debt & Taxes

1. *Hansard,* 1 April 1993.
2. Source: British Columbia Ministry of Finance, Budget 1991.
3. "A $2 billion sales pitch," *BC Report*, 16 March 1992.
4. Source: British Columbia Ministry of Finance, Budget 1992.
5. Ibid.
6. Ibid.
7. Ibid.
8. Ibid.
9. Ibid.
10. Ibid.
11. Ibid.
12. "The price of broken promises," *BC Report*, 17 February 1992.
13. Source: British Columbia Ministry of Finance, Budget 1993.
14. Ibid.
15. Ibid.
16. Ibid.
17. Ibid.
18. Ibid.
19. Ibid.
20. Ibid.
21. Ibid.
22. Ibid.
23. Budget 1991, 1992 and 1993.
24. *Hansard,* 3 April 1992.
25. *Hansard,* 1 April 1993.

26. *Hansard,* 7 April 1993.
27. "The sorry fiscal legacy of discarded NDP promises," Vaughn Palmer, *Vancouver Sun,* 28 March 1995.
28. "'Luxury' tax on trucks is absurd," *Prince George Citizen,* 20 December 1999.
29. "Citizens' willingness to pay taxes NDP," Vaughn Palmer, *Vancouver Sun,* 7 December 1993.
30. "Taxing the Truth," *BC Report,* 25 January 1999. Clark's comments were excerpted from a summer 1998 edition of *Canadian Forum*.
31. "A fox in the henhouse," *BC Report,* 10 August 1992.
32. Ibid.
33. "The case for wealth taxation," Maureen Maloney, Canadian Public Administration, Summer 1991, p 241-259.
34. Ibid.
35. Ibid.
36. Ibid, 249.
37. Ibid, 252.
38. "Awakening the beast of a tax revolt," Vaughn Palmer, *Vancouver Sun,* 7 April 1993.
39. "The sure things in life are death, taxes, and increased 'fees,'" Vaughn Palmer, *Vancouver Sun,* 13 February 1997.
40. Ibid.
41. "Industrial users say Hydro rate 5% too high," *Vancouver Sun,* 7 December 1999.
42. 2000 Financial and Economic Review, BC Ministry of Finance, p 167.
43. BC Central Credit Union.
44. "Alberta's economy surges ahead to third-largest, ahead of BC," *Vancouver Sun*, 3 October 2000.
45. Clark, from the 1991 budget speech debate as quoted in "Big labour's best bet," *BC Report*, 22 January 1996.
46. Glen Clark, Budget Speech 1993, British Columbia Ministry of Finance, Budget 1993, p 12.
47. Hansard, June 27, 1994
48. Elizabeth Cull, Budget Speech 1994, BC Ministry of Finance.
49. "Premier in retreat after NDP's town hall downfall," *Vancouver Sun*, 24 February 1995.
50. "The sorry fiscal legacy of discarded NDP promises," Vaughn Palmer, *Vancouver Sun*, 28 March 1995.
51. "A billion here, a billion there," *BC Report*, 8 January 1996.
52. Budget Speech 1997, British Columbia Ministry of Finance, p 5.
53. "Poof! Half a billion in debt disappears in transit deal," Vaughn Palmer, *Vancouver Sun,* 24 February 1998.
54. Joy MacPhail, Budget Speech 1998, British Columbia Ministry of Finance, p 2.
55. Source: BC and Alberta Budgets 1999. Calculations on per capita debt based on total debt comparisons of the two provinces.
56. "Can't see the house for the mortgage," Mike Harcourt, *The Democrat*, November 1999.
57. Budget Speech 199, British Columbia Ministry of Finance, news release, 30 March 1999.
58. All debt figures from the *2000 Financial and Economic Review*, British Columbia Ministry of Finance.
59. BC Budget 2000 / BC Financial and Economic Review 1999. British Columbia Ministry of Finance.
60. Debt Management Report 1994-95 / BC First Quarterly Update 2000, British Columbia Ministry of Finance.

Chapter 3: Labour of Love

1. "State of the Unions," Paul Willcocks, *Victoria Times Colonist,* 12 February 2000.
2. "Names the NDP doesn't want you to know," *BC Report,* 25 March 1996.
3. "Following labour's lead," *BC Report,* 9 December 1991.
4. "Great Expectations, great disappointments," *BC Report,* 30 November 1992.
5. "Harcourt's Conflict Conundrum," *BC Report*, 25 November 1991.
6. "Following labour's lead," *BC Report,* 9 December 1991.
7. "Public union settlements are private and lucrative," Vaughn Palmer, *BC Report*, 4 March 2000.
8. Source: Business Council of BC, as quoted in *BC Report*, 30 November 1992.
9. "Friends of the party," *BC Report*, 15 June 1992.
10. *BC Report,* 27 July 1992.
11. *BC Report,* 27 July 1992.

12. "Tweedledum and Tweedledee," *BC Report,* 6 September 1993.
13. Source: Business Council of BC, as quoted in *BC Report*, 30 November 1992.
14. Budget Speech 1992, BC Ministry of Finance, p. 5.
15. "Labour peace we can't afford," *BC Report,* 5 April 1993.
16. "The newest ministry – sickness & injury," Vaughn Palmer, *Vancouver Sun,* 23 February 1994.
17. Sources: Memorandum of Understanding between the BC Ferry and Marine Worker's Union and the British Columbia Ferry Corporation, salary adjustments for November 1, 1992, November 1, 1993, November 1, 1994, and November 1, 1995.
18. "Government talks tough (!) to BGGEU," Vaughn Palmer, *Vancouver Sun*, 18 February 1994.
19. "Public union settlements are private and lucrative," Vaughn Palmer, *Vancouver Sun*, 4 March 2000.
20. Ibid.
21. See the Korbin Report, June 1993.
22. "The sorry fiscal legacy of discarded NDP promises," Vaughn Palmer, *Vancouver Sun*, 28 March 1995.
23. "NDP's wage guidelines threaten internal wage fight," *Vancouver Sun*, 1 April 1995.
24. "Big labour's best bet," *BC Report*, 22 January 1996.
25. Ibid.
26. *BC Report,* 25 March 1996.
27. "Big Labour's big man in Victoria," *BC Report*, 5 February 1996.
28. *BC Report,* 5 February 1996.
29. "NDP given $175,000 in frowned-on donations," *Vancouver Sun,* 10 April 1997.
30. "NDP still best bet for labor, unions told," *Vancouver Sun*, 26 November 1996.
31. "NDP's job-slashing in the civil service turns out to be a sham," Vaughn Palmer, *Vancouver Sun*, 2 March 1997.
32. Ibid.
33. "NDP's civil service arithmetic: 5,500 in cuts = an increase of 1,400," Vaughn Palmer, *Vancouver Sun,* 15 March 1997.
34. *Vancouver Sun,* 15 October 1998.
35. "Coming clean on the last big lie of the Glen Clark era," Vaughn Palmer, *Vancouver Sun*, 7 April, 2000.
36. "Liquor workers get free TVs just for showing up on job," *Vancouver Province,* 26 June 2000.
37. "State of the Unions," Paul Willcocks, *Victoria Times Colonist,* 12 February 2000.
38. Ibid.
39. "The case for fair competition," *BC Report,* 4 October 1993.
40. Office of the Auditor General of British Columbia, Vancouver Island Highway Project: Planning and Design, Performance Audit, December 1996.
41. *BC Report,* 4 October 1993.
42. "Taking taxpayers for a ride," *BC Report,* 3 April 1995.
43. *Vancouver Sun,* 22 March 1997.
44. "The power and the pork barrel," *BC Report*, 30 May 1994.
45. Ironworkers Local 97 versus Gordon Campbell, the Liberal Party, Southam Inc., and Brian Kieran, Reasons for Judgment of the Honorable Mr. Justice MacDonald, Supreme Court of British Columbia, Vancouver, 27 October 1997.
46. "Court rules against fair-wage policy," *Vancouver Sun*, 1 August 2000.
47. "Construction unions get more clout," *Vancouver Sun*, 14 June 1997.
48. *Business In Vancouver*, 8 July 1997.
49. "Cashore lets the Ken out of the bag on labor code changes," Vaughn Palmer, *Vancouver Sun*, 26 June 1997.
50. "Labour minister doesn't know why he changed the rules," Les Leyne, *Victoria Times Colonist,* 29 June 1997.
51. "Business groups growling as labor-law changes nears," *Vancouver Province*, 25 June 1997.
52. "It's back to hardball as the NDP pushes unions on BC businesses," Vaughn Palmer, *Vancouver Sun,* 21 June 1997.
53. "How the Bill 44 backdown played out in the back rooms," Vaughn Palmer, *Vancouver Sun,* 17 July 1997.
54. "Business boiling over B.C. law," *Globe and Mail,* 24 June 1997.
55. "Cost of housing could go up by 10 percent if changes to B.C.'s labor code go through," *The Kamloops Daily News*, 15 July 1997.

56. "The ideological cart before the enterprise horse," *Globe and Mail*, 27 June 1997.
57. "Why fix labor code if it wasn't broken?" *Kamloops Daily News*, 27 June 1997.
58. "Payoff to unions will cost dearly," *Victoria Times Colonist,* 26 June 1997.
59. Ibid.
60. "Unions are useful, but these changes aren't," Hubert Beyer, *Chilliwack Progress,* 2 July 1997.
61. "Should I leave B.C.?" *Vancouver Province*, 26 June 1997.
62. "Labour minister doesn't know why he changed the rules," Les Leyne, *Victoria Times Colonist,* 29 June 1997.
63. "Labour shared its wealth with individual candidates," Vaughn Palmer, *Vancouver Sun,* 5 September 1996.
64. Ibid.
65. "Defeat the Recall and Defend Democracy," CAW Local 2301 Bulletin, 26 November 1997.
66. Teamsters Local 213, letter from Mike Croy, 22 January 1998.
67. Prince George & District Building and Construction Trades Council, letter from Jim Welsbrodt and George Seggie, 6 January 1998.
68. "NDP ran covert operation to defeat recall petitions," *Vancouver Sun,* 17 September 1998.
69. Investigation into the Recall Campaigns in Prince George North, Skeena and Comox Valley, Ron Parks; Lindquist, Avey, Macdonald, Baskerville, 24 February 1999.
70. "Hypocrisy of it all," *Prince George Citizen,* 20 September 1998.
71. "Recalls come up short," *Victoria Times Colonist*, 4 February 1998.
72. "State of the Unions," *Victoria Times Colonist,* 12 February 2000.
73. "Two minutes for mediocrity," Keith Kalawsky, *Canadian Business*, 30 October 2000.

Chapter 4: ¿Habla Español?

1. *Vancouver Sun,* 23 October 1997.
2. "Once again, NDP's message to investors: drop dead," Vaughn Palmer, *Vancouver Sun*, 14 October 1998.
3. "Hong Kong's investors wait for NDP to go," *Vancouver Sun*, 13 October 2000.
4. Ibid.
5. Author interview with Mike Geoghegan, October 3, 2000.
6. "BC's big chill," *Globe and Mail*, 22 June 1996.
7. *Vancouver Sun,* 10 September, 1997.
8. "BC forest policies hammered," *Vancouver* Sun, 6 October 2000.
9. "The Premier misses a point in his pulp mill musings," Vaughn Palmer, *Vancouver Sun,* 24 July 1998.
10. From the 1972 NDP election platform: "New ground rules of what constitutes 'good corporate citizenship' in the resource sector will outline the minimum conditions companies must meet to assure British Columbians that our resources are being managed in the public interest. An NDP government will be prepared to place firms unwilling to meet those conditions under public ownership." Quoted in Power Without Glory, Paul Hurmuses, Balsam Press, Vancouver, 1976.
11. Hansard, 24 September 1973.
12. "A fox in the henhouse," *BC Report*, 10 August 1992.
13. Ibid.
14. Ibid.
15. "The high cost of going green," *BC Report,* 5 July 1993.
16. The average compensation package per mining employee in 1998 was $77,800 according to a 1998 study by PricewaterhouseCoopers. *Vancouver Sun,* May 13, 1999.
17. Mary Webster, *Fraser Forum,* The Fraser Institute, January 1998.
18. "How BC blew $50 billion," *BC Report*, 4 July 1994.
19. "'Mining's 'crucial crossroads,'" *BC Report*, 16 March 1992.
20. *BC Report,* 4 July 1994.
21. *BC Report*, 16 March 1992.
22. *BC Report,* 5 July 1993.
23. "It was all my fault," *BC Report*, 27 September 1993.
24. Webster, *Forum,* January 1998.
25. "Mining and recreation can co-exist," David Barr, *Vancouver Sun*, 23 March 1996.
26. Webster, *Forum,* January 1998.
27. Ibid.
28. *Vancouver Sun*, 23 March 1996.

29. Survey of Mining Companies Operating in North America 1998/1999, The Fraser Institute, 1999.
30. "Mining industry withdraws from land-management deal," *Vancouver Sun*, 23 January 1999.
31. "Mine bosses carry message to Victoria," *Vancouver Sun*, 15 April 1997.
32. "Low level of exploration imperils mining industry," *Vancouver Sun,* 13 May 1999.
33. *Sun*, 16 May 1996.
34. "Mining industry withdraws from land-management deal," *Vancouver Sun*, 23 January 1999.
35. *Globe and Mail*, 10 January 1994.
36. *Vancouver* Sun, 23 January 1999.
37. *Vancouver Sun,* 6 October 1972.
38. *Vancouver Sun,* 16 May 1996.
39. *Vancouver* Sun, 23 January 1999.
40. "Negativity damaging recovery, Ramsey laments" *Vancouver Sun*, 22 December 1999.
41. "Mining industry optimistic about Miller's offer," *Vancouver Sun*, 26 January 2000.
42. "British Columbians to be owners of the economy, not simply tenants within it," Gordon Wilson *Vancouver Province,* 1 August 1999.
43. Author interview with Ken Drushka, 20 September 2000.
44. "BC 'going out of business', *Vancouver Sun,* 28 March 2000.
45. "BC sinking rapidly new council boss warns," *Vancouver Sun*, 6 April 2000.
46. "BC forest policies hammered," *Vancouver Sun*, 6 October 2000.
47. "A look at incomes in British Columbia," Policy Perspectives, Business Council of British Columbia.
48. As reported by CKNW 980, Vancouver, 16 October 2000.

Chapter 5: Three 'F's and You're Out

1. *Vancouver Sun,* 11 June 1994.
2. "Clark's night of the long nose," *BC Report,* 11 November 1996.
3. *Victoria News*, 1 November 1996.
4. "Roasted for a cooked budget," *BC Report*, 13 May 1996.
5. Ibid.
6. Ibid.
7. Ibid.
8. Treasury Board documents, as quoted in "NDP budget forecasts were optimistic at best. And at worst..." Vaughn Palmer, *Vancouver Sun,* 25 September 1996.
9. Ibid.
10. "Abracadabra! How the NDP got the budget figures it wanted," Vaughn Palmer, *Vancouver Sun,* 13 September 1996.
11. "The memo that did not lie and the government that did not listen," Vaughn Palmer, *Vancouver Sun,* 5 October 1996.
12. Ibid.
13. "Watchdog probes BC budget errors," *Vancouver Sun*, 16 October 1996.
14. "Legal decision comes as Morfitt inquiry enters a delicate phase," Vaughn Palmer, *Vancouver Sun* 8 July 1997.
15. A Review of the Estimates Process in British Columbia: Office of the Auditor General of British Columbia, 1998/1999 Report 4, February 1999, p. 189
16. "Lawyer in election hearing claims group using court for political ends," *Victoria Times Colonist*, 1 October 1997.
17. "Court case forces NDP into an embarrassing line of argument, Vaughn Palmer, *Vancouver Sun*, 7 February 1997.
18. Reasons for Judgment of the Honourable Madame Justice Humphries, Leonard Friesen, Holly Kuzenko, Mildred Umbarger versus Sue Hammell, Graeme Bowbrick, Ed Conroy, in the Supreme Court of British Columbia, 3 August 2000, Vancouver, paragraph 88.
19. Friesen et al. vs. Hammell et al., par. 87.
20. Ibid, p.140.
21. Ibid, p.165.
22. "A Review of the Estimates Process..." p.5.
23. Ibid, p.185.
24. Ibid, p.139.
25. Ibid, p.142.

26. Ibid, p.176.
27. Ibid, p.189.
28. Ibid, p.151.
29. "Petter set to dip fingers into forest fund," *Vancouver Sun*, 17 July 1996.
30. Ibid.
31. "BC minister won't rule out using forest fund to aid budget," *Globe and Mail*, 17 July 1996.
32. Forest Renewal BC: Planning and Accountability in the Corporation / The Silviculture Programs; Office of the Auditor General of British Columbia, Victoria, November 1999, p. 15.
33. "Clark admits forest funds may help balance budget," *Vancouver Sun*, 18 July 1996.
34. "Forest agency suffers from an embarrassment of riches," Vaughn Palmer *Vancouver Sun*, 18 July 1996.
35. "NDP grab hints at deficit near $1 billion," *Vancouver Sun*, 13 September 1996.
36. "NDP raid dampens forest takeover speculation," *Vancouver Sun*, 14 September 1996.
37. "Provincial grab of forest funds denounced," *Vancouver Sun*, 19 September 1996.
38. "NDP grab hints at deficit near $1 billion," *Vancouver Sun*, 13 September 1996.
39. "NDP supporters 'uneasy' about cash handover," *Vancouver Sun*, 14 September 1996.
40. "Clark backs off raiding forest fund," *Vancouver Sun*, 25 January 1997.
41. "FRBC rethinks worker-training strategy," *Vancouver Sun*, 19 July 1999.
42. "FRBC's death can't come soon enough," Ken Drushka, *Vancouver Sun*, 2 June 1999.
43. *Vancouver Sun*, 19 July 1999.
44. *Vancouver Sun*, 2 June 1999.
45. *Vancouver Sun*, 19 July 1999.
46. Ibid.
47. "FRBC, union accused of subverting program," *Vancouver Sun*, 27 August 1999.
48. Ibid.
49. "FRBC's death can't come soon enough," Ken Drushka, *Vancouver Sun*, 2 June 1999.
50. Forest Renewal BC: Planning and Accountability in the Corporation / The Silviculture Programs; Office of the Auditor General of British Columbia, Victoria, November 1999.
51. *Vancouver Sun*, 29 October 1999.
52. Ibid.
53. "Fast ferries boon to shipbuilders, Harcourt says," *Vancouver Sun* , 30 June 1994.
54. As quoted in the *Vancouver Sun*, 18, October 1997.
55. A Review of the Fast Ferry Project: Governance and Risk Management – Report 5 1999/2000; Office of the Auditor General of British Columbia, October 1999.
56. "Fast ferry project a Glendoggle out of control," Vaughn Palmer, *Vancouver Sun*, 29 October 1999.
57. A Review of the Fast Ferry Project, the Auditor General of British Columbia, October 1999.
58. "BC's fast ferries project, year by year," *Vancouver Province*, 19 January 1999.
59. "Fast ferries boon to shipbuilders, Harcourt says," *Vancouver Sun*, 30 June 1994.
60. *Vancouver Sun*, 28 June 1994.
61. "Fast Cats We Can't Afford," *BC Report*, 12 December 1994.
62. "Will Loose Lips Sink Ships?" *BC Report*, 19 June 1995.
63. Ibid.
64. "Executive, engineer at odds over fast-ferries horsepower," *Vancouver Sun*, 21, June 1995.
65. "BC's fast ferries project, year by year," *Vancouver Province*, 19 January 1999.
66. *Vancouver Sun*, 7 February 1996.
67. *Vancouver Sun*, 13 January 2000.
68. Ibid.
69. "Ferries sputter in the wake of a foolish decision," Vaughn Palmer, *Vancouver Sun*, 11 February 1999.
70. Ibid.
71. "Ferries chief says plan 'a recipe for disaster'," *Vancouver Sun*, 28 January 1999.
72. Ibid.
73. "The sorriest episode of the sad fast ferries story," Vaughn Palmer, *Vancouver Sun*, undated.
74. *Vancouver Sun*, 8 November 1997.
75. As quoted by Vaughn Palmer, *Vancouver Sun*, 24 March 1998.
76. *Vancouver Sun*, 26 March 1998.
77. "Ferries sputter in the wake of a foolish decision," Vaughn Palmer, *Vancouver Sun*, 11 February 1999.
78. "BC's fast ferries project, year by year," *Vancouver Province*, 19 January 1999.
79. *Vancouver Sun*, 29 October 1999.

80. Ibid.
81. Ibid.
82. Ibid.
83. Ibid.
84. Ibid.
85. "NDP were 'ruthless' when in Opposition," *Vancouver Sun*, 29 January 1999.
86. Ibid.
87. "Fast ferry cost expected to be up to $57 million over budget," *Vancouver Sun*, 19 January 1999.
88. "Clark says he didn't know key detail of ferry contract," *Vancouver Sun*, 20 January 1999.
89. "What?!! Clark didn't know about the ferry contracts?" Vaughn Palmer, *Vancouver Sun*, 20 January 1999.
90. *Vancouver Sun,* 29 October 1999.
91. "Fast ferries needed better planning, ex-chief says," *Vancouver Sun,* 29 January 1999.
92. "Victoria sinks fast ferries: We all paid a price MacPhail says," *Vancouver Sun,* 14 March 2000
93. "Fast ferries prove a taxpayer nightmare," *Vancouver Sun,* 18 May 2000.
94. "Aluminum poltergeists," *Victoria Business Examiner*, August 14 – Sept. 4, 2000.

Chapter 6: Jealousy in the Election Sandbox: The NDP Gag Law

1. Then NDP Attorney General Ujjal Dosanjh, on CKNW's Rafe Mair program, 21 April 1997.
2. "Election gag law ruled unconstitutional," *Globe and Mail*, 26 June 1993.
3. "British Columbia's gag law," *Globe and Mail*, 3 June 1995.
4. *Victoria Business Examiner*, 1-14 April 1997.
5. "Election Act adviser wanted no labor loophole," Vaughn Palmer, *Vancouver Sun*, 5 July 1995.
6. "Challenge to BC Election Act advertising curb begins today," *Vancouver Sun*, 31 May 1999.
7. "Election reform legislation branded 'gag law' by critics," *Vancouver Sun*, 2 June 1995.
8. "A Review of the Estimates Process of British Columbia," Office of the Auditor General of British Columbia, February 1999.
9. Hansard, July 11, 1995.
10. "Ordinary citizen shut out of politics, critics charge," *Les Leyne*, *Victoria Times Colonist*, undated clipping.
11. Then NDP Attorney General Ujjal Dosanjh, on CKNW's Rafe Mair program, 21 April 21 1997.
12. Hansard, 11 July 1995.
13. Ibid.
14. Ibid.
15. "Elections BC ponders criminal charges," *Victoria Times Colonist*, 5 September 1996.
16. "Unspecified offences against gag law leave 'offenders' dangling," *Vancouver Sun,* 19 March 1997.
17. Ibid.
18. "Free speech, gag the Election Act," *Vancouver Sun*, 21 October 1997.
19. "Elections BC: 'Ball-peen hammer' style of enforcement," *Victoria Business Examiner*, 1-14 April 1997.
20. Ibid.
21. *Victoria Business Examiner*, 1-14 April 1997.
22. "17 papers defy rules on election ads," *Vancouver Sun*, 23 May 1996.
23. Ibid.
24. "Prosecution urged for election-ad violators," *Vancouver Sun*, 28 May 1996.
25. "NDP critics fined $220,000 over election ad spending," *Vancouver Sun,* 18 March 1997.
26. "BC Elections law faces court challenge," *Vancouver* Sun, 25 November 1997.
27. "A union-made campaign," *BC Report,* 6 May 1996.
28. "Ottawa's gag law struck down again," *Globe and Mail*, 7 June 1996.
29. Pacific Press & Garry B. Nixon v. Attorney General of British Columbia, Reasons for Judgment, Honourable Mr. Justice Brenner, 9 February 2000, par 167.
30. Ibid, par 156.
31. Ibid, par 176.
32. Ibid, par 157-158.
33. Ibid, par 183.
34. Ibid, par 183.
35. Ibid, par 27-39.
36. Ibid, par 40-47.

Chapter 7: Gagging Mother Teresa

1. Re-printed in "Gunning for 'fascists' and Socreds," *British Columbia Report*, 20 June 1994. The original quotation appeared in the Health Employees Union newsletter, *The Buchanan Bugle.* The quote was later denied by Clark in the Legislature. He produced a letter from the *Bugle's* editor Geoff Meggs, who claimed the attribution was a mistake. Meggs was later appointed Clark's chief communications spokesperson.
2. *British Columbia Report*, 6 April 1992.
3. Ibid.
4. "Puncturing the Bubble," *British Columbia Report*, 15 January 1995.
5. Ibid.
6. Ibid.
7. Ibid.
8. "NDP strangely mum on Port Alberni," Vaughn Palmer, *Vancouver Sun,* 28 November 1994.
9. "Interfor discovers damaged machinery," *Vancouver Sun*, 30 August 2000.
10. *BC Report,* 29 May 1995.
11. *BC Report,* 6 April 1992.
12. Access to Abortion Services Act, Bill 48 – Third Reading Passed 27 June 1995, Legislative Assembly of British Columbia.
13. "Rights Group Judges Bubble Zone Goes Too Far," BC Civil Liberties Association, 20 June 1995.
14. "Rights Group Supports Bubble Zone Legislation," BC Civil Liberties Association, 18 September 1995.
15. *BC Report*, 5 December 1994, quoting Stephen Hume.
16. "NDP strangely mum on Port Alberni," Vaughn Palmer, *Vancouver Sun,* 28 November 1994; "NDP shows double standard in handling protesters," Jamie Lamb, *Vancouver Sun,* 6 January 1995.
17. "I rest my case," Joey Thompson, *Vancouver Province,* 23 June 1995.
18. "Bubble Bath," *Vancouver Province*, 21 June 1995.
19. Ibid.
20. "An excessive law on abortion protests," *The Globe and Mail*, 22 June 1995.
21. "Standing on guard against illegal prayer," *BC Report*, 2 October 1995.
22. "Abundance of evidence but Crown doesn't care," Susan Martinuk, *Vancouver Province*, 15 March 2000

Chapter 8: Witch Hunt Anyone?

1. "Human rights of children in BC are being ignored," Human Rights Commissioner Chairman Mary-Woo Sims, Commission website, 15 August 2000.
2. British Columbia Human Rights Code, consolidated 1997.
3. See "A Call for Action: Combatting Hate in British Columbia," British Columbia Human Rights Commission, undated, p.14.
4. "A left-wing exit," *BC Report,* 10 July 1995.
5. Jan Pullinger, quoted in Hansard, 17 June 1993.
6. "Hagen's bill delivers an Orwellian punchline to an old April Fool's joke," *BC Report,* 21 June 1993.
7. Ibid.
8. *Hansard,* 26 July 1996.
9. "Gagging on NDP censorship," *BC Report*, 21 June 1993.
10. Liberal MLA Wilf Hurd, quoted in Hansard, 17 June 1993.
11. Jan Pullinger, quoted in Hansard, 17 June 1993.
12. Mayor says gay pride fight is over," *Kelowna Daily Courier,* 20 April, 2000.
13. Okanagan Rainbow Coalition v. City of Kelowna, Reasons for Decision, BC Human Rights Tribunal, March 21, 2000.
14. Mayor says gay pride fight is over," *Kelowna Daily Courier,* 20 April, 2000.
15. Okanagan Rainbow Coalition v. City of Kelowna, Reasons for Decision, BC Human Rights Tribunal, March 21, 2000, par 32.
16. Ibid, par 32-34.
17. Ibid, par 25.
18. Ibid, par 26.
19. George Orwell, 1984, Penguin Books, New York, 1954, p.200-201.
20. Okanagan Rainbow Coalition v. City of Kelowna, Reasons for Decision, BC Human Rights Tribunal, March 21, 2000, par 112.

21. Ibid, par 115.
22. "A Call for Action: Combatting Hate in British Columbia," British Columbia Human Rights Commission, undated, p. 5.
23. Thomas Sowell, The Quest For Cosmic Justice, The Free Press, New York, 1999, p. 32-33.
24. Ibid.
25. "A Call for Action…" p.15.
26. Ibid.
27. Petter, Andrew. Immaculate Deception: The Charter's Hidden Agenda, *The Advocate*, date unknown.

Chapter 9: The NDP v. the Law

1. In the Supreme Court of British Columbia between: John Patrick Sheehan, petitioner, and British Columbia Hydro Authority, respondent. Reasons for Judgment of the Honourable Mr. Justice Brenner, Vancouver, 6 June 1999.
2. "NDP wants to put brakes on suit by ex-Transit boss," Vaughn Palmer, Vancouver Sun, 30 May 1995.
3. In the Supreme Court of British Columbia between: Frank Dixon, petitioner, and British Columbia Transit, respondent. Reasons for Judgment of Mr. Justice Hamilton, Vancouver, 5 September 1995.
4. *Vancouver Sun*, 24 February 2000.
5. Ibid.
6. In the Supreme Court of British Columbia between: British Columbia Lottery Corporation, petitioner, and City of Vancouver, respondent. Reasons for Judgment of the Honourable Mr. Justice Williamson, Vancouver, 19 December 1997.
7. In the Supreme Court of British Columbia between: Nanaimo Community Bingo Association, petitioner, and the Attorney General of British Columbia, respondent. Reasons for Judgment of the Honourable Mr. Justice Owen-Flood, Vancouver, 14 January 1998.
8. Ibid.
9. In the Supreme Court of British Columbia between: John Patrick Sheehan, petitioner, and British Columbia Hydro Authority, respondent. Reasons for Judgment of the Honourable Mr. Justice Brenner, Vancouver, 6 June 1999.
10. "Democrat Publications guilty in charity bingo," *Vancouver Sun,* 15 October 1999.
11. *Vancouver Sun*, 24 February 2000.
12. Ibid.
13. In the Supreme Court of British Columbia between: Robert Ward, plaintiff, and Glen Clark, defendant. Reasons for Judgment of the Honourable Mr. Justice Owen-Flood, Vancouver, 22 June 2000.
14. "Clark charged in casino scandal," *Vancouver Sun*, 21 October 2000.
15. "NDP easy with tax money in paying for lawyers," Vaughn Palmer, *Vancouver Sun*, 15 October 1999.
16. "Gunton gets government money to go after media," *Vancouver Sun,* 22 April 1999.
17. In the Supreme Court of British Columbia between: Carrier Lumber, plaintiff, and Her Majesty the Queen in Right of the Province of British Columbia, defendant. Reasons for Judgment of the Honourable Mr. Justice W.G. Parrett. Prince George, 29 July 1999, par 398.
18. Ibid, par 34.
19. Ibid, par 239.
20. Ibid, par 243.
21. Ibid, par 299.
22. Ibid, par 333.
23. Ibid, par 337.
24. The case is, as of the writing of this book, under appeal by the NDP government.
25. Ibid, par 338.
26. Ibid, par 340.
27. Ibid, par 342.
28. Unlike civil servants under Glen Clark, Philip Halkett never suffered any repercussions for his blunt assessment of the Premier's action. In fact, Halkett was later tapped by Dan Miller to head up BC Ferries in early 1999, a promotion that lasted 18 days after he released an error-riddled technical report on the fast ferries. By 2000, he was deputy minister in Premier Ujjal Dosanjh's office.
29. Ibid, par 343.
30. Ibid, par 352.
31. Ibid, par 365-366.
32. "Hidden paper costs $150 million," Ken Drushka, *Vancouver Sun*, 11 August 1999.
33. Carrier v. the Queen, par 314.

34. "Hidden paper costs $150 million," Ken Drushka, *Vancouver Sun*, 11 August 1999.
35. In the Supreme Court of British Columbia between: Carrier Lumber, plaintiff, and Her Majesty the Queen in Right of the Province of British Columbia, defendant. Reasons for Judgment of the Honourable Mr. Justice W.G. Parrett. Prince George, 29 July 1999, par 366-370.
36. Ibid, par 373.
37. Ibid, par 370.
38. Ibid, par 375.
39. Ibid, par 375.
40. Ibid, par 375.
41. Ibid, par 376-378.
42. Ibid, par 125.
43. Ibid, par 152.
44. Ibid, par 166.
45. Ibid, par 387-388.
46. Ibid, par 389-390.
47. Ibid, par 398.
48. Ibid, par 487.
49. Ibid, par 490-491.
50. "Cleaning up blots on the new man's copybook," *Victoria Times Colonist*, 23 August 1999.
51. Carrier Lumber Decision Appealed, 24 August 1999 News Release, Ministry of Attorney General, Government of British Columbia.
52. "Hidden paper costs $150 million," Ken Drushka, *Vancouver Sun*, 11 August 1999.

Chapter 10: Congratulations, You're Fired

1. Hansard, 8 December 1998.
2. Quotation taken from Our Home Or Native Land? Smith, Mel; Crown Western, 1995, p.79.
3. Ibid, p.79.
4. Ibid.
5. Ibid, p.80.
6. *The Aboriginal Peoples of British Columbia: A Profile* (Victoria, Ministry of Aboriginal Affairs, 1992.)
7. Our Home Or Native Land? Smith, Mel, Crown Western, 1995, p.78.
8. "In the fast lane on the road to self-government," *British Columbia Report*, 14 December 1992.
9. *Reasons for Judgment of Chief Justice Allan McEachern,* Supreme Court of British Columbia, Delgamuukw vs. A.G., 8 March 1991.
10. "Too successful for the NDP?" *British Columbia Report*, 23 March 1992.
11. Ibid.
12. Ibid.
13. Ibid.

Chapter 11: Provincial, Discriminatory & Illiberal

1. Premier fears fallout if deal were to fail," *Vancouver Sun*, 29 July 1998.
2. "Nisga'a settlement is a 'Glen Clark' deal," *Vancouver Sun*, 29 July 1998.
3. "Although opposed by many in BC, the Nisga'a treaty has profound implications for the rest of Canada. It shows how one aboriginal self-government, might work," Thomas Walkon, *Toronto Star,* 5 December 1998.
4. "Clark voices Nisga'a doubts," *Vancouver Province*, 9 October 1998.
5. "NDP sets spending record promoting Nisga'a treaty," Vaughn Palmer, *Vancouver Sun*, undated 1999.
6. "Get 'em while they're young," *BC Report*, 2 November 1998.
7. Theoretically, the Nisga'a will own the land in "fee simple," but unlike normal definitions of private property, the fee simple ownership of the Nisga'a will not be subject to normal expropriation rights of either the federal or provincial government. "This estate is not subject to any condition, proviso, restriction, exception, or reservation set out in the *Land Act*, or any comparable limitation under any federal or provincial law. No estate or interest in Nisga'a Lands can be expropriated except as permitted by, and in accordance with this Agreement." Nisga'a Final Agreement, August 4, 1998, 31, Chap. 3, par. 3.
8. Nisga'a Final Agreement, Ch. 3, par. 19.
9. Size of estimated land affected from Richardson, R.M., A Comparative Cost Analysis of the Nisga'a

Treaty, February 1999, p. 26.
10. NFA, Ch. 5, par. 3-4.
11. NFA, Ch. 3, par. 20.
12. NFA, Ch. 8, par. 69.
13. NFA, Ch. 15, p. 212, par. 8.
14. NFA, Ch. 15.
15. NFA, Chapter 2, paragraphs 19, 34, 35; Ch. 3, paragraphs 77 and 84; Ch. 6, paragraph 9, Ch. 7, paragraphs 42 and 45; Ch. 8, paragraphs 20, 21, 44, 58, 83, and 115; Ch. 8, par. 115; Ch. 9, paragraphs 11, 28, 50, 53, 76, 77, 82, 85, 95, 96; Ch. 10, paragraph 1, 5, 6 and 15; Ch. 11, par. 19, 28, 30, 64-67, 68, 80, 81, 85, 92, 102, and 141; Ch. 12, paragraphs 18 and 24; Ch. 15, paragraphs 3, 7, and 14; Ch. 16, par. 17; Ch. 17, paragraphs 17 and 31; Ch. 18, par. 3 and 7.
16. NFA, p. 220, Ch. 16, par. 17.
17. "Your guide to the Nisga'a Treaty," Government of British Columbia, 1998.
18. NFA, Chapter 11.
19. Ibid.
20. Ibid.
21. Ibid.
22. Ibid.
23. Ibid.
24. Ibid.
25. NFA, Chapter 5.
26. "Opposition to Nisga'a treaty fraught with misconception," Aboriginal Affairs Minister Dale Lovick in a letter to the *Vancouver Sun,* 1 November 1999.
27. NFA, Ch. 2, p.18 par. 13; Ch. 8, p. 113 par. 71; Ch. 9, p.139 par. 38; Ch. 11, p. 166 par. 36; Ch. 11, p. 167, par. 38, 40, 43; Ch. 11, p. 168 par. 45; Ch. 11, p. 169 par. 49; Ch. 11, p. 170, par. 51; Ch. 11, p. 174, par. 84, par. 87; Ch. 11, p. 175 par. 91; Ch. 11, p. 176, par. 99; Ch. 11, p. 177, par. 101; Ch. 11, p. 177 par. 105; Ch. 11, p. 179 par. 116.
28. Hansard, 13 January 1999.
29. UBC political scientist Paul Tennant made this argument in an interview with the *Vancouver Sun* in "Nisga'a treaty empowers band," 25 July 1998.
30. "Opposition to Nisga'a treaty fraught with misconception," Aboriginal Affairs Minister Dale Lovick in a letter to the *Vancouver Sun,* 1 November 1999.
31. NFA, Ch. 11, par. 19-20.
32. NFA, Ch. 11, par. 21, sub-section c.
33. "Opposition to Nisga'a treaty fraught with misconception," Aboriginal Affairs Minister Dale Lovick in a letter to the *Vancouver Sun,* 1 November 1999.
34. Premier fears fallout if deal were to fail," *Vancouver Sun*, 29 July 1998.
35. "Voting rights on Nisga'a lands divisive issue," *Vancouver Sun*, 30 August 1998.
36. "Clark lashes out at Liberals over Nisga'a talk," *Vancouver Sun*, 15 December 1998.
37. Hansard, 1 December 1998.

Chapter 12: Sweden or Switzerland?

1. *Hansard,* Volume 1, No. 8, 24 March 1992.
2. Canadian Press, 21 January 2000.
3. "NDP need Miller's advice but may not heed it," Les Leyne, *Victoria Times Colonist,* 21 September 1999.
4. Quoted in Freedom of Information and Privacy Association bulletin, January-March 2000, p.23.
5. Noted in Letter to Jon Havelock, MLA (Alberta), from Mel Smith, Q.C. Smith argued that, based on upon past judicial decisions, "provinces have the unfettered right to shape their own constitutions. Within their own sphere of jurisdiction, and to tailor their operation and conduct of their executives as they see fit. A province could for example, establish a provincial Senate and constitute it as a part of the law-making process." Smith goes on to argue that as long as the legislation for citizen initiated referendum provides for a role for the Legislature and the Lieutenant Governor, it would be wholly constitutional.

Appendix A: Turning Tommy Douglas in his Grave

1. Her Majesty the Queen against David Daniel Stupich, Reasons for Sentence, Mr. Justice Josephson, 3 September 1999, The Supreme Court of British Columbia, Vancouver.
2. Investigation of the Affairs and Conduct of Nanaimo Commonwealth Holding Society and Related Societies, The "Parks Report," 31 May 1995. Lindquist, Avey, Macdonald, Baskerville. p. 14.
3. "NDP minister has bingo memory lapse." Mark Hume, *National Post*, 14 December 1999.
4. Ibid. p. 14.
5. Parks Report, p. 62.
6. Ibid, p. 63.
7. Ibid, p. 15.
8. "The 'stiffed nun' will be a witness at bingo inquiry," Vaughn Palmer, *Vancouver Sun,* 1999.
9. Ibid.
10. Parks Report, Ibid, p. 24.
11. Ibid, p. 25.
12. Ibid, p. 25.
13. "Officials knew bingo society broke rules, but little was done," *Vancouver Sun*, 2 February 1995.
14. Parks Report, p. 25.
15. Her Majesty the Queen against David Daniel Stupich, Reasons for Sentence, Mr. Justice Josephson, 3 September 1999, The Supreme Court of British Columbia, Vancouver, par. 8.
16. The NCHS clues lead straight to the premier's office," Vaughn Palmer, *Vancouver Sun*, 28 October 1995.
17. "Audit proves NDP 'didn't get aid' from illegal bingo," *Vancouver Sun*, 4 April 1995.
18. "Anatomy of a cover-up," *BC Report*, 30 October 1995.
19. "My questions about the premier's knowledge and responsibility," Vaughn Palmer, *Vancouver Sun*, 17 October 1995 and "Harcourt leadership in question," *Vancouver Sun*, 21 October 1995.
20. "Anatomy of a cover-up," *BC Report*, 30 October 1995.
21. "My questions about the premier's knowledge and responsibility," Vaughn Palmer, *Vancouver Sun*, 17 October 1995.
22. "Cover-up or repayments was a mistake," *Vancouver Sun*, 16 October 1995.
23. "My questions about the premier's knowledge and responsibility," Vaughn Palmer, *Vancouver Sun*, 17 October 1995.
24. "Pattern of next Nanaimo scandal cover-up can already be discerned," Vaughn Palmer, *Vancouver Sun,* 15 October 1999.
25. Ibid.
26. "Cull 'has not committed any crimes,' premier says," *Vancouver Sun,* 18 October 1999.
27. "Ms. Cull's mishandling has badly misfired," Vaughn Palmer, *Vancouver Sun,* 15 June 1995.
28. Ibid.
29. Parks Report, p. 102.
30. Parks Report, Appendix 12.
31. "The money trail between the NDP and the NCHS," *Vancouver Sun,* 8 May 1998, based on information contained in the Ron Parks Report.
32. Ron Parks, from the Parks Report as quoted in "Report points to NDP coverup," *Vancouver Sun,* 14 October 1995.
33. "How pathetic, the premier and his 'I don't knows'," Vaughn Palmer, *Vancouver Sun*, 24 October 1995.
34. "Harcourt digging into the NCHS scandal with a teaspoon," Vaughn Palmer, *Vancouver Sun*, 3 October 1995.
35. Ibid.
36. Ibid.
37. "NDP minister has bingo memory lapse," Mark Hume, *National Post*, 14 December 1999.
38. Ibid.
39. Ibid.
40. "Democrat Publications guilty in charity bingo," *Vancouver Sun,* 15 October 1999.
41. Parks Report, p. 38.
42. Parks Report, p. 39.
43. Ibid, p. 85.
44. Ex-cabinet minister Stupich gets 2-year sentence," *Vancouver Sun,* 26 June 1999.
45. Ibid.

46. *Vancouver Sun*, 2 December 1999.
47. Parks Report, p. 8.
48. "Judge unwraps Commonwealth report," *Vancouver Sun*, 14 October 1995.
49. "Under the D. Dementia? Deceit?" *Vancouver Province,* 10 September 2000.

Appendix B

1. "Watchdog probes BC budget errors," *Vancouver Sun*, 16 October 1996.
2. "NDP budget forecasts were optimistic at best. And at worst…" Vaughn Palmer, *Vancouver Sun,* 25 September 1996.
3. "A Review of the Estimates Process…", p.181.
4. "Cock of the (legislative) walk takes his cookware to the people," Vaughn Palmer, *Vancouver Sun,* 1 May 1996.
5. "A Review of the Estimates Process…", p.178
6. "Clark's night of the long nose," *BC Report*, 11 November 1996.

Quick Order Form

Please send me ______ copies of Barbarians in the Garden City – The BC NDP in Power (ISBN 0-9687915-0-6)

1-4 books
Quantity ______ x $19.95 = ... ______________

(BULK: 5 or more books)
Quantity _______ x 15.95 = ... ______________
Discount price only applies to orders of 5 or more
Postage $4.00 first copy .... ______________
(+ .50 per each additional copy) .... ______________

Sub-total .... ______________

G.S.T. (7%) (on books and postage) .... ______________

Total .... ______________

Ship to:

Name: ____

Address:____

______________________________Postal Code __________

Payment:
❐ Cheque / ❐ Money Order / ❐ VISA / ❐ Mastercard
(No C.O.D. or cash orders)

Card Number:___________________________Exp Date:____________

Name on Card: ______________________________________

Signature (required for card processing)_____________________

☎ **Fax orders:**
250-598-1870 - Send this form. Orders shipped same day.

✉ **Postal orders:**
Thomas & Black Publishers, PO Box 8095 Victoria, BC, V8W 3R8

Quick Order Form

Please send me ______ copies of Barbarians in the Garden City – The BC NDP in Power (ISBN 0-9687915-0-6)

1-4 books
Quantity ______ x $19.95 = ... ______________

(BULK: 5 or more books)
Quantity _______ x 15.95 = ... ______________
Discount price only applies to orders of 5 or more
Postage $4.00 first copy .... ______________
(+ .50 per each additional copy) .... ______________

Sub-total .... ______________

G.S.T. (7%) (on books and postage) .... ______________

Total .... ______________

Ship to:

Name: ____

Address:____

______________________________Postal Code __________

Payment:
❒ **Cheque / ❒ Money Order / ❒ VISA / ❒ Mastercard**
(No C.O.D. or cash orders)

Card Number:____________________________Exp Date:____________

Name on Card: ____________________________________

Signature (required for card processing)_____________________

☎ **Fax orders:**
250-598-1870 - Send this form. Orders shipped same day.

✉ **Postal orders:**
Thomas & Black Publishers, PO Box 8095 Victoria, BC, V8W 3R8